THE REAL CAPTAIN

REAL-WORLD LESSONS FOR ASPIRING BUSINESS ANALYSTS

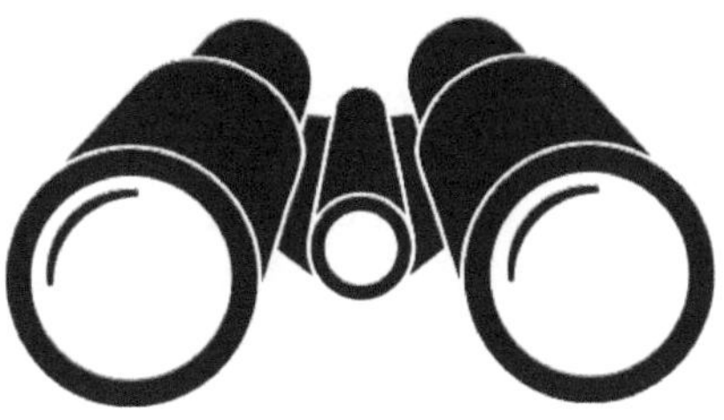

JAYAKISHOR BAYADI

Made with ♥ on the Notion Press Platform
www.notionpress.com

This book is dedicated to ***My Beloved GOD.***

This book is dedicated to my parents, **Shivarani and Dr. Thirumaleshwara Bhat**

to my wife, **Vidyalakshmi,** *and my son,* **Ved.**

CONTENTS

FOREWORD

Do these skills and abilities sound like a future business leader in the making: make informed (i.e., data-driven) decisions and recommendations, identify trends, opportunities, and potential problems, collaborate with business stakeholders to understand requirements, optimize processes, solve problems, documentation & reporting, etc.? You might be thinking about the role of a business analyst, who needs to possess these valuable skills to be successful.

Successful business analysts are future business leaders, period. In my professional journey, which has a bit of developer, entrepreneurial, operational leader, and strategy consulting stints, I couldn't have done those without business analysis skills or the help of internal or external business analysts. The way I see it, every profession in any business today is either a flavour of business analyst or is heavily dependent on another business analyst.

How did some of these skills help me throughout my journey?

Data-Driven Decision-Making: This is the most essential skill of all. Business analysts excel in collecting and analysing data to identify trends, opportunities, and potential problems, optimize processes, understand employee engagement, etc. Every meeting in a business setup depends on data-driven decision-making. This data-driven approach aids organizations in making informed decisions, which leads to increased profitability and efficiency. Every facet of my professional journey, be it the merger of my company or advising a client on a health insurance product, required the skill of data-driven decision-making.

Requirements Gathering: Business analysts are skilled at eliciting and documenting business requirements. This is crucial for product development, process improvement, and project management, ensuring stakeholders' needs are clearly understood and met. I see this process more as orchestrating innovation. It's not only developing something that your customers need, but it's also creating an environment where customer creativity is at its best!

Process Improvement: Business analysts identify inefficiency within an organization and work on optimizing processes. Innovations happen not only in product development but also in process improvement! Implementing this approach can lead to reduced expenses, enhanced efficiency, and higher levels of customer contentment. This particular skill helped me during my stint as an operational leader focused on improving profitability.

Project Management: Many business analysts have project management skills, which allow them to plan, execute, and monitor projects effectively. Their assistance can guarantee the timely completion of projects while staying within budget. Jayakishor has dedicated a part of his book to discussing who is the real captain - it's actually the business analysts with project management skills, not the other way around.

Stakeholder Communication: Business analysts act as intermediaries between different stakeholders in a project, such as business users, IT teams, and management. They ensure clear communication and alignment of project goals with business objectives. This skill is fundamental to growing as an entrepreneur or as a C-suite executive, where you tend to interact with diverse folks such as customers, investors, employees, competitors and peers.

Strategic Planning: Business analysts often participate in strategic planning processes. Their ability to analyze data and provide insights helps organizations make long-term plans and set strategic goals.

Problem-Solving: Business analysts are adept at identifying problems and finding solutions. They apply their analytical and evaluative skills to address complex issues and propose methods for improvement.

Market Research: Business analysts may conduct market research to understand industry trends, customer preferences, and competitive landscapes. This information can be used to make strategic decisions and stay competitive.

Cost-Benefit Analysis: Business analysts evaluate the costs and benefits of various options, helping organizations make financially sound decisions. One critical task involved is assessing the return on investment (ROI) for various projects or initiatives.

Documentation and Reporting: Business analysts create clear and comprehensive documentation, such as business requirements, project plans, and reports. This documentation is essential for tracking progress and ensuring accountability.

Change Management: Business analysts often play a crucial role in change management by helping organizations adapt to new processes, technologies, or strategies. They can develop change management plans and facilitate the transition.

Continuous Improvement: Business analysts promote a culture of continuous improvement within organizations. They monitor the performance of implemented solutions and make adjustments as needed to achieve better results.

One of my favourite quotes in the book is, "It's not just about doing things right, but about doing the right things". This captures the essence of this book and sets the tone for mindset, going beyond what the customer is asking and taking ownership.

In summary, developing yourself as a business analyst or developing some of these skills early in your career sets you up for long-term success. The book you hold is a pragmatic guide to becoming a business analyst and a must-read for all professionals.

Jayakishor's ability to simplify the complexity of the role and capture the essence of the journey will significantly impact anybody who picks up this guide.

Girish Ramachandra

Entrepreneur, Technology Consulting & Delivery Leader
Greater Chicago Area, USA
10/10/2023

in/in/girishramachandra/

FOREWORD

I am delighted to pen down this foreword as I have seen a writer within Jayakishor ever since we met as part of a business analysis workshop. I am glad he has written this book with great interest and covered the nitty gritty aspects of Business Analysis.

This book is a step-by-step guide for anyone aspiring to be a Business Analyst and reassuring for experienced BAs.

Jayakishor has thoughtfully presented real-world scenarios and practically feasible techniques to handle those scenarios.

I am impressed with how Jayakishor has articulated the steps to read and consume this book. Regarding the number of pages, this is a simple test for aspiring BAs to check if they have the appetite to read tonnes of documents and assimilate them into any projects.

The diagrams and process flow charts are very handy to keep the reader intrigued and apt for all the scenarios depicted in the book.

All the best to Jayakishor on this new journey as a writer, and I am looking forward to more books from him.

Raghavendra Krishnamurthy

Expert IT Consultant & Leader
California, USA
10/10/2023

in/in/raghu-krishnamurthy/

PREFACE

BEING A BA!

Many times, I felt that "I might no longer be an efficient Business Analyst (BA)".

The ever-changing business scenarios, demanding and complex projects, and technology needs have made my work as a BA challenging and demanding. Hence, I often get the feeling that "I am no longer an efficient BA."

Nonetheless, embracing the distinctive "BA mindset" has consistently strengthened me during such challenging situations.

Being a BA has taught me the benefits of working hard, working smart, and continuous learning. Being a BA gave me the required intellect to upgrade myself continuously. Being a BA allowed me to see a problem in multiple angles and dimensions and interact with diverse people. Above all, a whole unique mindset. Each time, the BA mindset made me take the situations positively and learn many new things, and as a result, I became wiser each time.

Each time I felt that I was no longer an efficient BA, the 'BA mindset' guided me to do what is needed and regain my efficiency. I would say, that's the power of 'Being BA'.

This book is all about my learning, mindset, tools, and much more in relation to Business Analysis.

Every day, a BA needs to learn and unlearn. Continuous learning is just the nature of the BA job.

I read somewhere that retention increases by five times when one writes about what they know and learn. Sharing what you know and learn is even better. This Book is the result of that thought.

I've witnessed many projects fail due to incorrect requirements or, to put it rightly, inefficient business analysis. Business analysis always begins with understanding what the business and business users genuinely need, which isn't always straightforward. Your users might not provide a clear picture. As a BA, you need to dig deeper. If you can't do that, it doesn't matter how fancy your solution is; your system won't be used, leading to project failure.

I have sincerely tried to discuss many practical problems and tactics for discovering users' needs. This Book explores how you, as a BA, can uncover genuine requirements. It also discusses numerous valuable methods, tools, and tricks for analysis.

Being a BA has enriched my learning experience. I'm not implying that you won't learn in other roles. Still, as a BA collaborating with internal teams, customers, and beyond, there's a significant opportunity to expand, lead, understand and contribute to solving business problems. Being a BA opened up many challenging and rewarding "growth" opportunities as well.

It was a couple of years ago. One fine evening, my manager suddenly called and asked: "Will you be a Program Manager for this project?"

I was at the peak of my BA career, loving and enjoying the job. Though there was some hesitation initially, I agreed because, I knew, I can work hard to learn new things. However, though I agreed to be the Program Manager, I never wanted to lose touch with my BA skills. Hence, I kept one of the modules for myself to handle the Business Analyst responsibilities.

It was a multi-million-dollar project. Team size was 30+. I was responsible for managing the project team, customer stakeholders and delivering the project. Suddenly, as usual, I felt inefficient, so I had to focus. Though the role of a BA is also overwhelming at times, the Program Manager role was new for me as the responsibilities are a little different in this role.

I used to be the bridge between the Customer and Project team, earlier as a BA. Now, I am owning the project in terms of delivery. Any miss would have economic impacts, and I must answer hundreds of questions from customers and my Management.

So, the question that kept me up at night as I went from BA to Program Manager role was: How can I show the value? Can I adapt my experience to my new role?

That's what the "BA mindset" taught me. It taught me apply and adapt experience to new situations. Work hard. Learn the tricks. Try again, fall again, rise again. Above all, it taught me to apply common sense.

As a Program Manager, essentially, I need to keep predicting the worst that can happen and plan accordingly—essentially a Project Manager or Program Manager should be able to imagine worst possible RISK that can happen and mitigation plan for the same. Again, I adapted many BA skills to overcome all such new Program Management challenges. In fact, I adapted my BA skills and mindset wherever I went.

That is why my transition to Program Manager, Delivery Manager, and now to a Leadership role was always smooth. I owe this success to my business analysis skills and mindset.

My BA mindset helped me to think creatively about how operationally I can bring in new technologies, innovative methodologies, and strategies to delight customers and, at the same time, add value to the deliverables. I realised, along with customers, that I needed to care for my team members well. Keeping them cheered became my utmost responsibility.

The skill of BA has given me everything I am today—a kind of all-round experience. Whether it is as a BA, Program Manager or Consultant, I get to learn every moment. I have that mindset to learn every day. Again, I owe this to my business analysis skills and mindset.

People may call me a jack of all—but it brings me great joy to share my experience with all of you. I have been sharing my knowledge and expertise in these areas in the form of LinkedIn posts and now as this Book and perhaps as courses in the coming times.

This Book represents an endeavor to help aspiring BAs navigate the correct and practical path to achieve success as a BA. I hope you will find this book useful and valuable.

I thank Girish, who mentored me, and Raghu, with whom I worked and learned many aspects, for agreeing to write Forewords for this book.

I thank my family (My wife Vidya; Son Ved; my Parents Shivarani Bhat and Dr. Thirumaleshwara Bhat) and my LinkedIn connections who have supported me so far directly and indirectly.

Jayakishor Bayadi

Experienced BA, IT Consultant, Leader
Bengaluru, India
10/10/2023

in/in/jayakishorbayadi/

TO WHOM THIS BOOK IS FOR?

As per publicly available info, Business analysis has been practised since the 1940s but gained rapid importance in the early 90s with the rise of IT. As the field of Information Technology (IT) and software development lifecycle (SDLC) matured, it embraced a more structured approach by incorporating established project management and analysis methodologies and best practices. This evolution gave rise to the role of the BA, whose primary function is to facilitate effective communication between the business stakeholders and the IT teams.

Today, Business Analysis is a crucial profession that analyses business processes, identifies improvement areas, and facilitates IT solutions development. The key objective of the BA is to ensure that technological solutions are closely aligned with the specific requirements and goals of the business. The BA acts as a single point of contact between the company and IT teams, providing an accurate definition of IT requirements to align with business needs. The profession has evolved to become an integral part of any IT project.

The fundamentals of Business Analysis will remain unchanged even with technological advancements like Artificial Intelligence (AI) and related aspects that enable increased efficiency and automation.

However, the role of a BA cannot be fully automated as it requires high energy, analytical and critical thinking capabilities, and, most importantly, basic "common sense". To achieve and master these skills it takes effort and dedication. If you have a natural gift for these abilities, that's great. Otherwise, you need to learn the tips and tricks through training and practice.

Hence, I guarantee that if you put effort into acquiring and mastering 'BA' skills now, those skills will be with you for a lifetime. Also, this Book's content is formulated in such a way that the Book remains evergreen as a guide or reference book for a lifetime. Tools or methodologies may change. But fundamentals of Business Analysis will remain the same.

You will only evolve and mature over time as you gain experience. Once you get more experience, you will start applying your logic, skills and common sense to solve the problem Infront of you. Nevertheless, I guarantee that this Book holds immense value for you, serving as a convenient and reliable quick reference guide at your disposal!

I am confident that the forthcoming chapters are brimming with power, knowledge, intensity, and meticulous details to fulfil your thirst for learning. If you commit yourself and truly grasp the concepts and processes presented in this Book, I am certain that you will be well-prepared to excel as a "Business Analyst."

It's essential to note that this Book is intended for individuals engaged in IT projects, aspiring to become BAs who concentrate on business functions and processes. These BAs are responsible for identifying business needs, Requirements, issues, and gaps and suggesting solutions, typically working within IT projects. It is important to clarify that this Book is not tailored for those focusing on data, analytics, and reporting; such professionals are also called BAs for Business Analytics.

This Book is Ideal For:

- Freshers Who Just Joined an IT Organization and want to pursue a BA career
- People with some experience working on a Project & want to pursue a BA career.
- People with Good experience in the technical area & now want to pursue a BA career.
- Just Freshers from college who want to explore BA as a career option and prepare for the same. (From day one, they can't become a BA as it requires a lot of learning and experience.)

Of course, you may find upcoming chapters a bit overwhelming. If you are inexperienced (Freshers), you may find it difficult to understand the context in many instances as you might not have worked in a typical IT project/IT Company environment. However, do not worry; you may have to use your power of imagination to visualize and understand the context and concepts. However, if you have little experience working on an IT project, you will be able to understand the context, and your job is to learn the techniques and processes – so you can be ready for the role of a BA.

As stated earlier, a BA Job just requires common sense, above all. A BA aspirant must develop or possess or enhance the nature of asking questions like a kid. No doubt, experience is required to become a great BA, but without working on a project, you won't get experience, and that's where real-life experience/ knowledge in the form of a book like this will help you.

In this book, I have made every effort to incorporate my experience and knowledge in a manner that transforms it into an indispensable guide for newcomers aspiring to enter the BA profession. Unlike mere theoretical accounts, this Book delves into the real-life experiences of BAs in action. It goes beyond abstract concepts and offers practical anecdotes and scenarios, all presented in clear and accessible language. I aim to equip readers with the insights and preparation they need to excel in this field. It's not just theory; it's the authentic and relatable narrative of BAs at work.

This Book will guide people with some IT experience who want to enter the BA profession. This Book could be a real guide for people who are in non-IT sectors and want to get into the BA profession. This Book could be a refresher for people who already have good experience as BAs. Simply put, the Book aims to assist individuals currently working in the IT industry or those interested in pursuing a career in IT as a BA. It helps them grasp industry jargon and processes (In the Business Analysis area), boosting their confidence for future interviews. By combining theory with practical scenarios, the Book provides a well-structured understanding of Business Analysis, equipping readers to easily tackle complex situations in their professional journey.

I do not have any issues with people pursuing courses in Business Analysis or any other area. I believe that courses are beneficial for gaining a good understanding of the fundamentals and theory, and they offer an opportunity to learn and refresh one's knowledge. On the other hand, books are valuable resources as they allow you to refer to them at your convenience and absorb the information at your own pace, providing a unique and profound impact.

Once you have that solid basic understanding, you can learn tactics considerably from people who share their real experiences or by talking to the people who have been there and done that. The best way to learn is on the job. To learn on the job, one should have an open mind and a basic understanding of Business Analysis. That's where this Book will come in handy.

To perform jobs like BA, one needs an open and unbiased mind. Without an open mind, learning becomes difficult – this is applicable not only for BAs but for people in every profession.

Hence, be open. Put your 100% to become an exceptionally good at what you want to learn. Like Warren Buffet says: "The best thing one can do is to be exceptionally good at something. Whatever abilities you have, can't be taken away from you. They can't actually be inflated away from you. The best investment by far is anything that develops yourself, and it's not taxed at all."

Hence, always try your best to become exceptionally goad at things that you want to pursue.

What do you say?

Switching Your Profession to Be A BA

Whether you are an IT Developer or Technical Architect, if you think you can do a BA Job and want to get into the BA domain, it's great. You can do it. However, before you decide to switch, as a first step, you should ask yourself whether you have a suitable "mindset" to be a BA.

As they say, the grass is always greener on the other side. That's why you should always ask yourself, "Why" do you want to become a BA? List down the reasons. Be honest with yourself. If you are convinced, get into the second step.

Ask yourself the questions below first:

- Can you talk to people and build and maintain a good relationship with them?
- Do you like meetings/workshops, etc.? Do you even like continuous/back-to-back meetings? Can you lead a meeting/workshop?
- Do you have confidence in yourself that you SPEAK and WRITE clearly?
- When you talk to someone, do you also listen to them actively?
- Can you resolve a problem independently (ownership)by figuring out what is required (by researching, asking people, etc.)?
- In a crisis (escalation/major issue, etc.), you don't panic but feel like, "Let's understand the issue first"? True?

If "YES" is your answer to all the above questions, it's time to look for opportunities as a BA. Else, see if you can improve on any area where you answered as NO.

If you do not have any experience as BA, see if you can get some experience or knowledge within your organization itself. While you perform your existing job, take up some extra work (by helping your BA, working with BA, attending calls with BA) within your Project, and get the feel of being a BA. Are you enjoying it? Do you feel like this is what you want to do?

If yes, then great! Ask for any opportunities within your Project or organization. Remember. Your transformation will take a few months to a couple of years. A BA should have the mindset of "NEVER GIVE UP", even to succeed in his/her regular job. Hence, during the transformation, "You Should Never Give Up."

Being a BA entails a leadership role where the true responsibility lies. While the Program Manager may hold the title of project leader, the BA assumes the role of the real leader—The Real Captain.

As a BA, your foremost responsibility is to ensure that your work aligns with the organizational vision, business needs and business requirements. Should any issues arise during a project, the first course of action will be to investigate whether the requirements captured by the BA were accurate. If any inconsistencies are discovered, the responsible party will be the BA. Consequently, BAs face constant pressure to perform flawlessly, as they carry the weight of ensuring correctness. They must consistently get things right, as their actions directly impact the Project's success.

If a system is implemented and fails to meet business expectations, the BA will bear responsibility for the outcome. This underscores the importance of BAs being capable of handling such pressure and delivering successful results.

Are You Ready to Do "Bagiri"?

It is always better to envision what type of BA you want to become - Just an order taker BA or a proactive BA and trusted advisor to your customers?

Becoming an order taker BA, who just talks to the customer, documents requirements, follows instructions and moves on—it's easy to become one. If you want to achieve real success and get real experience, you need to get deeper and become a trusted advisor—that path is not very easy. This requires real "Jigar" or "Courage".

When you are new, there may be instances where nobody gives a damn to your advice, approach, or suggestions. Such situations may be demotivating; however, make it a point to convey your opinion to the entire team – whether it is wrong or right. Perhaps document it by sending an email to all the people involved. Do not get demotivated. This happens even to the veterans in the field.

To avoid such situations, you must be prepared – because you are just a beginner as a BA – preparation is crucial to convince big sharks of your Project team – including customers.

In your regular office internal meetings, you hear one person's name very often— "Yeah, we should ask him/her. Let's get him/her for at least a call to get the advice". How did he/she create such a reputation for him/her? Is it something that was created deliberately, or it just happened?

Actually, it's a mix of both. He/she is the person who was prepared and dared to do that real "BAgiri"—recommending things that were contrary to popular opinion without any fear and thus earning the trust. Just talk to such people, and you will get some good insights. Meet people – this is a must for a BA.

When you are new, you may feel uncomfortable having some tough conversations. Due to a lack of experience, you cannot answer many questions. Above all, your self-doubt would be trying to take control of your mind. But don't fret. Prepare and practice before any meetings. Get as much knowledge about the Project as possible—all this will save you. Every time you cross your comfort zone, you will stretch the muscle holding you back. As you keep doing this over time, you will find that it no longer holds you back.

If you want to learn to swim, just jump onto the water—not blindly, but with all necessary preparations and precautions. Happy "BAgiri"!

Note: *The Word "BAgiri" is inspired by the word "Dadagiri" in Hindi, which means using strength and power to frighten or hurt weaker people. The word "BAgiri" should be taken in a positive connotation.*

HOW TO READ THIS BOOK?

This book offers deep learning about Business Analysis and requires a different approach than reading for leisure. Without your effort and dedication, no learning will be fruitful and complete. Here is how you should read this book:

- **Preview The Book:** Before diving into the book, take a few minutes to preview it. Look at the table of contents, chapter titles, subheadings, and any diagrams or charts. This act will give you a broad idea of what the book covers and help you focus on the most relevant sections to your learning goals.
- **Set Goals:** Set a goal to finish this book within 30 days or determine what you want to learn from the book and set specific goals. Each chapter in this book offers practical scenarios and concepts about Business analysis. Plan and set goals to study and learn from each of those.
- **Take Notes:** Read ONE chapter a day. Take notes on key concepts, ideas, and terms as you read. This act will help you retain the information and provide a reference for future learning. Use a notebook or a note-taking app to organize your notes.
- **Highlight And Underline:** Use a highlighter or underline essential passages and sentences. This will help you focus on the most critical info and make it easier to review later.
- **Practice What You Learn:** Learning something new requires practice. As you read, look for opportunities to apply the concepts and skills you are learning while you perform your job.
- **Review & Answer Questions:** After finishing a chapter or section, take a few minutes to review what you have learned. This act will help reinforce the information and make it easier to recall later. At the end of each chapter, there are a set of questions. Try to write answers to those questions in a notebook. This act will help you absorb the concept and prepare yourself for interviews.
- **Take Breaks:** Reading a book about learning can be mentally taxing. Take breaks when needed to rest your mind and avoid burnout.

All The Best!

CHAPTER 1

WHO IS THE REAL CAPTAIN?

- *Who Is a Business Analyst (BA)?*
- *Role of A BA In a Project Team?*
- *Why BA Role Is Still Relevant?*

In project management, the role of a Project Manager/Program Manager is often compared to that of a **Captain of the Ship**. The Project Manager is entrusted with the overall responsibility of planning, organizing, and directing the successful completion of specific projects for an organization. They are accountable for ensuring these projects are executed within the designated timeframe, allocated budget, and defined scope. Essentially, the Project Manager assumes complete ownership of the project's delivery.

On the other hand, the BA plays a crucial role in driving and controlling the deliverables of a project—analysis, scope, requirements, design, testing, demo and more, in alignment with the stakeholders' expectations. The BA is responsible for collaborating with customers and the project team to ensure that the delivery aligns seamlessly with the defined requirements and maintains an unwavering commitment to quality. In some instances, the BA may unofficially assume the role of a Project Manager if needed, demonstrating the breadth of power and skill sets they possess.

Thus, the BA can be considered the actual or "**The Real Captain**", assisting the official Captain (the Project Manager/Program Manager) in steering the project towards success—yes, you heard it right, the BA, in a way, assumes complete ownership of the project's "success".

Who is a BA?

I have been practising business analysis for over 19+ years. If I ask my project teammates or colleagues about what I do, they'll say, "I am the person who bridges the gap between business & developers". If I ask my mentees in my organisation who just joined the IT workforce, they say, "I create Requirements by working with Customers". If I ask my parents or in-laws, they will tell me, "I create software".

Look at how each of them views my job and role. While they are accurate regarding my responsibilities as a BA, there is a deeper dimension to it. The part of a BA is always confusing because they are famous for multitasking. Some people see them as custodians of requirements, some as custodians of scope, and some as a person who is the real captain helping the official captain of the project—the Project Manager.

From a technical standpoint, a BA performs business analysis duties, which include comprehending customer requirements and aiding in their fulfilment. The primary function of a BA is to structure, categorise, and strategise requirements to ensure successful project delivery.

In the context of an IT project, BAs assume responsibility for unearthing, synthesising, and analysing the essential information needed. They elicit the genuine needs of stakeholders, often involving thorough investigation and clarification of their expressed desires to identify underlying issues and root causes. Additionally, BAs are vital in aligning designed and implemented solutions with the stakeholders' specific requirements.

BAs are vital communicators and facilitators in projects, responsible for gathering and conveying requirements to the technical team amid vast amounts of information. This role is crucial but comes with unique challenges that BAs should be aware of and overcome. Understanding these pitfalls helps BAs address them effectively.

The primary contribution of BAs is to spare organisations from difficulties arising due to poorly implemented strategic decisions and project deliveries. They achieve this by producing precise requirements based on various business scenarios, defining implementation scopes for each release, and conducting testing to deliver the captured requirements successfully. Accomplishing these tasks demands extensive planning and adaptability, which we will explore in subsequent chapters.

In essence, a BA is an individual who assists businesses in analysing their processes, products, services, and systems to improve existing processes or implement new processes and make informed decisions based on business requirements insights backed by data. BAs also aid organisations in documenting business processes by evaluating the business model and its integration with technology.

What is Business Analysis Really?

If you go back to history (Search Online), as per the information available in the public domain, Business Analysis has a long-standing history, dating back to the 1940s when the first programmable computer emerged. During that time, computer systems were primarily used by government entities, universities, and the organisations that pioneered them. However, these systems were inefficient, and data storage posed challenges due to its significant space requirements.

Inevitably, a change occurred. In the early 1990s, there was a rapid surge in the need to incorporate IT into businesses. Enhancements in data storage, user-friendly programs, and interfaces emerged. Consequently, the demand for software programmers increased substantially. While the value of technology became apparent, significant amounts of money were being spent on software rewrites, updates to meet business needs, maintenance costs, and resolving software defects.

Despite the expertise possessed by business users and programmers in their respective domains, effective communication between them proved difficult. Business users struggled to articulate their needs in technical language, while programmers faced challenges in interpreting the business users' requirements and this gave rise to the field of Business Analysis.

In the 1980s, as computers became prevalent, companies began converting paper-based processes into automated electronic processes. BAs entered the scene during the early 1990s to combine this emerging technology with business acumen.

So, what does Business Analysis entail in an IT project context? It involves analysing current systems and processes within an organisation, enabling change, and planning for new and efficient processes that leverage the latest technologies. Through Business Analysis, an organisation can precisely articulate its needs and subsequently design and develop solutions that fulfil those needs.

In simple terms, the Business Analysis process is employed during the development or updating of computer systems to address an organisation's business requirements. The BA captures these requirements accurately and works collaboratively with the IT or project team to implement the new system while supporting testing and system implementation.

What Does A BA Do?

Imagine you are visiting a Tailor shop. You tell him your requirements. He clarifies, confirms your requirements, takes proper measurements, and notes them. Here, the tailor is doing a kind of BA job. You are, of course, his customer. Now, if the tailor delivers what you want, you'll be happy and happily wear his stitched shirt/dress. If not, I don't need to explain any further! That's why a BA's role is crucial in any IT Project.

To further illustrate, imagine you are an entrepreneur building a mobile app, such as a Grocery ordering App. How would you convey your requirements to a developer? This is where Business Analysis comes into play: understanding, analysing, and accurately capturing the needs, developing and implementing a suitable solution. Initially, it may seem complex, but it becomes more straightforward once mastered.

So, in a nutshell, what BA does & should do in a Project is as below:

Discover the Business Needs/Problems → Understand Current State & Future State → Identify & Define Scope → Define Require ments → Support Design/Dev/ Testing & Deployment → Asses the Value

In simple terms, a BA is a bridge between the business users and the technical IT people within the project and customer team.

The key activities that a BA performs are:

- Understanding Organization's pain points, Vision & Mission
- Capturing the Requirements in a Crystal-Clear manner
- Define a clear project Scope & Scope Management
- Facilitate System Integration testing, User Acceptance & other Testing as required
- Work with Customers & Project team for Solution design
- Work with Customers & Project team for implementation
- Stakeholder Management
- Collaborating on Change Management

To do the above, the BAs should possess a great degree of soft skills including communication, facilitation, and strategic thinking as well as a set of hard skills including ability to understand the business dynamics (business acumen), data analysis, technical diagramming, and technical design.

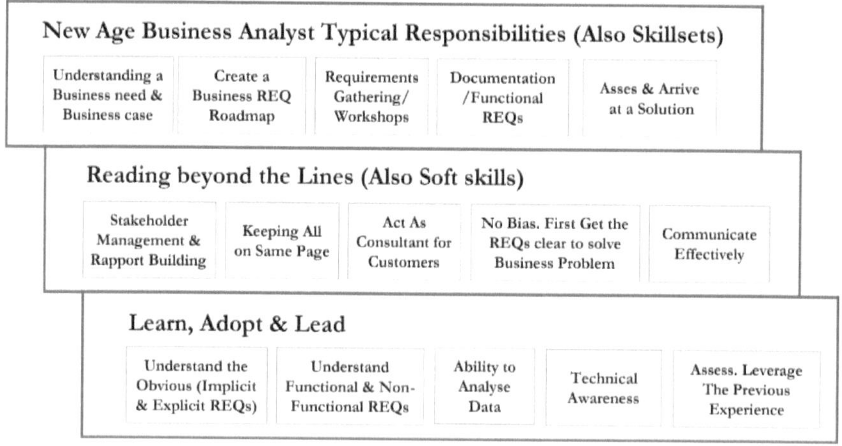

[REQs =Requirements]

Above all, he/she needs to have common sense and an ability to work with the required team to get the job done—In many areas a BA's job is more of taking ownership than personally doing the tasks on his/her own. Ex: The technical design responsibility may sometimes lie with the BA, although the Technical Lead or Team handles the delivery. The BA ensures the technical design aligns precisely with the specified requirements.

What's in A Name?

The designation "Business Analyst (BA)" has gained immense popularity in the last two decades. BAs are also now present in every department of every organization, serving as moderators, communicators, contributors, analysts, and more. Their role is crucial in ensuring the smooth functioning of other departments.

It is very interesting to note that a BA has several names. People gave him/her several titles. They are also called analysts, Systems Analysts, Business Architects, Enterprise analysts, Management consultants, Process analysts, Product owners (as sometimes he becomes a dummy Product owner), Requirements engineers and others.

In some cases, we also get to see Technical BAs, in a Project, who usually perform technical activities. A Technical BA (This person is sometimes called a Solution Architect/Technical Architect) is one such role that analyses system and enterprise architecture. They interpret the technical model and information; and know to develop an improved model whenever a requirement arises. It, however, is not necessary for them to be able to design the models themselves. All they need is knowledge of system architecture.

Usually, nowadays, a Technical Architect does all the above tasks. Hence, the "Technical Business Analyst" role is becoming extinct in IT. However, an awareness of technical aspects is important for a BA.

People are often confused with the two popular roles: BA and Consultant. However, please note there is a subtle difference between a BA and a Consultant.

A BA mostly works for a Project. Hence, he/she will be responsible for finding the root cause of the problem, which has led to the beginning of the project he/she is working for. A BA's knowledge may be limited to a certain technology or maybe not.

In a nutshell, a BA will analyse the problem → if required analyse the current state & Future state analysis →Work with customer to elicit requirements → Understand the Requirements → Work with internal technical teams → Suggest a best possible solution (if customer is not already sure of that) → Control/Manage the scope → Thus acts as Gatekeeper (for requirements) so that only scoped requirements are delivered (as much as possible!!).

However, consultant (or a management consultant) is one level above. He/she may not work for a project. He may be an influencer for a project that may begin in future. When a customer has an issue in certain area and customers are not sure about what to do—that's where consultant comes into the picture. His audience mostly also involves C-level executives. So, a consultant will listen to the problem → Analyses the problems using various tools and data to suggest a Process improvement, if required→ Suggests process improvement→May or may not suggest a Product/technology for that improvement → Suggests an overall measure to overcome the problem and hence improve the overall business performance, leading to an improvement in bottom line.

Though it sounds BA and Consultant are two jobs that are kind of similar with overlapping skillsets, functions, and responsibility, they are different. Typically, a BA is more of a business/ technical/product expert who uses certain techniques and tools to do his/her job while a consultant is more of an industry/financial/process/business and best practices expert who suggests the best strategy or way forward for an organization.

Certainly, A BA also can play the role of a consultant (Provided he/she has that wide experience to be a consultant), and consultant can also play the role of a BA too (provided the consultant possesses required Business Analysis skills and tools).

Where A BA Stands?

Being in a crucial role, we need to understand where the BA stands in a typical organizational structure. Look at the organization structure below.

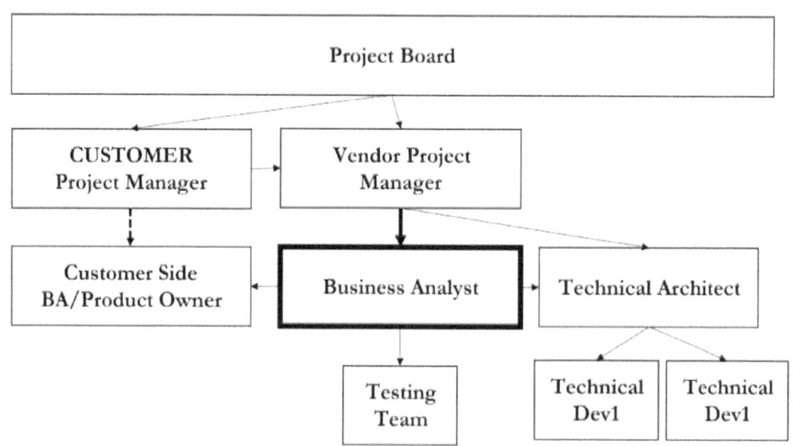

Normally, a BA will report to the Project Manager or in some cases, BA himself/herself will be doing the duties of Project Manager as well as Technical Architect (This usually happens in smaller projects, not in large projects).

Typically, a Project Board is led by top management representatives from both the Customer and Vendor sides. For instance, if BMW is the customer, and Infosys serves as the vendor responsible for executing their IT projects. The entire project team reports to this Project Board. In most cases, a project will have one or two Project Managers—one from the Customer side and one from the Vendor side. Similarly, there might be two Business Analysts assigned to the project—one from the Customer side (often serving as a consultant or Product Owner) and one from the Vendor side.

Typically, the Customer side BA will work with Vendor side BA (Who could be a Product Owner too) for requirements and its management. Vendor side BA (Who could be a proxy Product Owner in the absence of Customer side BA) usually will take help from Customer side BA in terms of requirements/product backlog and to get all required support from the customer for the smooth execution of project requirements.

Why A BA is Important for a Project?

Often, people think that a BA's role ends after requirement elicitation and documentation. However, this is untrue.

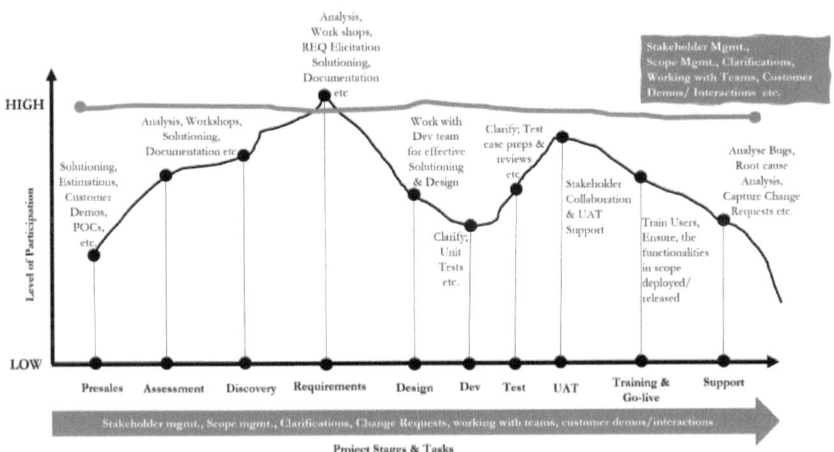

If you observe the diagram above, which illustrates the various typical stages of a project and tasks involved, you'll notice that a BA is involved in all of these activities—although the level of participation varies in each stage.

Whether the project is being delivered in a Waterfall or Agile way, the presence of a BA in a project is always important. The BA is a Full-time Employee in a Project. In addition to the scheduled activities during project stages, such as Requirements, Design, Testing UAT, etc., a BA has a handful of responsibilities for the entire project duration.

These responsibilities include stakeholder management, scope management, clarification sessions with customers and development teams, unit testing, handling change requests, scope management, customer demos/interactions, and many other tasks.

Hence, the project team benefits from the involvement of the BA in various ways. Firstly, the BA enhances the overall quality of work within the team. This enables team members to concentrate on their particular tasks and the technical aspects of the project.

The BA effectively communicates the project assumptions, providing clear and concise explanations and addressing any questions related to the tasks at hand. Additionally, the BA plays a crucial role in ensuring that the delivered solution perfectly aligns with the business requirements and project objectives, thereby supporting the verification process.

So, it is important to note that the BA's involvement extends beyond providing substantive consultations, which are typically part of project work. As stated earlier, the BA often acts as a liaison between the dev team and the customer, facilitating effective communication and collaboration.

Furthermore, the BA builds relationships within the project team, with stakeholders, within the IT department, and between the business and IT. These positive relationships contribute not only to efficient project management but also to the day-to-day work dynamics.

Why the BA Role is Still Relevant?

In agile software implementation, there is a perception that Business Analysis might not have a place anymore. Some suggest that BAs are no longer necessary, as their role primarily involves documenting requirements and bridging the gap between businesses and developers. The Agile Manifesto, which prioritizes working software over extensive documentation, influences this perception.

However, Agile principles also emphasize the importance of daily collaboration between business people and developers, favouring face-to-face communication as the most effective means of sharing information. Given this perspective, it is clear that even BAs' responsibilities align with agile values.

Reflecting on these points, examining the value that BAs bring to the agile context becomes crucial. Can a team implement changes faster without the presence of BAs? Are there specific burdens that BAs could shed to enhance agility? Are there new techniques or approaches that BAs should adopt to keep pace with the dynamic nature of agile?

Let's understand and assess the core activities of BAs. By eliciting information from multiple stakeholders and transforming it effectively, BAs enable change and deliver value to stakeholders. While the most tangible outcome is the creation of requirements for IT solutions, BAs play a broader role in facilitating efficient communication and collaboration within the team. In essence, it is the BA who faces the customer. The BA works with various stakeholders while allowing the technical team to do their work peacefully.

The International Institute of Business Analysis (IIBA) defines Business Analysis as facilitating change within an enterprise by identifying needs and recommending value-driven solutions for stakeholders. In simpler terms, BAs gather extensive information from various stakeholders and transform it into a usable format for the rest of the team. The tangible outcome of this process is a set of requirements that serve as the foundation for developers to 'create/develop' the IT solution.

Now, let's understand two major methodologies used in the delivery of projects—Waterfall and agile. As you may know, in the age-old Waterfall, the requirements are defined initially, before implementation even starts—see the picture below.

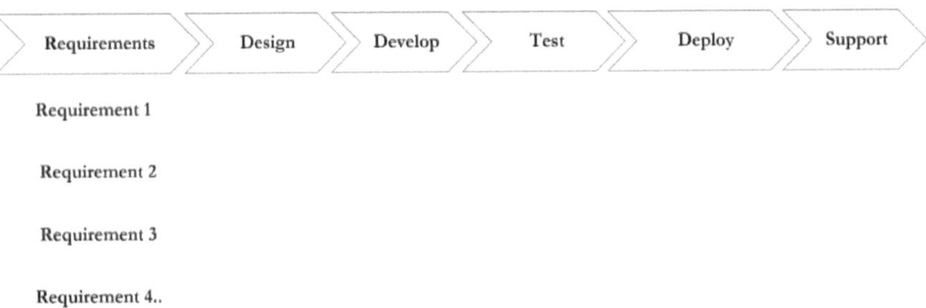

In the modern agile inspired approach (Let's take an example of SCRUM here), requirements are continuously defined and refined to enable short and rapid delivery cycles (Ex: Sprints). The primary objective is to collect feedback after each cycle, and adopt it subsequently. This iterative process allows for adjustments to be made to the requirements for subsequent cycles, ensuring a focus on delivering value and achieving desired outcomes. See the picture below:

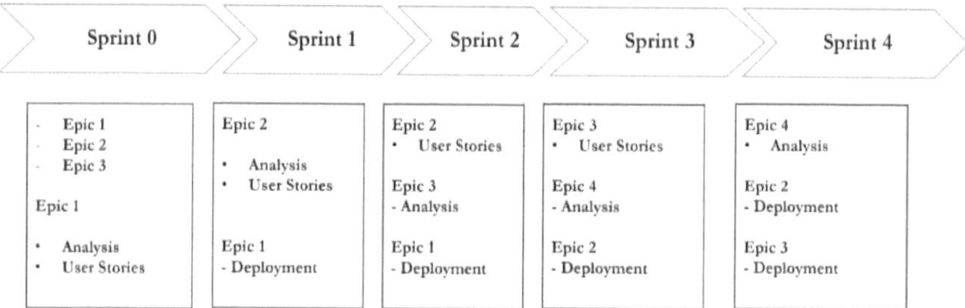

Agile methodology also has pain points when not done correctly, such as unclear requirements, the team struggling with obstacles, underwhelming delivery due to insufficiently refined product backlog items, and a lack of clarity of requirements for development. And this is exactly where BAs can contribute; that's what their role is all about. That is why the role of "BA" is also still relevant in agile teams.

However, how an agile BA should work could be different in an agile setup. In Agile, when BAs adhere to traditional practices, there can be various possibilities:

- **Over-analysis**
- **Implementation of unnecessary elements**
- **Underutilization of implemented features due to changing business needs**
- **Producing copious amounts of documentation that quickly becomes outdated**
- **Engaging in predominantly individual work. Agile is all about collaboration**
- **Focusing on solutions or features without fully understanding user needs**

Hence, as a BA, he/she should adopt the skills to suit Agile needs. We will discuss those in upcoming chapters. In this new way of working (Agile), BAs cannot solely concern themselves with how requirements align with the final solution.

As part of agile or SCRUM teams, a BA should emphasise achieving understanding and fostering collaboration. Agile is all about iteration, incremental delivery and value. This entails comprehending user needs, understanding the scope, and then breaking it down into individual increments for implementation.

Hence, when you are in "Agile", be Agile. Adopt the new approach:

- Produce "just enough" at the appropriate moment.
- Understand the need and ensure shared understanding within the team.
- Collaborate through agile sessions rather than relying on extensive documentation for information exchange.
- Leverage your BA skills, techniques, tools and visual models as per the need to facilitate conversations and enhance clarity.

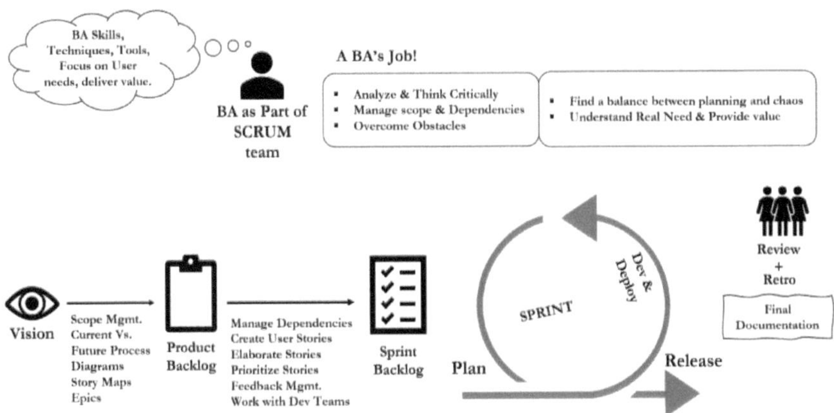

In my opinion, BAs are extremely important no matter how a project is done. BAs do more than just write documents and translate information. They analyze problems, think critically, manage scope and dependencies, overcome obstacles, and find a balance between planning and chaos. Their main goal is to understand what is needed and provide value. BAs should recognize their importance, especially in agile projects where teamwork and organization are key to success.

At the same time, BAs should regularly update their knowledge of Business Analysis and stay informed about new technologies. They should learn new techniques and actively practice their skills. Transformation happens gradually with each passing day, meeting, and modelling session. By staying updated and continuously improving, BAs can adapt to changing needs and deliver better results.

Can BAs maintain the speed as per the new age "Agile" situations?

Certainly, by preventing chaos and contributing their expertise, BAs can increase the overall speed. At certain points, slowing down, assessing the bigger picture, verifying positions, evaluating dependencies, anticipating roadblocks, and determining the correct course is beneficial.

It is a delicate balance. Ultimately, agile is not solely about speed but about providing value, albeit as quickly as possible.

Top 25 Terms a Every BA Must Know!

- **Business goal**—A predetermined target an organisation must meet to achieve its intended vision
- **Stakeholder/User**—Anyone who is part of a project/who may be affected as a result of project execution or a beneficiary who interacts with a solution
- **Business case**—Justification/Reason for initiating a project or program
- **Use case**—A use case is like a sequence of events a system should perform.
- **User story**—User Stories are written from an end-user standpoint
- **Requirement**— In an IT context, a requirement is a functionality a user needs
- **Verified requirement**—A requirement that is unambiguous, complete, correct, and testable
- **Validation**—Check whether the defined requirements meet customer and business needs.
- **Validated Requirement**—A requirement that meets user needs & delivered business objectives
- **Elicitation**—Process steps to get info/requirements from stakeholders/users
- **Scope**—Set of specific project goals, deliverables, tasks, and requirements that will be a part of the project as agreed by all the stakeholders
- **Change Request**— Request for an alteration to an already developed product functionality based on previously agreed upon requirement
- **Requirements traceability**—The requirement Traceability matrix is used to map the journey of a requirement till its implementation
- **Requirements management**—Process of analysing, documenting, tracing, prioritising, validating & controlling change, and communicating to stakeholders/users
- **Process analysis**—Technique used to assess the effectiveness of a process to come up with a possible improvement
- **Prioritisation**—Organise requirements so that the most important thing is done first
- **Functional requirements**—Description of Requirements that a solution should offer as expected by its users

- **Non-functional requirement—**Constraints/Requirements imposed on the system to enhance the solution's functional requirements
- **Estimation—**Technique used to arrive at an effort required to complete a task or a project.
- **Current Vs. Future State**—Present set of circumstances | Visualisation of the desired future state
- **Assumption**—A belief based on which a requirement or solution is created/designed
- **Change Management**—A systematic approach to deal with transition/transformation
- **Business Constraint**—A business situation/event that prevents the full delivery of a project
- **Variance**— [Expected outcome – Actual outcome]
- **Model/Wireframe**—Visual representation of a topic, process, or requirement

Bonus:

- **Workshop—**Well-structured meeting, guided by a facilitator, to perform elicitation, define and refine requirements
- **Active or Attentive listening—**Act of listening and interpreting what the other person is saying – which facilitates the mutual understanding
- **Project Sponsor—**A stakeholder guiding a project or product
- **Business problem—**Either market, organisational, or managerial challenges that a business face
- **Unified modelling language (UML)—**UML is a versatile visual modelling language designed to offer a standardised method for visually representing the design of a system.

What did You Learn in this Chapter?

- What are the roles played by a BA?
- Why a BA is important in an Agile Project?
- What is the difference between a BA & a consultant?
- Who is according to you the "Real Captain of the Project"?
- Why A BA is important for a Project?

CHAPTER 2

THE RIGHT BA MINDSET

- *The Right BA Mindset Challenge*
- *The BA: The Big Picture Person*
- *Principles of the Right BA Mindset*

What is a Mindset? The Oxford dictionary defines the Mindset as: "the established set of attitudes held by someone". In essence, your mindset defines your mental attitude. It's the way you think. Your mindset constitutes your thoughts and beliefs and determines what and how you focus on.

Indeed, how you think and act matters more than ever before, especially if you want to be a successful BA. The difference between being good and being great depends on your mindset and your skill set. Acquiring a skill is relatively easier than developing a mindset. Though you have the required skillsets, it is your mindset that sets you apart. By cultivating the right habits and mindset, you can demonstrate excellence in every way by utilizing your skills accordingly.

So, what is the right BA mindset? Like whom he/she should think? How should he/she think? How his/her actions should be?

The BIG PICTURE Person

Often, a BA is referred to as the "BIG PICTURE" person due to their unique ability to visualize project needs from a high-level perspective, akin to viewing them from 10,000 feet above, while also being capable of examining them in intricate detail at a micro level. Unlike other roles, being a big picture person requires a distinct "skillset" and the right "mindset" to ensure the successful delivery of expected outcomes.

Let's begin by focusing on skillsets and gradually understanding the importance of mindset. Skillsets serve as the tools that enable you to deliver results, while mindset helps in analysing situations and planning and executing the delivery effectively. For a BA, two critical skillsets are domain understanding and stakeholder management. These skillsets play a significant role in acquiring the right BA mindset.

How does this happen?

By increasing their domain understanding, BAs are able to grasp the broader context surrounding detailed requirements. Consequently, they can apply critical thinking not only to the functional and technical aspects of a functionality but also evaluate whether it adequately addresses the underlying business needs. When combined with improved stakeholder management skills, this empowers BAs to take on a more strategic role in client communication and contribute at a higher level.

What that means is that a BA's job is not just "take order—deliver it" kind of job. It requires an ability to understand the customer's business, what is best for customer's business and how to make those needs technically feasible to deliver, while managing various stakeholders, impediments, and Risks.

When you see this layer of responsibilities, and when you realize that there is no specific way to execute things, certainly possessing a right mindset is essential to execute. That's called a "The Right BA Mindset"—always ready to Analyse the problem → Propose Solution → Execute delivery.

Let me make it even simpler. Let's compare a Software engineer role with BA role in a project. A software engineer will be more technically oriented and will always think about how he can develop the logic technically, to develop a certain requirement. Whereas a BA needs Business, Functional, and a hint of technical consulting skills to grasp requirements from multiple angles and understand underlying business needs.

The BA also plays a crucial role in developing the logic in collaboration with technical team. Generally, a BA will look at the problem or solution from all aspects of the Product development (Project Implementation/Requirement fulfilment) life cycle, whereas the software engineer will most probably be taking care of coding/development, unit testing and some technical documentation, if required.

It is certainly true that a BA can make or break the system. Imagine a BA, captures a requirement wrongly and communicates the same to Developer and developer develops the system accordingly. What will happen? Obviously, the developed system will not meet the customer requirement. Hence it is imperative that a BA should have a multi-dimensional thinking capability as his/her work involves dealing with entire project organization structure—entire Project team including stakeholders at all levels.

In simple terms, the BA is involved in multiple things, which include understanding business needs, converting them into requirements, and collaborating with the technical team for solutions. A BA collaborates extensively with the Project Manager and team to define and manage scope, monitor risks, test and demo requirements, maintain traceability, assist testers, train end-users, and support the Change Management team.

While the BA does all of these, it is very important for him/her to always maintain a cordial relationship or rapport with customer and the project team. Just imagine the multi-faceted responsibilities a BA has! And this list is not exhaustive.

Certainly, a BA must have a "self-starter" and a "go-getter" mindset. It's all about taking ownership by leading & running the show to identify solutions for business problems while involving and collaborating with stakeholders involved in a project. You need gain the confidence of everyone.

Remember, a BA with the right mindset resembles a leader who possesses a clear understanding of what is correct, consistently takes appropriate actions, communicates effectively, remains unafraid of making mistakes and taking calculated risks. Efficiently managing risks allows them to handle mistakes effectively.

If you are just starting out, all these jargons and expectations could be overwhelming. However, with calm and firm mind, this is achievable—the right BA Mindset. If one learns to set a process for each aspect of the responsibility, the job will become quite easier.

Now, let's learn to develop the right mindset by understanding various practical situations[1]. What is important to know is that one cannot develop the "the Right BA Mindset" using tools or techniques. This comes by practice, experience, and eagerness to do the right things and finding a solution that makes sense as part of the big picture for his/her customer.

Simply put, "common sense" is essential to develop the right BA Mindset.

If you observe the successful people—be it in business, career or anything, they have that "common sense". Common sense refers to practical knowledge and reasoning applied to everyday situations.

To cultivate common sense, observe and learn from your surroundings, seek diverse experiences, think critically, reflect on past experiences, and learn from mistakes. Engage in active observation, broaden perspectives, and use practical wisdom to make informed decisions.

Most important of all, the kind of mindset a BA should possess or should develop is that—a mindset to think and adopt to a situation. A mindset of

[1] Please note that you may feel that some topics and scenarios described are repeated across the book. This is intentional because repetition makes learning more effective.

always being ready to solve the problem! That is what makes a BA's job exceptional.

The Mindset Challenge

How can a BA develop an exceptional 'Mindset'? How do BAs handle challenging problems, difficult customers, and stakeholders? Why do some BAs navigate complex situations effortlessly while others feel intimidated?

Books and courses may teach you tools and techniques, even guiding you on how to develop the "Mindset." However, in the end, it is "you" who need to put in the real effort. That effort begins with delving into the human side of business problems, recognizing that customers and problems are inherently human creations.

The right BA mindset goes beyond techniques or toolkits; it is akin to a code of ethics, being passionate not just about doing things right, but about doing the right things. It involves seeking solutions that align with the big picture, solving business problems, and driving changes that help the client or organization achieve strategic goals. It requires looking beyond politics, individual viewpoints, and departmental agendas, understanding clients, users, and stakeholders, and working with them to bring about positive change.

The right BA mindset is about determining the right course of action, not merely following explicit directions. It involves questioning, analysing with passion, and an innate drive to understand and improve efficiency. It means seeing what makes sense, even if you stand alone in your perspective. It's about embracing being different and standing out without fear.

Let's explore some common scenarios BAs encounter and how they should approach them with the "Right BA Mindset".

Scenario: BA is forced to document as per stakeholders wishes

What is the Problem for a BA here? The perception that a BA role is solely to document requirements provided by the business is a significant issue. This misconception is risky and undermines the value of business analysis.

How can a BA, possessing the right mindset, manage such a situation? They should start by establishing transparent stakeholder expectations regarding the objectives and process of business analysis. Educating stakeholders on the significance of information gathering, current state analysis, and requirement definition as the outcomes of analysis activities is crucial. To foster successful collaboration, BAs must emphasize that their role goes beyond documentation to primarily focus on analysis. Taking a firm stance and asserting the value of their analytical contributions is essential. It is important to remember that BAs are not mere order takers.

Scenario: Unreasonable request from a powerful stakeholder

What is the challenge for a BA? Managing influential stakeholders, especially when lacking access or communication to question or challenge their requests.

How should a BA with the right mindset handle this situation? In such cases, the BA should consider that the request may be a result of misunderstanding or misinterpretation. Politely seeking clarification and rationale usually helps. If necessary, the BA can facilitate communication or establish a new line of contact. Persistence and understanding the underlying reasons behind the requirements are crucial. This justifies having a conversation with the stakeholder to foster shared understanding and find the best solution. Additionally, involving PMO and management can be helpful, seeking support from higher-ups if needed.

Scenario: Dealing with disagreements among key individuals

The challenging situation arises when important individuals/stakeholders disagree, and the side with more power prevails despite having a weak argument. Challenging authority can be intimidating, and acting as a referee between conflicting parties can be emotionally draining for a BA.

How should a BA with the right BA mindset handle this situation? A BA with the right mindset should perceive this as an opportunity to improve negotiation and leadership skills. While complete agreement might not be achievable, the BA should aim to find common ground on project-specific matters. Making decisions based on factual analysis and real business data to validate assumptions is crucial. Objectively assessing pros and cons helps avoid biased choices. Diplomacy, assertiveness, and objectivity remain essential, even in high-pressure situations.

In summary, the "right BA mindset" refers to a way of seeing, thinking, and reasoning that enables BAs to perform their best in analysing, resolving business problems and delivering value.

Principles of the Right BA Mindset

The right BA mindset is centred on understanding and solving business problems effectively. It involves being diplomatic, assertive, and objective, while handling disagreements among key stakeholders. BAs focus on finding common ground, making decisions based on factual analysis, and avoiding biased choices to ensure successful project outcomes. Here are the principles you should keep in mind while you develop the right BA mindset.

Understand Business and Focus on Business Needs: The right BA mindset must emphasize a deep understanding of the business context and its specific needs. BAs must prioritize on gaining insights into the underlying requirements and challenges faced by the organization or clients/stakeholders. By focusing on the core business objectives, BAs can align their efforts to deliver valuable solutions that address real business problems effectively.

Get to the Business Problem first: Solving problems is a key role for BAs. However, it is important to recognize that the issues presented to you might be symptoms or pain points rather than the actual problem. Before attempting a solution, invest effort in understanding the true problem. Analyze, investigate, and break down the problem into its root causes. By asking "why?" repeatedly, you can uncover the genuine problem and apply your BA mindset to solve it effectively.

Ensure the solution is aligned to the business needs: BAs carry the responsibility of solution design. Despite accurately capturing requirements, there is always a risk of misinterpretation by the technical team and hence BAs must collaborate closely with the solution design team and customers to ensure that the design aligns with the captured requirements. Maintain a requirement traceability matrix to track the progression of each requirement throughout its implementation.

Think Independently: BAs must possess independent thinking skills. Evaluate, categorize, establish relationships, and compare information from various sources. Recognize and discard irrelevant information while exploring hidden but relevant insights. Instead of accepting information at face value, think critically and consider alternative explanations. Analyze the bigger picture and encourage the team to think independently.

Don't Afraid to Ask questions: Asking questions is foundational to business analysis. Use questions to gain knowledge, investigate, and comprehend complex situations. Instead of making assumptions, rely on questioning. Your ability to ask the right questions significantly impacts the success of any change. Even the unasked questions can hold significant importance, potentially altering the project's course. Keep asking questions until you and the customer are aligned and have a comprehensive understanding of the requirements.

Start Owning things: As a BA, take responsibility for managing relationships, clarifying expectations, and ensuring effective communication. Assume leadership roles in planning and leading requirements analysis processes, organizing diverse groups, and preparing business units for upcoming changes. Embrace the accountability associated with being a BA and adapt to the various responsibilities that come with the role.

Manage Shared Responsibilities: Conduct knowledge-sharing sessions to ensure everyone is informed of significant developments while maintaining a degree of abstraction. Assign clear owners and decision-makers for each task to avoid bottlenecks. As a BA, act as a coach and facilitate a smooth transition process.

Drive Change: Change management is a significant risk in any project. BAs should take the initiative in driving change management activities. Take a lead in bringing together all change management stakeholders and work towards achieving successful outcomes. Collaborate with Change Management teams, customers, project managers, and other stakeholders to develop comprehensive change strategies.

5 Tips to develop an effective Strategic Mindset—

1. **Big Picture:** Look beyond your project and understand how it contributes to the overall success of the organization. Ask yourself why you're doing something and justify it.
2. **Get out of the usual pattern:** Thinking strategically often requires being innovative and thinking outside of familiar patterns.
3. **Ask tough questions:** Even though they may bring uncertainty and confusion, they are necessary to find better solutions that will make the project or organization more sustainable. Asking questions helps prevent narrow thinking and encourages seeing the organization as a whole system, rather than just one part.
4. **Understand overall industry trends:** Learn about and understand trends outside of your project. Some industry standards and best practices can be customized to fit your project and contribute to its success.
5. **Focus on you, always:** Improve your presentation skills. Learn to present your ideas in a clear and organized way. When you communicate and present innovative ideas effectively, it helps your customers and they will appreciate you for it.

The BA and the Entrepreneurial Mindset

A BA and an entrepreneur exhibit identical mindset. Do you Agree?

As far as I understand, the BA is almost like an entrepreneur. If you dig the mindset of an entrepreneur, deep down, he/she is a BA. They both possess same skills in varying degrees. The only difference I could see is, the BA is working for someone as an employee/freelancer, whereas Entrepreneur has invested some financial capital into his/her business.

The logic here is simple. What does a BA do? What does an entrepreneur do?

They both identify a problem first. They find a solution to the problem. While a BA/Consultant solves his/her customer's problem, an entrepreneur finds a business opportunity in the problem he/she is solving. While solving the problem, an entrepreneur leverages his/her skills to utilize the existing resources to market and sell the solution.

Hence, if you want to be an entrepreneur, you should possess the right mindset—ability to identify, analyse and solve the problem by providing relevant solutions. Again, this applies to BA profession too!

Every BA may not have such mindset initially. However, such mindset can be developed. It will require a bit of behavioural change. That is, the way you look into a situation, or a problem will require a change. How?

Do you have an "Achievement" oriented mindset? Do you always dream of "I want to achieve something?"

Not Just dreaming – do you also have a determination to prepare for that achievement? Are you ready to take up pain of obstacles that may come in your way? Will you be able to own and take accountability for your decisions? Can you prioritise what needs to be done first and what next? If required, can you go and talk to anyone to get your issues resolved? Are you ready to take at least some calculated risks?

If yes, you are well equipped from a "mindset" standpoint. If no, you need to work on these aspects. How?

- ✈ Look, all of these are about "mindset". Hence, we should get ready within our minds first. We should get organized first on what to do—which involves identifying, planning, and prioritizing tasks, mentally rehearsing the future negative situations, hurdles, and strategies to address such hurdles (Plan A/Plan B/Plan C…) etc.

- Just think that you need to execute a task and to do that you need to figure out a way. Leaning on colleagues for help for every small task will not work. That's how you can begin—learn to figure out things (solve problems) on your own. Being focussed on one task at a time—for effective planning and execution.

- Being "positive": If you are positive, all people working with you will be positive. Being positive and calm always attracts positivity.

Developing That BA's Thick Skin

It is crucial for a BA to develop a thick skin to handle external criticisms effectively. Without this resilience, they may find themselves overreacting to minor situations, such as receiving feedback from stakeholders or facing uncooperative behaviour. In such instances, maintaining a mindset of indifference, thinking calmly, and devising suitable strategies to handle stakeholders becomes extremely important for a BA.

Do you possess a resilient attitude?

If not, it is advisable to cultivate one, especially if you are a BA or aspire to pursue a career in Business Analysis. Similar to life, a Business Analysis career is akin to a roller coaster ride, filled with unforeseen and unpredictable situations.

As you are aware, being a BA entails comprehending the current situation, empathizing with stakeholders to understand their pain points, needs, business requirements, and providing solutions to address their issues. Being the owner of Project requirements and stakeholder communications, primarily, you should be ready to shoulder the blame if something goes wrong and also be open to receiving compliments when everything goes well. Developing a thick skin is beneficial, regardless of whether the situations are positive or negative. Being immune to both good and bad circumstances is always advantageous. Most importantly it will help your mind to keep calm and think about coming out of such situations.

Is managing customer feedback making you anxious? Then probably you need to face it. Get that damn feedback. If there is negative feedback or any improvements suggested—act on it. It will be a learning experience for you.

If you have concerns about a difficult stakeholder or find yourself puzzled by a particular approach suggested by a stakeholder, handle these situations in a different manner. Schedule a one-on-one meeting with the stakeholder to discuss and explain your viewpoint. Additionally, bring up the matter in larger forums for further discussion. Your goal should be to reach an optimal solution that aligns with the business needs. As a BA, it is important not to be swayed solely by someone's opinions. Ensure that any solution you propose is backed by valid logic. As a BA you should be open, and there should be no ego.

For a BA, self-introspection is essential. It goes beyond merely fulfilling responsibilities, which are, in any case, expected. Instead, focus on delivering genuine value to your customers.

Every now and then, step out of your comfort zone, and without a thick skin, you'll only stay in the safe zone. Always, strive to expand yourself to grow further. Never settle.

Top 5 Myths About BA Job!

BAs Are Just Proxy Project Managers: Not true. I agree some projects have BAs who handle Project Manager responsibilities too. But that does not mean that BA and Project Manager roles are same, and BA is just a proxy Project Manager. A BA is responsible for understanding the business need and hence come up with relevant requirements and solutions for the same in collaboration with stakeholders. A BA is responsible for managing the scope, working with technical and testing teams too. Whereas a Project Manager is responsible for the execution of a Project in terms of timeline, scope, resources, and budget.

BAs Do Not Need People Skills: This is an absurd notion. Business analysis is a mindset. A BA needs to interact with stakeholders and hence requires all the skills to extract required information from them, be it Interviewing, Listening, analysis etc. In addition, a BA needs a skill to build that rapport with a stakeholder. Once the requirements are drafted a BA should closely work with his/her dev team to get the output as per the requirement. In addition, a BA needs to interact with many external team members, management and more. In a way they are entrepreneurs.

BAs Are Not Required During Dev & Go-Live Stage: It may appear like a BA might be less loaded during a dev and deployment stage of any project or teams (Waterfall or SCRUM or Agile), but he/she will be busy with several other activities. He/she will be constantly working with dev teams to ensure a quality deliverable as per the requirements. A works with testing team during QA stage and business users during UAT and ensures the team involved in testing understands the intended requirements and its development correctly. During deployment, it is generally the BA who works with deployment team to prepare deployment documents, strategy in collaboration with technical team. The BA leads resolution of any bugs/issues post deployment and during warranty phase.

BAs Should Be Technically Strong: This is wrong perception. Even customers get confused with the role, sometimes. If you have a technical background and know some basics of SQL etc., it "may" help. However, technical or developer skills are not at all necessary for a BA. A BA should know about design of functional architecture of a system, how a system works and how a logic behind a program or workflow works. Above all, a BA should be thinking about business needs and problems that need to be addressed and come up with an efficient solution for the problem.

BAs Are Just Requirements Writers: While writing Requirements is one of the key jobs the BAs do, it's NOT just that. Even if it is, do you think writing a document is an easy job? Without a skill you cannot even write a single sentence which will be understood by all. A lot of analysis, interactions and hard work goes into that documentation. In addition, a BA does many activities as already described above.

Living with Uncertainty and Ambiguity

I am, not a Guru. I am not quoting any Gurus here.

However, what I have realized and is a common fact is that our life is mortal. When our life is mortal, should we really worry about uncertainty, ambiguity, and failures of life/work/our projects?

That's the mindset a BA should cultivate.

Of course, you must take care of any issues or problems within a project, including in your life. No one else will do it for you. However, there is no point in living life or working on a project and always worrying about something, right? I agree it's tricky to live with uncertainties and ambiguities. However, somewhere we must make peace.

In a project, sometimes, all is going well, customers are happy, and developers are happy. All look happy…happy. That's when usually I start getting that feeling—is it a kind of lull before the storm?

Unfortunately, the BA role itself is full of uncertainties. Anything can change in a Project at any time, despite a solid risk mitigation plan, Change request procedures, and more.

Based on my experience, cultivating the "mortal" mindset has helped me a lot. In my view, BAs should approach failure with a growth mindset, recognizing that it is a natural part of the process and an opportunity to learn and improve.

Mistakes happen! And it is unrealistic to expect that your initial requirements documents, mock-ups, or use cases will be perfect on the first or even 10th attempt. However, instead of giving up when things don't go as planned, BAs should embrace the opportunity to understand their customers' needs better and strive to deliver the actual needs of the customer.

At ground level, BAs should have this goal in their mind. Never ever, give up.

This "never give up" until you deliver attitude comes only when you are internally calm. When you are internally calm, it is easy to manage uncertainty, ambiguity, etc. To maintain that internal calmness, the "Mortal" concept really helps. It really helped me, without a doubt.

Criticism is one of the most important things which many BAs are unable to handle. First off, why criticism comes? When there is ample area for improvement in your work, or there is some mistake or any gap that need to be filled, correct? (Leave aside criticisms that come due to internal politics!!).
So, why there is a mistake or gap or still room for improvement? Perhaps, in that situation and at that point of time (obviously which might ambiguous or uncertain) you could only come up with only that much. You know this. Then, why worry about criticism?

So, if something has to be changed, some feedback needs to be included, include it. What's wrong in it?

Do you know what great leaders think? The leaders or experienced BAs who are skilled at managing uncertainty or ambiguity, recognize that mistakes are inevitable in complex and uncertain situations, but they see failure as a chance to learn from the experience. By being open to making mistakes and viewing criticism as an opportunity for learning, BAs can develop their skills to live with uncertainty or ambiguity.

Making Peace with Situations

Sometimes, things can get really tough, and no matter what you try, it might not work out. Just like life has its ups and downs, a project can have tough times and regular times. But no matter what, it's important to keep your mind in a good place. This is the most important quality a business analyst should have. Over time, I've found that if we let stress get to us, think negatively, and don't try our hardest to fix things, we can end up in even worse situations. Here are the top 4 things you should always keep in mind to make peace with situations.

- Be Honest and Straightforward
- Be Clear. Ask Questions. Seek Help
- Always Give Your Best
- Don't Take Things Personally

- **Be Honest and Straightforward**: As a BA, you being honest, straightforward, open, without ego, and transparent is really important. With your team members or stakeholder, speak with integrity. Communicate regularly. Be open about what you are going to do and if something changes communicate with the relevant people, ASAP.

- **Be Clear. Ask Questions. Seek Help:** As a BA, you should have the courage to ask questions. Clarify things that are not clear. Don't imagine or make assumptions. Understand things clearly. Even if you have the slightest doubt, don't just assume it, clarify it. Strictly no room for any ambiguity. Do not hesitate to seek help, when needed. Remember, in a team everyone should help each other.

- **Always Give Your Best:** Whatever the situation may be, give your best to resolve the issue or situation. There is no need to te Whether you are a newbie or experienced, don't break your head about why a plan did not go well or if requirements need to be rewritten. Always think about what is that you can learn from this situation. Never blame anyone, including yourself.

- **Don't take things personally:** First-off, understand that the world will not listen to you, just because you are saying. As BAs, it's your duty to ask questions, assess business needs and suggest what is really needed for business. During this process, you will get a lot of resistance, knee-jerk reactions, and not-so-good behaviours from stakeholders. To keep your sanity, just always be aware that all those reactions are not intended for you. Obviously, you are an agent of change, and the change will have repercussions. The person on the other side may have his/her own concerns with the project or impending change. Hence, as a BA, your duty is just to "listen" and "understand" to them and act in such a way that whatever your output should become a real value for them. This will benefit a lot for your project and for your mental health.

What Did You Learn in This Chapter?

- How will you ensure you have a required "the right BA Mindset"?
- What are the four Agreements that a BAs should make with themselves?
- What are according you are Top 5 Principles of the right BA mindset?
- Why BAs have to be the BIG PICTURE person?
- What is the difference between an Entrepreneur and a BA?
- Why Project scenarios are always uncertain?
- You need to own the project but should not get attached to it. Do you have such a mentality (I am not talking spirituality here)? Yes/No
- Do you have a mentality of NOT taking any feedback personally? Yes/No
- Do you have a mindset to manage the project from an execution standpoint? Yes/No
- Can you manage a team? Are you good at delegating or getting the work done from your team members? Yes/No

CHAPTER 3

SKILLS OF A BA

- *Essential BA Skills*
- *Attentive Listening*
- *Decision Making*

In the previous chapter, we have learned about the BA Mindset. Let's understand the BA skillsets in this chapter. The mindset refers to one's attitude, beliefs, and thinking patterns. In contrast, skillset or skills refers to a collection of specific abilities and competencies—that are required to perform a given task. For example, good communication skills are mandatory for effective stakeholder management.

In this chapter, I've explored a scenario where you are the sole BA working on the Project, also serving as the product owner, and I've summarized my key learnings below. Following each skill, I've included self-assessment questions, allowing you to honestly test whether you possess these skill sets.

While this chapter contains theoretical content, I've tried incorporating practical approaches and examples. I've highlighted the significance of certain skills for a BA's career advancement. Additionally, I have covered some topics at a high level, and we'll delve deeper into them in upcoming chapters.

While it is possible to dedicate individual books to each skill discussed in this chapter, my approach here is to provide a practical and concise guide to enhancing these essential skills.

Communication Skills

The most crucial skill for BAs is effective communication. Since their main role involves providing solutions to business problems, they must listen to customer pain points and articulate their ideas, opinions or solutions clearly and precisely (via speaking and writing) to their customers and the team. Hence, communication skills encompass speaking, writing, and attentive listening abilities.

BAs look at data and tell the bosses what it means, so they must explain things clearly. BAs don't just work with their team; they also talk to important people involved in the business. Hence, BAs use talking, listening and writing skills in different situations, like collecting information, starting a new project, or checking if a solution works.

BAs also meet with clients and important people every day. They are the face of the Project, interacting with customers, always. BAs must ensure the clients understand what they are saying or have written. Hence, a good speaking or writing ability helps a BA to convey his/her idea clearly, while attentive listening always demonstrates a BA's willingness to understand others' perspectives. In today's world, communication no longer solely relies on face-to-face interactions. It has extended to online meetings and calls, making communicating effectively in virtual settings equally crucial. So, how can one improve our communication skills?

Listening: You may excel at understanding the language used by people in a familiar work environment or, let's say, in your home country or location. However, the situation becomes more challenging when you communicate with clients from various parts of the world. Dealing with different accents and diverse ways and tones of speaking can make it difficult for many BAs (Especially entry-level BAs) to fully comprehend their customers' messages. This is a common obstacle, especially for new BAs entering the realm of global IT projects.

Here is a tip for you to tackle such situations. Read Novels or any literature aloud. When you read, you should hear it. Or here is a great tip I used, which you also might like. If you want to get better at listening and speaking, watch movies! For example, if you want to understand the American accent better, watch American English movies with subtitles. Read subtitles while you hear their dialogues. This can help you get better at understanding the nuances of their way of speaking, and in turn, this will help you understand your customers from such global locations better and communicate with them better. Feel free to ask your customers to repeat if you cannot follow what they said initially.

When you hear new words or sentences, it's a good idea to look up their meanings and try to use them. Talking to people who know a language better than you can be useful. Remember, getting used to global accents may take time, requires continuous effort and practice, and cannot be mastered overnight. However, there's no need to excessively worry about these challenges. Maintain your determination and exert effort; eventually, you'll conquer them through perseverance and time.

Speaking: When engaging with customers or delivering presentations, it is essential to be well-prepared. Avoid rushing to respond to customer inquiries or requests during the interactions in a call or meeting. It is perfectly acceptable to take a few moments to gather your thoughts before continuing the conversation. If you're unsure of an answer, communicate that you'll provide the correct response within a few hours or a day. However, once you commit, ensure you follow through and provide the answers as promised. Consistently missing such follow-ups can lead to trust issues with customers or team members. Building trust through reliable and timely communication is crucial for fostering positive relationships.

As a new BA, it's normal to experience difficulty or nervousness before meetings or workshops, especially with unfamiliar customers or stakeholders. If you find it challenging to interact with people you don't know, maintaining a positive mindset is the key to overcoming this. Start by offering a warm smile and a friendly greeting, then gently initiate the conversation. After all, they are also humans, just like us, right? So, don't worry. Despite the initial challenges, make an effort to engage with more people. With time, you will gradually conquer your hesitations and become more comfortable in such situations.

Please note that, having excellent speaking skills, including a rich vocabulary and correct grammar, is not the sole factor that matters as a BA. It is essential to ensure that your communication is clearly understood by the intended audience, whether customers, developers, QA teams, users, or others.

Writing: The main objective of communication is to establish collaborative relationships, as stakeholder involvement is essential for successful project implementation. As discussed earlier, writing skills are crucial for BAs to communicate efficiently with stakeholders, document various artefacts, and provide clear and concise responses. As BAs work closely with people, having clarity in their thinking process is vital for ensuring smooth project management—writing helps you communicate and document your thoughts more clearly and concisely.

It is important to remember that in the age of AI, tools like ChatGPT or Google Bard (and there are many nowadays) can assist in writing flawlessly, but being a skilled communicator is still paramount. While AI tools can be helpful in offline settings, when engaging with stakeholders in live BA activities such as workshops or brainstorming sessions, no tool can replace your ability to speak and write effectively. Your proficiency in communicating with clarity and effectiveness remains unwavering.

Self-Assessment [If the answer to any of the questions is NO, then improve in that area]:

1. Can I write an Email clearly which can be understood by my recipients? Yes/No
2. Can I put across my points orally without any difficulty? Yes/No
3. Can I note key points discussed in a meeting and assign action items? Yes/No
4. Can I ask questions? Do I get questions to ask? Yes/No
5. Am I preparing myself before any meeting? Yes/No
6. Can I go & talk to a customer without any inhibitions? Yes/No

Attentive Listening Skills

A key trait of a BA is the perfect listening skill—Attentive Listening. They don't just listen for the sake of it. They listen to understand and gather essential information and details from what they hear or converse. Hence, they must be vigilant and observant, ensuring no chance is missed.

Not only this, but they also understand the body language, tone, and context to get the message clear and loud. So, if you are also planning to start a career as a BA, start working on your listening skills.

Being an Attentive Listener: Listening with an open mind influences the ability to solve problems and, above all, builds trust. By listening, we can better understand the people we contact and support them more effectively. Above all, it is worth realizing that listening is a gift. By listening, we devote our time and attention to others; everyone can learn this skill. We know from experience that listening is important in personal and professional relationships. It is the foundation of success, as it helps to improve efficiency, creativity, and the ability to express ideas.

So, you are not only a good listener but an attentive listener?

Attentive listening is vital in effective communication, enabling individuals to connect and understand one another. By actively engaging with the speaker and showing genuine interest, attentive listeners create an environment where open dialogue can thrive. Rather than simply hearing words, attentive listening involves delving deeper into the speaker's message, uncovering underlying meanings, and fostering meaningful discussions.

Improving your capacity for attentive listening requires posing logical and conversation-driven questions that motivate speakers to divulge their insights and viewpoints. For instance, instead of asking a generic question like, "Did you enjoy the book?" a more engaging approach would be to inquire, "What specific elements of the book resonated with you and why?" Such open-ended questions elicit more detailed responses and encourage speakers to express their thoughts and emotions.

Attentive listening also requires setting aside judgment and criticism, creating a safe space for speakers to express themselves freely. By showing empathy and understanding, listeners can establish a rapport with the speaker and forge a deeper connection via non-verbal cues, such as maintaining eye contact, nodding in affirmation, and using facial expressions, further conveying active engagement and reinforcing the speaker's sense of being heard and valued.

In various personal and professional contexts, attentive listening yields numerous benefits. It allows for effective problem-solving as listeners comprehensively understand the speaker's concerns, needs, and perspectives. This way, you are becoming empathetic towards speakers speaking with you. Being empathetic is indeed a valuable trait for a BA. Attentive listening is also instrumental in building stronger relationships, fostering trust, and promoting a collaborative and inclusive environment. BAs can uncover hidden insights and discover innovative solutions by attentively listening and engaging with stakeholders and team members.

For a BA, practising the "Attentive Listening" habit is a must. Let's consider some examples of how attentive listening can be practised by asking engaging and connecting questions:

Asking exploratory questions:

- What motivated you to pursue this project?
- Can you elaborate on the challenges you encountered during the implementation phase?

Using open-ended questions:

- How would you describe vision for the future of the company?
- In what ways do you believe we can improve our customer service experience?

Employing reflective questions:

- If I understand correctly, you suggest we streamline our production process. Is that accurate?
- So, you're saying that we need to prioritize sustainability initiatives within our organization.

Encouraging further elaboration:

- Could you provide some specific examples to illustrate your point?
- Can you share any personal experiences that have shaped your perspective on this issue?

Summarizing and paraphrasing:

- Let me ensure I've understood correctly: You're proposing a shift in our marketing strategy to target a younger demographic.
- I gather that your main concern is improving cross-team collaboration to enhance project efficiency. Is that accurate?

By actively practising attentive listening, individuals can strengthen their communication skills, foster deeper connections, and gain valuable insights from others.

Top 4 Tips to Become a Great Attentive Listener:

1. Jot down key points, demonstrating your commitment to actively engaging with the speaker.
2. To become an attentive listener, having the desire and genuine interest in understanding others is essential. Stay attentive and focused.
3. Maintain your presence in the conversation. If you find yourself losing track, it's acceptable to interrupt and seek clarification before proceeding.
4. Listening is akin to a holistic meditation practice, engaging your ears, eyes, heart, intuition, and mind. Embrace the multi-dimensional nature of attentive listening.

Attentive Listening Framework: Here is a kind of mental framework that you could use in your daily life as a BA. Whenever you interact or have communication (Meetings, workshops, etc.) with someone, these aspects will help you engage with customers, Project team members and the management:

- Be open to Listening to others. Empathize and drive deeper into what the other person is saying. Try to hear their perspective and dive into their world without any judgements. Ask what caused it, why they think so, and get to the root.

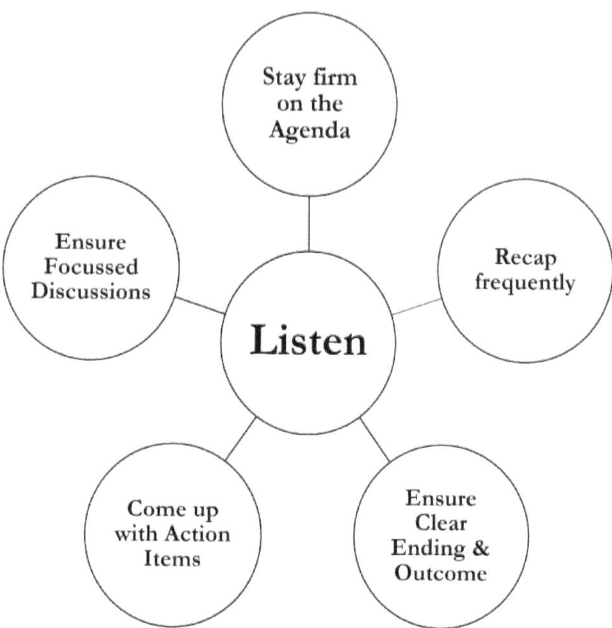

- Imagine you set up a meeting with customers and other stakeholders. Always remember your goal and agenda for the meeting. We often get carried over by responding to a conversation and forget our goal without any outcome. Listening plays an important role in making your meeting effective.

- Have focussed discussions—sometimes the entire conversation loses its track. Only Listening can help you quickly gain control back.

- Recap repeatedly at every opportunity in a meeting is a listening technique, ensuring whatever you understand is correct. It also proves to other parties that you were listening to them. Recapping lets both parties stay on track and dive deeper than spread into unrelated topics.

- Finally, don't forget about Takeaway from a meeting. Be firm to note the key takeaways and action items of a meeting without fail. Always leave the conversation with a clear ending and action items—this becomes measurable progress and creates trust, leading to a better outcome.

Self-Assessment [If the answer to any of the questions is NO, then improve in that area]:

1. Do I interrupt others during meetings? Yes/No
2. Will you be able to lead & drive a meeting? Yes/No
3. Are you an observer? Can you sense beyond what is being discussed? Yes/No
4. Do you just ask whatever questions you prepared or questions based on the context of the ongoing discussion? Yes/No
5. Do you probe other people's opinions in depth so that you can get further insights? Yes/No

Negotiation Skills

A BA's role involves liaising between different departments, including clients, developers, and management. Good negotiation skills are necessary, and sticking to your goals while keeping all stakeholders satisfied is important. A significant aspect of successful negotiation involves changing (or making them aware of) people's perspectives.

In an organization, a BA must have negotiation skills to mediate between Customers and the Project or IT/Tech and business teams. The business and IT teams must reach a consensus on the requirements and solutions proposed to implement any business idea or solution. To do that, a BA should have the skills to negotiate with both teams to implement the best possible solution for the business problem.

As a BA, you would need this skill in the first stage of a project when deciding about the project vision. The BA determines which requirements should get acknowledged first and which requests would only prove to be a waste of time. Moreover, to give a cost-effective solution to the team, the BA also needs to perform a proper cost-benefit analysis.

Conflicts and disagreements can arise during the project lifecycle, whether about conflicting requirements, limited resources, or project scope. Negotiation skills enable BAs to address conflicts diplomatically, find mutually agreeable solutions, and maintain positive stakeholder working relationships. In some scenarios, areas like resource management may come under the BA's purview (when the BA is also handling Project Management responsibility or a Project Manager also handling the Business Analysis). Still, normally, the Project Manager manages it.

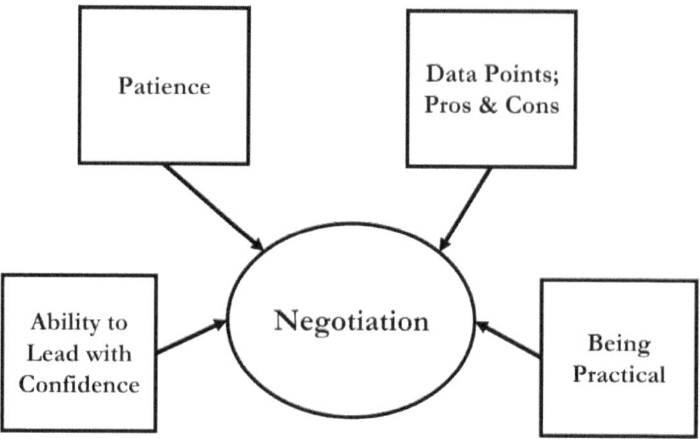

Negotiation plays a crucial role in managing project scope. BAs must negotiate with stakeholders to define project boundaries (Scope), prioritize requirements, and effectively manage scope creep. Negotiation skills help set realistic expectations and ensure that the project stays within agreed-upon constraints.

BAs often encounter changes in project requirements, timelines, or resources. Negotiation skills assist in managing these changes by engaging stakeholders, understanding their concerns, evaluating trade-offs, and reaching a consensus on revised project plans. For example, when there is a change in requirement and if that change is crucial, then the BA can negotiate a trade-off (moving other planned requirements to the next phase/Sprint to accommodate the new change) with stakeholders to maintain the same timeline as before.

To negotiate with individuals from different teams, the BA needs to cultivate several qualities:

- Patience is crucial when explaining your ideas and persuading colleagues or clients to accept your ideas and proposals. This can be a rare skill, but some people possess it naturally, and it is an essential quality for a BA.
- Some people generally do not possess negotiation skills. They are hesitant, especially when dealing with customers. If you are one of them, don't worry. But you need to put some effort into developing this skill. Negotiation in the IT world is not so complex. Importantly, you need to present your viewpoint to customers and explain why it is the best approach. Present them the data points,

Pros & cons. In essence, you should be confident enough to put across your points clearly and make your point.

- It's essential to be practical, as people only agree with feasible solutions.
- Creating a friendly environment while interacting with coworkers or clients can help persuade them to listen and agree with your point.
- Being firm and bossy on a few things is sometimes required, especially if the team is working on your idea—sometimes the team may not have the complete background information, or you may not have the privilege to explain all of those to the team in such cases, you may need to delegate responsibilities and lead the team. However, if the team's suggestions are valid, accept them.

Self-Assessment [If the answer to any of the questions is NO, then improve in that area]:

1. Can I talk to customers confidently? Yes/No
2. Can you put your solution clearly and will be able to explain why it is best? Yes/No
3. Will you be able to lead & drive a meeting? Yes/No
4. Are you an observer? Can you sense beyond what is being discussed? Yes/No
5. Can you comfortably delegate some of the work to your team members? Yes/No
6. If something is wrong, you need to inform your customer. Can you take such actions independently? Yes/No

Critical Thinking

What is critical thinking? Oxford Dictionary explains it nicely in a single line: "The objective analysis and evaluation of an issue to form a judgement". From a BA perspective, it's all about understanding the Problem, uncovering the true need and coming up with the best possible solution.

Critical thinking is crucial for BAs as they must meet client expectations by analysing requirements and prioritising business needs. The BAs can follow below steps to think critically:

- Clearly understand and write down the Problem
- Gather all necessary information
- Utilise the gathered information to arrive at a Solution(s)

- Evaluate the Solution options to solve the Problem
- Consider the potential consequences
- Take into account alternative viewpoints

BAs require strong analytical skills to comprehend and analyse business needs and stakeholder input, converting them into specific requirements. This involves examining various existing documents process flows, conducting user interviews and much more. Techniques like use case diagrams, visualisations, and SWOT analysis can aid further in requirement analysis.

Critical thinking allows business analysts to assess multiple options and select the most appropriate one to achieve the business goal. Like how a doctor diagnoses a patient's symptoms and history before deciding on treatment, critical thinking helps BAs evaluate requirements to uncover the core needs.

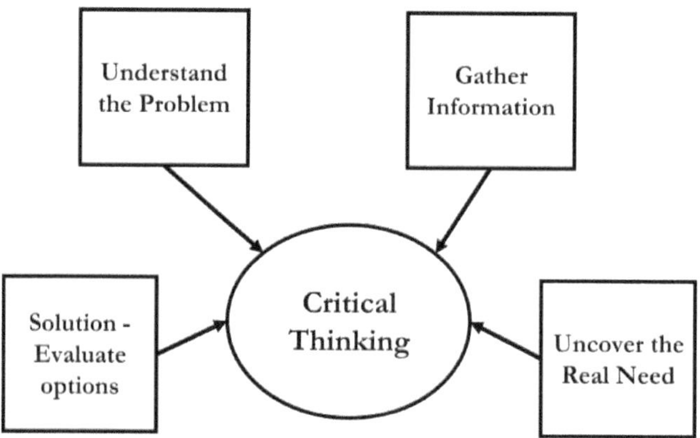

BAs evaluate multiple options and guide a team toward a solution. While identifying the Problem to be solved, BAs must attentively listen to stakeholder needs and critically analyse them, asking probing questions until the true need is revealed and understood. New BAs must possess critical thinking and evaluation skills.

Self-Assessment [If the answer to any of the questions is NO, then improve in that area]:

1. Do you have the patience to understand current customers' Business & Processes? Yes/No
2. A customer explains many things. However, will you be able to make sense of the actual need the customer might have? Yes/No

3. Are you an observer? Can you sense beyond what is being discussed? Yes/No
4. When you have multiple options, do you feel stressed to choose the best one? Do you have any method to choose the best one? Yes/No

Decision-Making

Effective decision-making skills are essential for a BA, particularly when their decisions directly impact the business. As a BA, you must carefully evaluate the current processes, the nature of the customer's business, various data sets, situations, plans, and circumstances. During this evaluation, assessing the potential consequences and making significant decisions that align with the business objectives is crucial. Developing a solid sense of judgment is vital so that your decisions contribute productively to the project and ultimately benefit the customer.

The success or failure of a project heavily depends on the BA's comprehension of the elicited requirements. Therefore, BAs must exercise caution and thorough consideration before finalizing solutions. They must ensure that the requirements captured are agreed upon by all stakeholders and, more importantly, that every stakeholder understands the requirements in the same way as the BA. Once the BA is sure of this, he/she should get into a solution mode. There may be multiple solutions that the BA and the team can devise. Therefore, it is crucial to consider multiple perspectives when contemplating various solutions in order to anticipate potential outcomes and make well-informed, precise choices, decisions, or recommendations.

Since the BA possesses the vision of the future system, he/she plays a pivotal role in solution design and implementation. Though the BA collaborates with the project team on every aspect of solution design, any decisions/recommendations regarding the functional/technical solution approach should be made by the BA in alignment with requirements. For instance, the BA can determine how a process is designed in a system, such as the Lead to Opportunity qualification process. Based on the requirements, the BA can propose a design, present it to the customer, and seek feedback. The BA also collaborates with customers to reach an optimal solution—establishing such shared understanding is critical.

Though BA must have decision-making skills, often, the customer is the decision-maker when it comes to major decisions like process changes, technical approaches, technology-related aspects and more. However, the

BA should be in a position to make recommendations to the customer on the best approach to address a particular problem.

To enhance decision-making skills, always consider the following factors:

- Have a clear understanding of the Business Objective
- Accurately assess & evaluate your available options
- Write down the Pros and cons of each available option
- Identify any associated uncertainties or ambiguities
- Recognize the value each option can offer
- Recognize the potential change impact of each option
- Identify Risks and Benefits
- Identify the cost impact of each option

Self-Assessment [If the answer to any of the questions is NO, then improve in that area]:

1. Do you have a confusing mind where for everything you go to customers or your seniors? Yes/No
2. Can you decide based on the particular purpose and then stick with the same and convince anyone about your decision? Yes/No
3. When you have multiple options, do you feel stressed to choose the best one? Do you have any method to choose the best one? Yes/No
4. Do you mind doing thorough research to arrive at that decision? Yes/No

Problem-Solving Mindset

The "mindset" of always being inclined to solve issues and problems is more of an attitude than a skill. If you don't naturally possess this mindset, it's advisable to learn it as a skill initially and gradually internalise it as a mindset is recommended to grow as a BA.

For example, an organisation could have several departments, each with unique sales processes. Digital transformation aims to unify these processes, inevitably bringing numerous challenges. Of course, the BA is responsible for gathering accurate requirements and spearheading the change management process. However, they may encounter hurdles such as insufficient stakeholder support, incorrect scenarios, non-cooperation from stakeholders who resist implementing a new process, and various other obstacles and problems.

In this scenario, once the BA engages with stakeholders and team members (assuming some support is obtained from stakeholders), they can gain a comprehensive 360-degree view of the problem and current processes. Armed with this initial information, the BA can develop a high-level solution that aligns with business needs and technical feasibility. As the BA, your next step is collaborating with all impacted teams, presenting the solution and seeking their input to refine and enhance it. Through this process, you build the stakeholders' confidence and foster a shared understanding of the proposed solution.

However, challenges, such as stakeholders not accepting the solution or potential escalations, may arise. It's essential to handle resistance effectively by understanding its true reasons. Exceptional problem-solving skills are crucial in persuading multiple team members about the advantages of adopting the new process. Remember, you act as an authoritative figure, implementing essential rules at this stage. If necessary, don't hesitate to seek management assistance to address any issues that may arise.

No project is without problems. The entire project is a solution to a problem. At the highest level, BAs facilitate a shared understanding of the problem and the possible solutions and determine the project's scope. You'll also find BAs facilitating teams to solve technical challenges, especially when negotiating between multiple business or technical stakeholders. Often, we start this by analysing the business process.

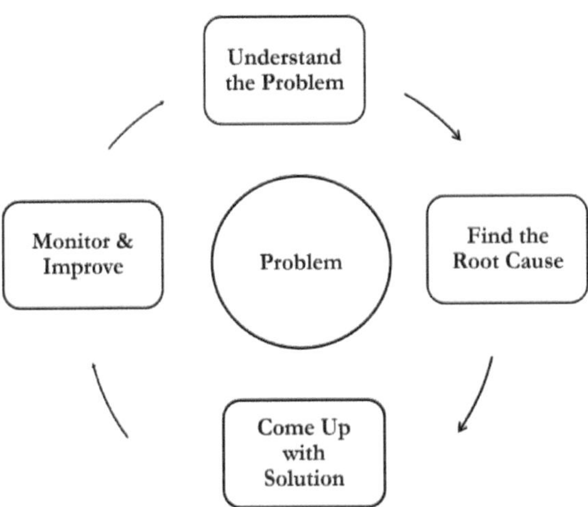

The role of a BA is challenging at every step, and they should be able to solve these challenges to overcome them. Thinking deeply about a problem's source and causation will lead to finding appropriate solutions. To solve any business problem, as a BA, you can follow these steps:

- Get to know the problem
- Determine the root cause of the problem
- Try examining the problem from different perspectives
- Find out a possible solution
- Identify the consequences of the solution
- Think about the solution from various perspectives
- Identify if this solution aligns with the Business objective
- Implement the solution
- Monitor and review to further improve the solution

I will explain a simple trick to get the "Problem Solving" mentality. Think of your product/project as your baby. Have that ownership. Do all the hard work in the back end, but make it SIMPLEST for the user. Customers will thank you later.

Self-Assessment [If the answer to any of the questions is NO, then improve in that area]:

1. Do you have a confusing mind where for everything you go to customers/your seniors? Yes/No
2. When do you have the mindset or patience to listen and understand a problem? Are you a good listener? Yes/No
3. Do you have a mentality of slowly gathering data and understanding a process rather than a "Somehow, I just want to finish it off" mentality? Yes/No

Essential Tool Proficiency

We will thoroughly explore this topic in the upcoming chapters. Nonetheless, this section will provide a concise overview of the "Tool skills" required for a successful BA.

- **Researching the Internet**: Research is the fundamental building block of a Business Analyst's role. It's imperative to recognise that conducting thorough internet research is a skill. Proficiency in utilising appropriate keywords and familiarity with various search engine tools are essential for effectively executing your responsibilities. Presently, advanced AI tools like ChatGPT might even offer assistance in enhancing your research endeavours.

- **Excel:** Excel, a time-honoured and exceptionally potent tool for analysis, sometimes analytics and reporting, is employed by BA for a myriad of tasks. They utilise it to perform diverse calculations, outline requirements, create Wireframes, generate reports, and execute budget analyses to reveal business trends. Excel stands as a fundamental instrument adaptable for virtually any conceivable purpose.
- **SDLC tools (Tools like JIRA or Azure DevOps):** Microsoft Team Foundation Server (TFS), now rebranded as Azure DevOps Server, was initially crafted to integrate seamlessly with the Microsoft Visual Studio development ecosystem. In contrast, beyond the realms of Microsoft, enterprises often opt for Atlassian Jira, a widely acclaimed Agile Project Management solution compatible with diverse development environments. These two platforms, TFS (Azure DevOps Server) and Jira stand out as the prevailing choices among major tech conglomerates for orchestrating and overseeing their project endeavours.
- **SQL:** Though an IT background is not one of the mandatory skills needed for BAs, it surely pays off to learn them. Tools like SQL can be a boon for a BA to analyse, slice, and dice the data with appropriate queries rather than depend on a technical team member. It is proven that if you want to do anything with a database, you need to learn SQL. It will make you skilled enough to process and analyse heavy data sets to derive relevant information.
- **Diagramming Tools:** For Diagramming, Wireframing, Flowcharts, etc., I have used Tools like Lucid Charts, Axure, and Balsamiq. Some of the Tools that are must learn for a BA are:
    - MS Visio (Or any Diagramming Tools like Lucid Charts, Axure, or Balsamiq)– This helps explain architecture and workflows.
    - MS Office (Excel, PPT Word, etc.)

Other Important Skills A BA Should Have

Asses yourself if you have these skills already. If not, it's time to master these. Don't worry. Start Practicing. Over time, you will become a pro in all of these.

- **Time management:** Time management is paramount and the most indispensable skill for a BA. Project deadlines are typically stringent, making timely delivery crucial. However, it is not just about meeting deadlines; the outputs must also adhere to the project's quality standards for success. Therefore, developing strong time management skills early on is vital for maximising your professional journey as a BA. You can ensure timely delivery while upholding quality standards by efficiently managing your time. This ability will greatly contribute to your effectiveness and productivity as a BA, enabling you to meet project requirements and exceed expectations. Here are the basics one should follow to do an effective time management:

- **Set clear goals:** Define specific, measurable, achievable, relevant, and time-bound (SMART) goals. Having clear objectives helps you prioritise tasks and allocate time accordingly.
- **Prioritise Tasks:** One helpful strategy is prioritising tasks by assessing their level of urgency and importance. This can help ensure that the most pressing tasks are addressed first. Focus on high-priority items first to prevent procrastination and ensure timely completion.
- **Create a schedule:** It is recommended that you create a schedule, either daily or weekly, outlining your tasks and activities. Use calendars, planners, or digital productivity apps to allocate time slots for different activities.
- **Break tasks into smaller steps:** When facing large, complex tasks, it is often useful to divide them into smaller, more achievable steps. When faced with complex tasks, dividing them into smaller, more achievable steps is often useful. This approach can make the task less overwhelming and easier to handle. This approach helps you make progress and reduces the chances of feeling overwhelmed.

Documentation: Documentation skills play a pivotal role for BAs in IT projects. The ability to effectively document requirements, processes, and decisions is vital. Documentation is a reference for stakeholders, promoting shared understanding throughout the project's lifespan. It facilitates collaboration and knowledge transfer among team members, mitigating the risk of misunderstandings and mistakes. Well-documented artefacts also aid in project maintenance, troubleshooting, and future enhancements.

BAs with strong documentation skills can efficiently organise and present information, ensuring clarity, consistency, and traceability. Ultimately, these skills significantly contribute to the success of IT projects by enabling effective communication and facilitating project management processes. Thus, it comes under the BA skills essential for every professional. You should know how to create sorted and elaborate documents and reports. It's a creative process. There are plenty of templates available online for free, which could be your starting point for documentation. Your documentation should be clear and thorough enough that a new team member can easily understand their role, even if they join the project midway.

Team Player/Management: As the BA works with multiple stakeholders, being a good team player is essential. Key qualities include collaborative working, conflict resolution, and shared ownership of team goals.

Presentation Skills: Presentation skills are vital for BAs when managing projects. As the face of the team, BAs are responsible for effectively offering insights to various audiences. This is where presentation skills come into play. Communicating ideas, conveying requirements, and influencing stakeholders requires clear, concise, and engaging information delivery. Strong presentation skills enable BAs to articulate complex concepts, facilitate productive discussions, and gain buy-in from key decision-makers. Effective presentations enhance the BA's credibility, create a positive impact, and foster collaboration within the project team. Developing and honing presentation skills is therefore crucial for BAs to effectively communicate their expertise and contribute to the success of projects.

Understanding of Organisational Dynamics: The BA must comprehend the political landscape and company dynamics that impact the product to proactively prepare for potential issues. That's why a BA should be a keen observer. The Organisational dynamics involve organisational structure, various business units, business models, key stakeholders, etc. Understanding organisational dynamics enables the BA to understand organisational relationships and politics.

Familiarity with Methodologies: Familiarity with different methodologies is valuable for BAs. Specialising or knowing such methodologies allows BAs to cater to the unique requirements of different approaches to change or software development. Some commonly sought-after skill sets include Agile Inspired processes like SCRUM, Waterfall, Hybrid Agile and various other project management skills. Expertise in one or more of these methodologies can give BAs a competitive edge even when searching for job opportunities. Additionally, quickly adapting to specialised methodologies within an organisation is crucial for new BAs to hit the ground running. By acquiring and honing these specialised skills, BAs can enhance their versatility and proficiency, positioning themselves for success in the ever-evolving landscape of business analysis.

Industry and Domain Expertise: Industry or domain expertise benefits a business analyst's career but is not mandatory. Trying to be an expert in every domain or industry is simply not feasible. However, many BA positions do require specialised knowledge in specific areas. If you possess expertise in a particular domain, you can leverage that knowledge to excel in your BA career and be known as a domain-specific BA. For instance, banking projects often require BAs who have an in-depth understanding of banking-related business processes instead of a generic BA who simply focuses on requirements gathering and subsequent processes.

On the other hand, if you do not possess specialised expertise in a specific domain, it does not mean that your skills as a BA are any less valuable. Instead, you should identify opportunities that appreciate your other business analysis skills. Emphasise your ability to analyse, problem-solve, communicate effectively, and facilitate collaboration. These core BA skills are highly transferable across industries and can still contribute significantly to the success of various projects.

Being Creative

Is being creative a skill or mindset? Even I do not have an answer.

Creativity is a gift. Some are born creative; some have to make an effort. If you are willing to make an effort, you can do a task much differently. The diagram below depicts what it takes to be creative.

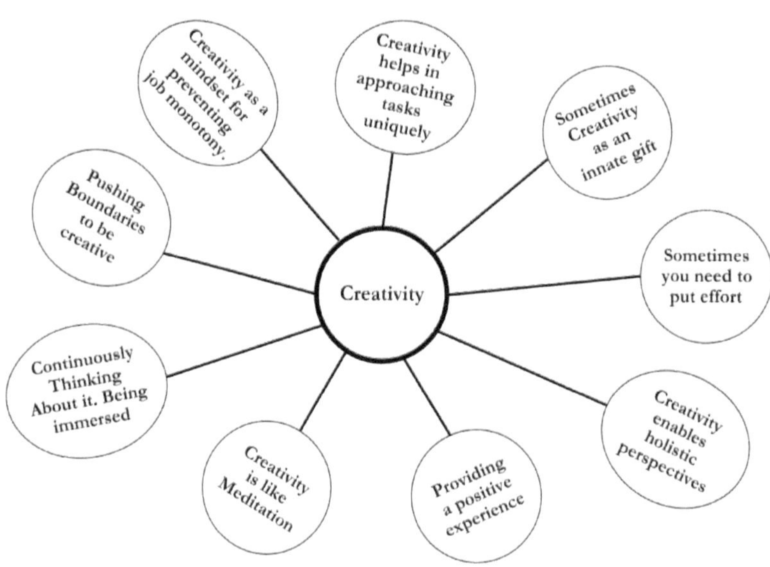

Hence, being creative is the key mindset one should develop to excel in any job – otherwise, the job will become mundane. If you try to push your limits, you will find a new "creative person" inside you. Have you ever tried doing that?

Being creative is important if you are in Business Analysis, Project Management, or technical developer roles. Creativity helps you to solve a problem differently and efficiently.

Here is a tip to get creative. If you are stuck in a problem or some issue, you can keep thinking about it in the back of your mind while performing other routines (Be careful when you drive or operate machinery). It's like your mind processing the information at the backend. Sometimes, you may have to do it for hours or even days.

And one fine day, suddenly, you will have that "Eureka" moment, for sure! But beware! While you are in this process of thinking, sometimes people around you may see you as worried, lost, or become mad, etc. So, if possible, try to be present while you are at it – it's a meditative state. Don't worry about what people say about you – mad, lost, etc. Creativity is about being immersed in your actions and being mad about something. BAs are generally Creators, and basically, they are mad people sometimes.

When you step into a car showroom, you don't see a vehicle as merely a collection of parts like the engine, tires, gears, steering wheel, lights, and more. Instead, you perceive it as a complete entity, a car, and this holistic view creates a vivid image in your mind, allowing you to understand its purpose and functionality. In essence, looking at a car is an experience in itself.

Similarly, as a BA, your approach to your customer organisation should mirror this holistic perspective. Rather than seeing it as an amalgamation of various departments, businesses, employees, processes, and customers, you should strive to comprehend it as a unified whole.

Your foremost task is to grasp how the project you are involved in, the business problem you are addressing, and the requirements you are fulfilling will impact the entire organisation. This broader view should always be at the forefront of your mind as you explore ways to provide a comprehensive and integrated experience by meeting genuine business needs and requirements. Your role as a BA is not merely about dissecting the parts but understanding how they come together to create a functioning and harmonious whole within the organisation.

Being Detail-Oriented

The devil is in the details. No one else would agree to it more than a person in the shoes of a BA. Attention to detail is paramount for a BA. It is through diving into the specifics that the scope expands, the need for additional clarifications arises, and ambiguity in client responses or missing documentation becomes apparent. BAs must drill down to gather those relevant details and leverage all available sources for support.

While communication, stakeholder management, and time management skills are vital, thriving as a BA would prove challenging without a keen eye for detail. The role of a BA revolves around processing vast amounts of data, emphasising the importance of meticulousness and clear articulation to avoid ambiguity in requirements.

BAs have a love-hate relationship with ambiguity – they're hired to handle it but don't like it. Ambiguities in specifications lead to unexpected defects, and conversation ambiguities result in unnecessary conflicts. Throughout a project, BAs continuously clarify and address ambiguities.

Yet, at the project's inception, BAs must embrace ambiguity and effectively navigate it before fully understanding the problem and deciding on a solution. Managing ambiguity involves embracing new information and learning as it arises, even if it comes later than desired.

What did You Learn in this Chapter?

- ✪ Why communication skills are important for a BA?
- ✪ How you can improve your "Attentive Listening" Skills?
- ✪ Do you think without the domain Knowledge BAs can deliver?
- ✪ How you will manage Requirements Ambiguity in a Project?
- ✪ What's your view on documentation skills at this AI Age?
- ✪ Which SDLC tools you have used so far?
- ✪ Name the popular tools you used for your BA tasks for documentation, diagram creation and more?
- ✪ How you will manage Ambiguity?

CHAPTER 4

CATAGORIES OF BUSINESS ANALYSTS

- *Three Main Categories of Business Analysts*
- *Role of A BA in an IT Services Company Vs. Product Company*
- *Proactive BA Vs. Order Taker BA*
- *Functional Consultant Vs. BA*

The key objective of this chapter is to help you understand the types of BAs and decide what kind of BA you want to become. This is an important chapter, and read them carefully.

We have learned that the BA is the person who identifies the business vision, needs and problems and helps determine solutions for the same. While this can be the simplest definition of a BA role, based on the complexity of a project, certain additional expertise and soft skills are also needed for a BA—be it people skills, domain expertise, technical skills and a special mindset.

For example, as an experienced BA, knowing banking fundamentals and how banking as a business run will be more beneficial if a project is about digital transformation for a Bank. Though domain Subject Matter Experts (SMEs) are available in the industry, sometimes, Organizations need such expertise from a BA as they may not have access to SMEs. This could be an opportunity for BAs to learn more if they are open to taking up challenges of additional learning, which may help them become an expert in the business aspects of that particular industry. Who knows, such learnings will open lucrative opportunities in the future. If you have worked in Banking or any such industry and want to get into IT as a BA, you can become a Domain-specific BA where you need to upskill yourself with BA skills.

A generic/Generalist BA/Functional BA who knows Business Analysis fundamentals is also suitable for the above-said project to carry out functional Business analysis tasks. However, he/she may need help from a domain expert as and when required. However, as a Generic/Functional BA, you must possess the ability to understand banking as a business and then do your BA work and add value.

Similarly, if a project is all about complete technical transformation, a BA who is also an expert in technical aspects can add value. However, nowadays, all the technical aspects are handled by Technical Architects or Technical Leads.

Hence, roles like Technical BA are almost non-existent nowadays. However, as a Functional BA or Domain-Specific BA, an awareness of fundamental technical aspects (In your chosen area, e.g., Microsoft technologies or Salesforce or SAP or Oracle, etc.) is advisable, and it will help you as a BA to grow further.

Hence, going by the above examples, in the industry, there are broadly three categories of BAs:

- Domain-specific BA
- Generic/Functional BA [Also called as Generalist BA]
- Technical BA

Domain-Specific BA

Domain pertains to various industry or business sectors, encompassing areas such as Banking, Insurance, Manufacturing, Telecom, and others. Domain knowledge denotes comprehension of industry-specific business elements, including processes, operations, necessary skills, and critical business process flows within that particular industry.

For instance, if you aim to excel in comprehending retail banking, you should have a grasp of the following (Not the complete list):

- The intricacies of transactions performed through the retail banking web application (e.g., funds transfer, etc.).
- The NEFT/online money transfer process involving messaging between front-end, back-end, and external systems.
- And various other aspects of day-to-day banking

The Value Domain-Specific BAs Can Bring: Imagine you're a BA in the Banking and Financial Services industry. So, when working for a customer in this domain, you, as a BA, need to interact with the customer to understand the business needs and requirements—essentially, you need to drive and own the entire requirements management process.

Now, if you have an understanding of how the industry works and understand the business processes, you will be able to achieve good results because:

- You know what your customers are talking about
- Your domain knowledge lets you communicate with customers in their language, facilitating better comprehension and ensuring you precisely understand what they convey.
- With your in-depth knowledge of the industry's workings, you can grasp the stated needs and identify the unstated ones, which are often critical to meeting their requirements.
- Your expertise in the domain empowers you to provide valuable recommendations and insights, enabling you to contribute to improving processes and enhancing your credibility as a BA.

As a practising BA, some domain knowledge becomes essential. Of course, by reading/self-study and interacting with industry people, you will be able to get a superficial understanding of the domain, and you may be able to work in any industry, but this is just a starting point.

However, becoming a domain expert is like beyond your BA work.

In addition to the BA job, you may be doing consulting, process mapping, and improvement suggestions. But you are becoming a specialist in that specific industry. Domain knowledge is a measure of your experience, which is not replaceable. An entry-level BA cannot replace you, as domain expertise comes with experience. Remember: Such domain expertise cannot be earned via any certification. It all comes from experience.

Becoming a Domain-Specific BA: As an entry-level BA, you are not expected to possess domain knowledge. Understanding requirements capturing techniques, UML modelling, requirements analysis and SRS/FS understanding are more important as an entry-level BA. Hence, if you are new to business analysis, you should not worry too much about the domain knowledge. But it would be best if you focused on gaining domain knowledge as you start working as a BA—because understanding the fundamental business aspects of your industry is essential.

For the experienced, if you want to take the next step (to become a Domain BA), from being a generic BA who takes requirements and helps in implementing the project and product roadmaps to someone who can advise a customer (within an industry or domain), and help grow their Business as a proactive partner, you can become a **domain expert**. You would already know how the industry works if you have worked chiefly on telecom projects. You will learn from your experience what needs to be done in certain situations, the suggested best practices, and more. As domain consultants, you can transition into industry consultants, offering guidance to your customers within that domain on process improvements and demonstrating how their offerings can give them an edge over competitors, leading to increased revenue.

Suppose you are already working in any of these industries (like Banking, telecom, etc.) and want to get into IT Business Analysis from a non-IT background (Or with some IT background). In that case, you can enter the BA arena as a domain BA. However, just having domain knowledge will not be sufficient. You should also know how a BA typically works in an IT Project. Once you acquire the requisite knowledge (and some experience), you need to tweak your Resume/CV and write and publish your CV highlighting your overall domain experience, BA experience and knowledge.

Your CV must clearly indicate that you possess 'x' years of experience working in the 'XYZ' industry. Additionally, highlight your knowledge of Business Analysis acquired through training and involvement in internal projects. It's crucial to powerfully communicate your role as a BA and emphasize your relevant experience. This approach will increase your chances of securing interviews. Subsequently, performing well during these interviews becomes essential for the selection process. However, it's important to note that this journey is not without challenges. You may face setbacks, but with each attempt, you'll gain confidence and expand your knowledge.

If you are dedicated and determined, one fine day, I am sure, you will get that success.

Therefore, whether you possess IT experience and are seeking to transition your Business Analysis role to a new domain, or if you're aiming to enter IT Business Analysis from a non-IT background, where should you seek to acquire this domain-specific knowledge and a fresh perspective? How should you initiate this process?

- **Explore Books and Blogs:** To gain surface-level knowledge of a business domain, many online resources such as e-books and blogs are available on the Internet.

- **Understand the Business and analyze the Customer Journey:** Take time to understand the typical customers in the domain and how the Business operates. For instance, if you're interested in the Telecom industry, study the entire journey that their customers go through, from initial contact to final engagement. Understanding the revenue streams in the domain is also crucial – what drives people or businesses to pay for the services.

- **Explore Opportunities Within Your Current Organization**: Explore if there are any suitable opportunities (Research, study, process improvement, etc.) that may help you gain domain-related knowledge within your current organization. This can be a great way to gain hands-on experience and learn about the industry.

- **Identify Leading IT Companies**: Explore and identify the top IT companies that excel in the specific domain you're interested in. This information is found on their websites, press releases, or sponsored articles.

- **Networking:** Utilize professional networking platforms like LinkedIn to connect with experienced Business Analysts working in the domain of your interest. Building these connections can be highly beneficial in understanding the intricacies of the domain.

- **Online Courses:** If possible and affordable, consider enrolling in trustworthy online courses. These courses can provide valuable insights and perspectives about your chosen domain or Business Analysis activities. Check if your organization can provide industry-specific training or alignment to further enhance your knowledge.

So, do you want to be a Domain Specific-BA?

Well, there is a catch. You should be aware that if you become a domain BA and target only to become a BA in that specific domain, the count of future job opportunities will be narrowed. If you are fine with that and have patience and confidence that one or the other day, you will be successful; you can continue and become that domain BA—as it may pay you well, sometimes.

However, I would generally suggest being a specialist in one or a maximum of two areas of your interest/domains (Let's, Insurance and Banking). Hence, when presented with opportunities, you will always know your choice.

However, if you get a chance, keep your option to work as a generic BA as well, as you might not always get an opportunity to work on a particular domain, especially if you are in the IT services industry and working in an IT services company. Sometimes, Jack of all – generic BA is very useful in downturns as it always improves your chances of being relevant.

As a BA, I believe having an in-depth domain understanding of at least one industry is essential, along with the required Business Analysis skills.

Who is a Generic/Generalist/Functional BA?

The Generic/Generalist/Functional BAs are highly skilled professionals with special abilities and adaptability, making them valuable assets in various industries. They are known for their flexibility and expertise across different domains. These BAs can take on multiple roles, providing numerous career opportunities.

Some of the roles a Generic/Generalist/Functional BA can excel in include:

- **Product Expert BA/Functional Consultant:** In this role, the Generic BA becomes an expert in a specific product or service, such as Microsoft Dynamics 365 or Salesforce. They offer valuable insights and recommendations to stakeholders.
- **Presales Consultant BA:** The Generic BA collaborates with the sales team to understand customer requirements and develop tailored solutions to meet their needs effectively.
- **Consultant:** As a Consultant, the Generic BA provides expert advice and guidance to clients, assisting them in making informed decisions and optimising their business processes. They play significant roles as Domain BAs/Consultants.
- **Testing BA:** The Generic BA can also take on the crucial responsibility of a Testing BA, ensuring that developed solutions meet the specified requirements and function flawlessly.
- **Data Analyst BA:** Sometimes BAs are often referred for the role of Data Analyst. Data Analysts specialise in collecting, cleaning, and analysing data to extract meaningful insights that inform business decision-making. Data Analyst BA is a versatile professional combining data analysis expertise and business acumen. The skillsets required for this role are slightly different, and I have not covered this role or the job in this book.

A remarkable characteristic of a Generic/Functional BA is their ability to apply their expertise across different industries. They possess a broad-level understanding of various domains, allowing them to adapt their skills to various contexts. This versatility gives them a competitive edge, enabling them to tackle various challenges.

Being a "Jack of all trades" in business analysis offers certain advantages. Generalist BAs, such as Generic/Functional BAs, have more opportunities because they are open to working in any industry and can quickly gain the required domain knowledge. Their adaptability and willingness to take on different roles make them highly sought after by organisations seeking flexible and knowledgeable professionals.

Whether aspiring to be an expert in a specific domain or adopting a more versatile approach, mastering the fundamentals of Business Analysis is crucial. Core skills and techniques like requirements elicitation, documentation, stakeholder management, and solution evaluation form the foundation of a successful BA career. Therefore, aspiring BAs should focus on honing these essential skills to thrive in the dynamic field of Business Analysis, regardless of the industry they choose to work in and you can rely on this book to learn about all these aspects.

Functional Consultant (FC) Vs. BA

Whose Job is better? BA? or FC?

I received this question from a couple of people in recent times.

I have answered this query to many career aspirants in these areas (BA or FC). Though the skillsets required to perform these two job roles overlap, some differences exist.

Who is a BA?

- The BA elicits, documents, validates, and manages requirements and scope.
- The BA comes up with relevant solutions to business problems.
- The BA Interacts regularly with business stakeholders as part of stakeholder management w.r.t managing requirements, scope, change requests, etc.
- The BA is a technology agnostic—he/she can work on any project; for him/her, analysing business problems, capturing requirements, proposing solutions, and fulfilling requirements becomes the key focus.

Who is a FC?

- An FC is a Product expert. Ex: Microsoft Dynamics 365 or Salesforce.
- An FC works with BA to understand requirements. Sometimes, both BA & FC are the same person!
- An FC and BA together decide on a relevant solution to the business problems
- An FC also interacts regularly with business stakeholders along with BA w.r.t design and other solution-related aspects
- An FC is technology-specific—this is where the key difference comes in.

The advent of software products in many areas (like CRM, ERP and much more) has given rise to many such product implementation projects. There are many products in the market in these areas, such as SAP, Oracle, Dynamics 365, etc., in the ERP area, and Microsoft Dynamics 365 CE, Pega CRM, Salesforce, etc., in the CRM area. An FC is a person who has significant expertise in any of these products or multiple products. Ex: While a BA, I am also an expert Dynamics 365 CE Functional Consultant.

As an FC, one needs to understand the requirements and analyse how those requirements can be implemented using the product he/she is an expert on. An FC's critical skill is mapping requirements to the capabilities of the product being implemented.

The BA is a Business Problem solver, and an FC is an SME of a software product. an FC may be an expert in that technology in complex developmental projects. An FC may not be a technical person, but he/she knows how a product can be configured/customised/ extended to fulfil requirements.

So, which role is better?

As a BA, your marketability is higher as your skills can be usable in any project. As an FC for a specific product, your marketability becomes limited—but no harm if you want to be in a niche. If you have BA skills and expertise in any of the hottest products in the market (e.g., Dynamics 365 CE or ERP, Salesforce CRM, Pega, etc.,) your marketability further increases, and it will help you do the Job better—you may become BA & FC for a project.

My take: If you are an expert BA, gain expertise on any of the hottest products/skills in the market. If you are just an FC right now, gain some

BA knowledge and experience—you don't have to struggle much, as your current skills are transferrable.

Who is a Technical BA?

Technical BAs bring together technical expertise and business knowledge. Like Functional BAs, they act as a bridge between business and technical teams, ensuring smooth collaboration and successful project implementations—but they mainly focus on technical aspects. In today's job market, these roles are often called Technical Architect, Tech Lead, or Technical Solution Architect. However, it's essential to understand the responsibilities associated with this position.

Traditionally, Technical BAs are found in the Information Technology department. They combine their understanding of business processes with technical skills to develop effective technical solutions. Their main goal is to identify opportunities for improving business processes using technology.

One of the critical responsibilities of a Technical BA is to act as a bridge between business and technical teams. They translate business requirements into technical artefacts that can be implemented by the technical teams efficiently. This requires them to understand the business needs and convert them into technical terms for accurate and efficient implementation. In essence, the key requirement of this role is the ability to understand the business problem and accordingly suggest the best possible technical solution for the business problem. Technical BAs expand on traditional Business Analysis, focusing on managing the complexities of modern enterprises. They often work alongside functional BAs within the team to achieve the desired outcomes.

Technical BAs facilitate effective communication between technical teams and business stakeholders. They articulate business challenges and requirements in a way that technical teams can understand. They also develop solutions to address business problems and guide teams in their implementation. Conducting system impact analyses is another crucial skill they possess, enabling them to anticipate challenges and identify the effects of proposed solutions before implementation.

To be successful in their role, Technical BAs need specific skills. They should have expertise in system analysis, which involves analysing system and enterprise architectures. While they may not design the models themselves, they interpret and improve existing models when necessary.

Data analysis is another important skill for Technical BAs. They work with the data team and examine, clean, transform, and interpret data to derive meaningful insights. They provide accurate and actionable information by distinguishing facts from assumptions and correcting faulty data.

As a Technical BA, proficiency in system integration analysis is also crucial. System integration involves merging different systems within an organisation to ensure seamless operation. Technical BAs must assess which systems can be integrated and work together effectively.

As Technical BAs, they are expected to deliver various artefacts. One primary deliverable is the Technical Requirements and Design document (High level, Low level, etc.), which defines the technical requirements of a project or solution. Deliverables vary for this role. They are also expected to contribute to Functional Specifications, which the Functional BA owns. They also produce data analysis artefacts, interpret and design data models, and define technical terms related to data analysis. Documentation of system and enterprise architecture is another essential deliverable.

Now, here is the truth. As conveyed earlier, a role like Technical BA is non-existent now. Anyone who is technical and wants to get into the above role is called a Technical architect or Technical Lead.

Categories of Bas Based on The Behaviour

As discussed in the previous chapter, the right Mindset is essential for a BA. If a BA has the right Mindset, the responsibilities of a BA can be executed without much fuss. The absence of the right BA Mindset will be problematic for a BA. Simply put, the absence of the right BA Mindset will result in BAs becoming mere order-takers rather than Proactive, confident, and authoritative BAs.

As the Delivery Manager, I am entitled to get feedback from customers very often. In this meeting, we often discuss Requirements, Projects, Schedules, Risks, contracts, and more. Regarding resources, I always hear a major complaint about BAs. However, considering the multi-layered nature of the job role, a BA can't satisfy everyone, so I often take a complaint with a pinch of salt.

However, when I hear the one complaint repeatedly: "Your BAs are not proactive", it's a major concern for me. Most of the time, "We want people who can drive things proactively rather than mere order takers" would be the next line of complaint that I usually receive from customers.

Imagine you are in a Restaurant. The waiter comes to you and asks: "May I take your order?" You will order what you think may be good, and the waiter records it. In some Restaurants, the waiters go one step forward and suggest the delicacies that are unique or bestselling, and you like it eventually.

Become a Proactive BA: I have seen BAs doing the Job of just order takers like the first waiter in the above example. Like the second waiter, some BAs ask right and high-impact questions to the customers, for which they go blank, forcing them to think, go back, come back, answer and conclude. That one question may change the course of the project. It would have solved an issue/a problem that would have come after the implementation. Projects where BAs are proactive have become successful and received good feedback from customers.

What is "Being Proactive"?

The essence of the 'Be Proactive' habit is taking responsibility. You take ownership. This can be applied to any aspect of your personal or working life you desire to be effective. For instance, you can keep blaming someone or the circumstances for your current situation. On the other hand, you could take a proactive approach and decide to take control of your situation and try to escape it.

BAs can learn from this habit by being proactive in their work. It's easy to take a passive approach and merely follow instructions from their customers or PMs without offering valuable suggestions or challenges to enhance the work's effectiveness. However, being proactive allows BAs to influence and control their work, leading to increased effectiveness.

Being a proactive BA means driving the conversation, asking relevant questions, and understanding the root cause of a problem during discussions with customers. It involves writing clear and concise requirements, even if the customer expects the BA to write what they want. A proactive BA critically analyses assumptions made during the presales phase and ensures they are still valid during the project phase. By doing so, they can propose alternative solutions and lead discussions with customers to minimise any potential impact on project execution.

To be effective, BAs must focus on value-add and bridge the gap between what the business articulates and what the technology department needs for successful development. They need not be experts in every business process but should possess techniques that add value and help articulate business needs. A proactive BA should attack the details of a project and ask the right questions to uncover information needed to support business processes and objectives.

Understanding requirements is not about gathering them like apples from a tree. Instead, BAs gather information about business pain points, needs, and objectives. This discovery phase helps BAs ask well-informed questions and provides a foundation for analysis. Through continuous refinement and analysis, BAs can discover root causes, dependencies, and factors that impact desired outcomes.

Data is not information, information is not knowledge, knowledge is not understanding, understanding is not wisdom. – Clifford Stoll

Order Taker Vs. Proactive BAs

Generally, a company win a Project by bidding for a Request for proposal (RFP) floated by the customer. This is called the Presales stage, where the company proposes a solution based on a limited understanding of the customer's business problems/requirements. From such presales RFPs/other documents, BAs get a high-level understanding of requirements. During presales, due to limited information and time availability, the team would have proposed a solution based on certain assumptions.

During the project phase, BA must check if those assumptions are still valid; if not, what's the next step? – This is where a BA's critical thinking skill is used. There might be a scenario where assumptions might not be valid, and the approach might have to be changed, impacting the timeline/cost of the project.

But now the customer says: "This is unacceptable. You said it can be done, now you are saying you can't".

Suddenly, hell breaks loose, and the BA will come under pressure from all the corners. However, a BA who cares about quality will not fret. He/she will build a case for why the approach should differ and lead proactive discussions with customers to convince them. Adamant customers won't listen, but most will agree to get into some trade-offs to minimise the impact on the project execution, time and cost.

Remember that, as a BA, your primary goal is to provide value to your customers. However, it's equally important to maintain awareness of your organisation's revenue and profitability throughout the project delivery process. This dual focus ensures that you can successfully deliver the project while contributing to your organisation's financial health and sustainability.

This is how a proactive BA can make or break a project:

- Instead of simply sitting and passively listening/typing/scribing to what the customer says, a proactive BA will steer the conversation by asking relevant questions to gather only the necessary information.
- Many BAs become order takers for several reasons–lack of experience, insufficient skill, or the "fear of customer" –making them believe whatever customers say they should do. They will never go in-depth into the problem statement; hence, the real problem remains as it is. Thus, creating ambiguous requirements, leading to a troubled or failed implementation.
- They make sure that real end users are consulted while drafting requirements. Ultimately, they will use the system–if they do not find it helpful, feedback will come immediately.
- Proactive BAs always showcase their experience, thus adding value to their work, which customers will respect. Above all, they apply common sense.
- Proactive BAs always follow a model/technique to discuss topics – well-prepared questions, whiteboarding, visuals (process diagrams, etc.) to incite your customer's thought process– this approach will reduce understanding gaps immensely.

Business analysis should be a conversation. BAs must bring their experiences into requirements workshops, even if the concept isn't perfect. This opens up discussions and unblocks creativity. As a BA, learn to ask questions, as there is no such thing as a stupid question.

Be creative. Create value. Be brave, Be free.

What did You Learn in this Chapter?

- Who is a Proactive BA?
- Who is a Domain Specific-BA?
- What is the crucial character a BA should possess?
- Are you a proactive BA? Introspect yourself

CHAPTER 5

PROJECT LIFECYCLES & ROLE OF A BA

- *Typical IT Project Lifecycle*
- *Top 5 Deliverables of A BA*
- *Waterfall Vs. Agile*

As we read so far, BAs play a crucial role in ensuring the success of IT projects by identifying and analysing the business requirements of stakeholders and translating them into technical requirements that can be implemented by the development team in collaboration with BA and customers.

How Does a Typical Project Lifecycle Work In IT?

Now, let's explore how a typical IT project starts and ends and how a BA contributes to each stage. These are typical scenarios/steps.

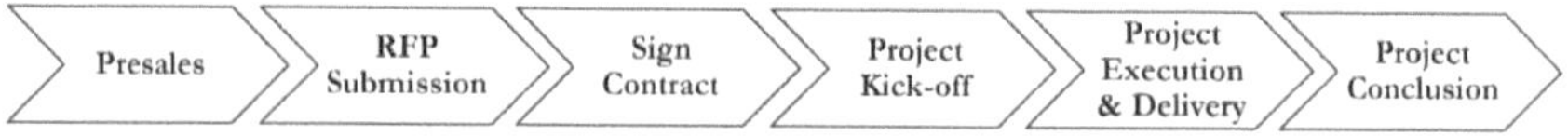

Presales Stage: This stage is the first stage of an IT project (typically), where an IT company's sales & presales team identifies potential clients/opportunities and discusses their requirements (or potential customers approach the company). In this stage, BAs work with potential customers to understand their needs and objectives and help the sales team create a proposal that meets their needs and budget. Typically, the IT company secures a project by participating in a bidding process for a customer's RFP and presenting a solution based on understanding the Customer's business problems.

Responding & submitting the RFPs: Sometimes, potential clients may request an RFP document outlining their requirements. In such cases, the BA works with the sales team to respond to the RFP. The BA evaluates the client's requirements, provides input on the technical feasibility, cost, and risk, and provides recommendations on meeting the client's requirements within the budget and timeline. The BA also works with the development/ technical team to get the effort estimations. The final proposal outlines the project's scope, deliverables, timelines, budget, assumptions, risks & mitigations, team structure, delivery methodology, delivery approach, Price and any other requested information. After the submission, if the Customer invites, BA also presents the Proposal/RFP.

Contract/SOW Signing: If the client agrees to the proposal/RFP, the project moves to the Contract phase. In this phase, BA prepares the Contract or Scope of Work (SOW) as per the organisational template in collaboration with the legal team, which includes the project's scope, deliverables, timelines, budget, and payment terms and legal terms and conditions—which are contractually binding for both the parties (Vendor & Customer). Of course, the legal aspects of the contract/SOW are completely taken care of by the legal team within the organisation. Ultimately, both parties will sign the finalised and approved contract or SoW.

Project Kick-off & Discovery: Once the contract/SoW is signed, the project moves to the kick-off and Discovery/Requirements phase. During this phase, the project team develops a comprehensive project plan. BAs help PMs and collaborate with the development team to create a detailed project plan outlining the system's design, development, testing, and deployment. The methodology of delivery will be finalised. The scope will be finalised. BAs play a vital role in this phase by translating the client's business requirements into technical requirements.

Project Execution: The development team implements the project plan during the project execution phase. BAs play a critical role in this phase by ensuring the development team meets the client's business requirements. BAs work closely with the development team to create use cases, business process flows, and data models used to develop the system. They also provide input on the system's technical specifications, such as the programming language, database technology, and deployment environment.

BAs are often indirectly involved in project implementation but are called upon when issues arise, requiring them to coordinate problem-solving meetings and engage stakeholders and development teams to devise new ways of achieving desired results while saving available resources. This support may include reviewing proposed processes and procedures during the implementation stage to address technological, functional, or compatibility issues and to communicate any new or additional needs to stakeholders.

Project Delivery & Testing: Once the system is developed, the project moves to the delivery and testing phase. BAs play a crucial role in this phase by ensuring the system meets the client's business requirements. They work with the development and testing team to conduct testing and ensure that the system is functional and free of bugs—testers test the system to raise the bugs. The development team fixes the bugs. BAs also train the customer stakeholders to ensure they can use the system effectively. BAs also work with customer stakeholders in User Acceptance testing (UAT), where a set of identified users (From the customer side) will test the system and give the go-ahead for final deployment to the production environment.

Project Conclusion: The project concludes with the delivery of the system to the Customer. BAs play a vital role in this phase by ensuring that the Customer is satisfied with the system and that it meets their business requirements. They work with the development team to address any issues or bugs during deployment. BAs also help the customer transition from the old system to the new one and provide support during the post-deployment phase.

Indeed, BAs play a vital role in the success of IT projects from the presales stage to the project conclusion. By working closely with the Customer, BAs ensure the system is delivered on time, within budget, and meets the Customer's business requirements. At the same time, he/she collaborates with the PM, Project team, Customer and other stakeholders.

Typical Top 5 Deliverables of A BA

Approach Document: This approach document outlines the key elements of a project, including background, business drivers, problem statement, vision, scope, dependencies, key roles and stakeholder engagement plan. It comprehensively explains the project's purpose, requirements, scope and outcomes. Though this is a TOP 5, many organisations suggest including these details in the Project Charter document, which outlines a project's purpose, scope, and stakeholders. Sometimes, this document is provided by the customers or customer side BA.

Business Requirements Specification: The Business Requirements Specification includes business drivers, problem statements, stakeholder models, business domain models, business use cases, business activity diagrams, and business requirements. The stakeholder model defines internal and external actors, while the business domain model represents the business's structural view. Business use cases and activity diagrams identify functional areas and their behavioural representation. Sometimes, this document is provided by the customer side BA.

Functional Specification Document: The functional specification includes contextual information—current status, to-be system use cases, user stories, traceable user requirements, mapping of requirements to business needs, system activity diagrams, functional requirements, process flow diagrams, class diagrams, wireframes, Integration requirements and mappings (source-to-target mapping of data etc.) and data migration requirements (Data Migration requirements sometimes would be a separate document), diagrams that show domain concepts, assumptions and any information that needs to be documented and agreed with stakeholders.

Non-functional Requirements Document: The non-functional requirements specify technical requirements associated with project functionality/deliverables, such as hardware, software specifications, performance, supportability, security, interface (integrations), availability, and compliance-related specifications. Depending on organisational preferences, these can be combined with functional requirements or delivered separately, but it is crucial to understand the client's required deliverables and terminology.

Requirements Traceability Matrix (RTM): This document clearly links project requirements and their fulfilment, ensuring comprehensive and successful outcomes. The matrix tracks each requirement from its inception through design, development, testing, and final implementation. This helps stakeholders monitor the project's progress, detect potential gaps, and verify that every requirement is addressed. By fostering accountability and transparency, the RTM minimises misunderstandings, enhances communication, and facilitates quality assurance. Ultimately, the RTM serves as a roadmap that aligns the project team and stakeholders, leading to a smoother development process and a higher likelihood of project success.

Basics of Methodologies: Waterfall Vs. Agile

As you already know, Agile and Waterfall are two project management approaches that aim to deliver a successful project, but their approaches differ.

Waterfall Way: This is a linear methodology that follows a strict sequence of phases, including requirements, design, development, testing, deployment, and maintenance. In Waterfall, each phase must be completed before moving on to the next, and generally, no changes are allowed once a phase is complete.

The BA plays a crucial role in the Waterfall methodology by writing the requirements document, which serves as the project's foundation. While providing structure, it can be rigid and less adaptable to changes compared to Agile methods.

Agile Way: Agile is an approach (SCRUM, SaFe, etc., are methodology frameworks inspired by Agile) that emphasises an iterative approach to project management. In this concept, in SCRUM, one of the popular agile frameworks, the project is divided into smaller, more manageable chunks called sprints, usually lasting for two weeks. The team works on each Sprint until it is complete before moving on to the next one.

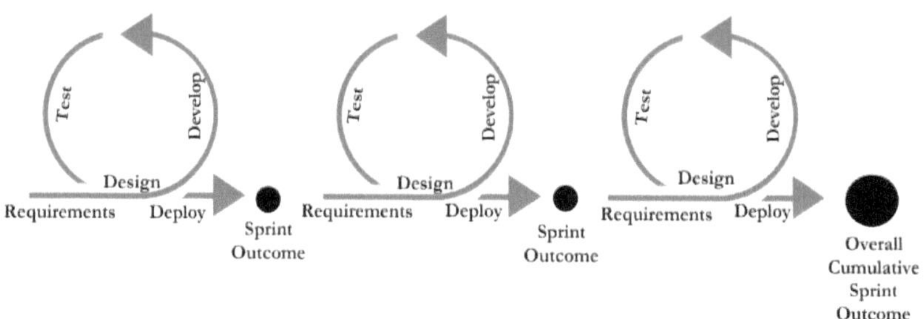

Throughout the project, Agile methodology enables the team to adapt their plans based on feedback. The three critical roles in Agile are the Product Owner, the Scrum Master (SM), and the Development Team. Although there is no "official" role for the BA in Agile, they still have a valuable role in the project.

The Product Owner works with the BA and development team to set project vision and priorities, ensuring it stays on track. Sometimes, BA and product Owner roles are handled by a single person—the BA. The SM is responsible for ensuring that the team follows the Agile methodology and promptly addresses any issues. The development team is responsible for completing the work on each Sprint. BAs collaborate with the Product Owner to define the project vision, prioritise user stories, manage the product backlog, and ensure the team is on track. They can also work with the development team to ensure their work meets the project's requirements.

Which one to choose when: Choosing the best methodology for a project depends on several factors, such as project requirements and team dynamics. Waterfall is suitable for projects with clear and well-defined requirements that do not require much change or iteration. Conversely, Agile is ideal for projects requiring flexibility, rapid development, and the ability to make changes and adjustments throughout development. Agile is more appropriate where requirements are not very clear or evolving. However, Agile necessitates active customer participation in project activities, a challenge numerous organisations encounter.

Role of A BA In an Agile Scenario

As discussed earlier, even though there is no exclusive role for a BA in Agile-inspired SCRUM or any other Agile approach-based projects, having a BA role in Agile is a must and beneficial. The success of any Scrum project heavily relies on the contributions of the BA.

As the skill of a BA is unique, they have their usual and core responsibility of identifying and analysing the needs of customers and stakeholders and providing solutions that address their problems. Additionally, they review user stories created by the Product Owner to ensure they meet acceptance criteria and cover all business rules and functionality. Depending on a project's complexity and size, a BA can join a Scrum team in two ways: as a Product Owner or as a team member. In some cases, the project can have BA & proxy Product Owner roles handled by a single person—the BA.

As a Product Owner, a BA mediates between the team and the stakeholders. They negotiate with stakeholders/customers to prioritise tasks and user stories. The BA can also be a Product Owner in less complex projects because the scope can be less manageable. Conversely, in complex projects, usually, there will be two professionals, a Product Owner and a BA.

As a team member, a BA plays a vital role in helping the development team understand the product and brainstorm new ideas to create the product increment. They collaborate with the QA team to analyse and test the coverage, use cases, hidden requirements, dependability, and effects. When complex projects have several modules distributed among teams, having the same BA for many teams is advantageous.

The importance of BAs in Scrum teams increases, especially in the initial phases of a new project and with large-scale projects. As Scrum has Sprints and, in each Sprint, there could be Requirements elicitation of clarification sessions, having a BA during the entire Project lifecycle is essential.

They serve as the primary contact for developers when they face any obstacles during the development process. They are the people who understand the product requirements and write stories, acceptance, and wireframes achievable by the technical team.

BAs are high-performing professionals with technical knowledge of the development process of a product. Their involvement in a project begins with understanding the customer's needs and extends to the sprint demo. With their critical role in the Scrum team, BAs are indispensable for any organisation or project that aims to deliver high-quality products, regardless of the methodology employed, whether Agile or Waterfall.

When there are lengthy Epics/Features or User Stories, BAs must break them down further and prioritise them according to the Sprint. This will avoid problems for the Developer, who may not have the skill set to do so and will help the Developer to understand the user stories better and deliver them more efficiently. If left unaddressed (lengthy Epics or User stories), this may result in ambiguity or unclear requirements, or one may not be able to accommodate them within a Sprint and, hence, a failed Sprint and, ultimately, a failed project. To prevent such scenarios, having a BA role within a Scrum team is always wise – and it is becoming a standard practice nowadays.

Role of A BA In a Waterfall Project

The Waterfall methodology sees software development as a linear process progressing steadily from project initiation through analysis, development, testing, and delivery. The BA plays an important role in ensuring project success with this approach.

During the project initiation phase, the BA may create a business case that involves problem analysis, goal and objective definition, and cost-benefit analysis and present it to senior management. BA is responsible for creating a Requirements Specifications document or something similar in the analysis phase, which captures, clarifies, and confirms the requirements. The BA elicits and analyses business and stakeholder needs expressed in natural language and/or models to accomplish this. Waterfall methodologies commonly use process and data models to improve stakeholder communication, enabling early identification of potential issues.

In the design phase, the BA and Subject Matter Experts, Technical Architects and Developers define solutions and technical specifications. The BA will also be involved in the testing phase and usually leads the acceptance testing with customer stakeholders. Although testing is not a recognised business analysis activity, many organisations assign the responsibility for acceptance testing to the BA, and the BA will drive the entire user acceptance testing activity by working with customers and the testing team. This is based on the recognition that no one understands the requirements better than the BA. In this situation, the BA needs different skills to verify and validate that the delivered software meets the business community's requests.

Change Management: Changes that arise after acceptance of a phase are managed through a rigorous "Change Management" process, where the BA works with the Change management team. Change management involves structured approaches and strategies to smoothly transition customers, individuals, teams, and organisations (users impacted by the project) from current to desired future states while minimising resistance and maximising the adoption of changes.

Scope Changes: Even though the Waterfall approach requires a lot of effort in managing requirements, it is necessary to do so to deal with changes in requirements that may arise during the development of the project cost-effectively. The Waterfall approach assumes that requirements can be clearly defined upfront and that changes to requirements (Scope changes or scope creep) are minimised.

However, requirements or scope changes can still occur, and effective management of requirements can help deal with such changes in a way that minimises costs and impacts on the project. Therefore, while the effort required for requirements management in the Waterfall approach may be high, it is necessary to ensure the project's success. The BA is "The Real Captain" of a Project team in that sense.

What did You Learn in this Chapter?

- What is key difference between Agile & Waterfall?
- How to decide if Agile is better or Waterfall for a Project?
- Do you think Agile methodology is "change" friendly? Why?
- What are the typical roles a BA can handle in a SCRUM (Agile) team?
- What are according to you Top 3 deliverable from a BA in a Project?
- What is the role of BA in a Presales Stage?
- Should BAs collaborate with testing team to execute testing – SIT, UAT etc.?
- Is Agile is a methodology or an approach (concept)?

CHAPTER 6

TECHNIQUES OF BUSINESS ANALSYS

- *What Exactly Is Business Analysis?*
- *Widely Used Business Analysis Techniques*
- *How Frameworks and Techniques Work & When to Use Them?*

[Disclaimer: *The detailed literature about each technique discussed in this chapter is available online in the public domain, and I did not invent these techniques. I do not claim ownership or copyright of these techniques, and the credit for creating these valuable techniques goes to the respective experts who originated them. The primary objective of this chapter is to share my experiences of utilizing these techniques. This is an endeavour to consolidate all the necessary information in one location for individuals new to Business Analysis, enabling them to learn and incorporate these techniques into their work.]*

Like anything, business analysis's power depends on how you do it.

Note, if you're a BA, you're not limited to working on projects. Depending on your organisation's role, you can be a consultant, a business advisor, or a strategist. Business analysis can be done for all kinds of initiatives within a company, whether they're big-picture plans or day-to-day operations. It's all about making the organisation better and better.

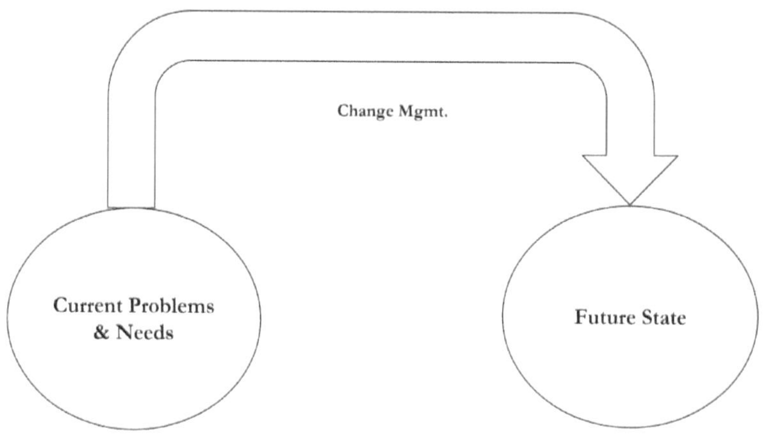

In this chapter, we'll explore some cool business analysis techniques, what each option brings, and how you can use them to analyse your processes based on your needs and goals. Business analysis techniques are important to analyse the organisation's current state (Current Problems and needs) and how a desired future state can be achieved based on the organisation's vision (Future State) leveraging various Business Analysis techniques.

Business analysis techniques are like tools for creating plans and making them work to determine what a company requires and achieve great outcomes. Since each business is unique, there's a single technique that fits all. Let's discover some key business analysis methods and how they contribute to a company's success in different situations. These approaches are widely recognised and applied both within and outside of projects.

Here is the list of business analysis techniques widely used in the BA world. As a BA, one should be familiar with most of them, if not all. This book will explore only basic and practical information about each technique, which is sufficient to understand the concept behind each. Note, each of these techniques has its purpose. Use them for the purpose.

Here is the list:

1. **Business Process Modelling (BPM)**
2. **Use case modelling**
3. **Brainstorming**
4. **Ishikawa Cause and Effect (Fish-bone Diagram)**
5. **SWOT Analysis**
6. **CATWOE**
7. **MoSCoW (Must or Should, Could or Would)**
8. **The 5 Whys**

Business Process Modelling (BPM): BPM is commonly used during or before analysing a project to figure out and study the differences between how things are done now in a business and how they want it to be done in the future. Business Process Modelling is about improving things and improving the way processes work. In this chapter & section, we'll cover only the basics of BPM and delve into the details in the upcoming chapters.

As per the International Institute of Business Analysis (IIBA), BAs perform the following tasks while performing BPM:

- Plan and Analyse

- Business Model Analysis (May include technical Analysis)
- Enhancing the process and modelling it
- Propose how to automate/make it better for higher productivity
- Monitor it and fine-tune it if required

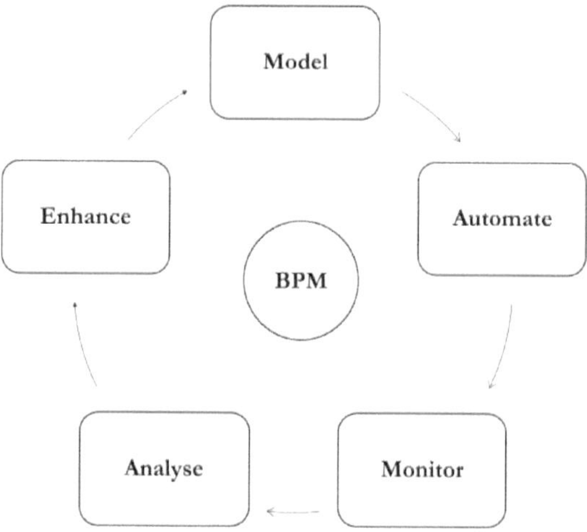

In the business world, BPM is often depicted in a diagram format where processes, decisions, and information flow sequentially. There are two standard notations used for BPM diagrams:

- BPMN (Business Process Modelling Notation)
- UML (Unified Modelling Language) Activity Diagram

The advantage of the BPM technique is its ability to visually illustrate how a business process will unfold with various roles. This makes it easier for people to grasp the sequential steps of the execution process. As a result, complex business analysis becomes more manageable for a BA. A BPM is a lively graphical representation of a business process or workflow, along with its related sub-processes. Process modelling generates vibrant activity diagrams and flowcharts that offer valuable insights into a particular process's operation. These diagrams capture:

- Events and activities within the workflow
- The individuals or entities responsible for initiating those events and activities
- Decision points & the different paths the workflow can follow based on the outcomes
- Devices involved in the process
- Timelines for the overall process and each step

- Success and failure rates of the process

Many industries, especially the dynamic IT sector, prefer this technique because it straightforwardly presents the execution process, highlighting the roles and responsibilities. These nifty visuals help BAs to document processes in a fun and pictorial way. BPM, a flow chart method, allows us to map out the steps of a planned business process from start to finish. It's like creating a roadmap for success!

An Example of a Simple Process Flow Diagram:

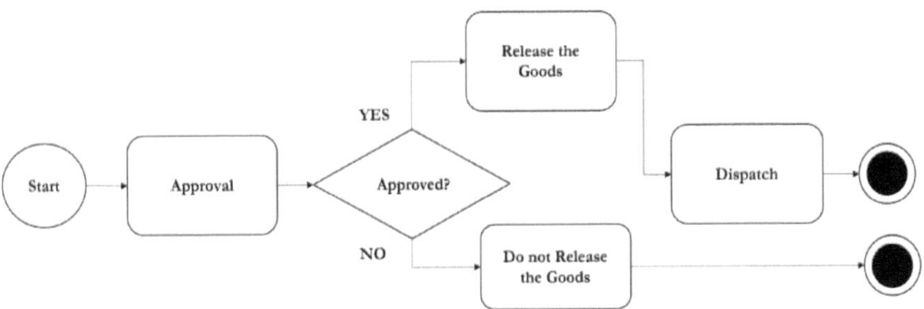

Now, here's the cool part. BPM helps us understand two different states of a process (Not shown in the diagram). You can create two diagrams. First, the "As-is" state represents the process as it currently exists, without any changes or improvements. Then, with the "To-be" state, which envisions the future after implementing those changes and improvements. And now, you have a clear comparison right before you; isn't that valuable?

Use Case Modelling: Another groovy technique we have is use case modelling. This is all about creating eye-catching illustrations of how the business functions should work in a proposed system through user interactions. It's like sketching out a blueprint for success! Use case modelling is particularly handy in software development projects during the design phase. It helps transform those awesome business requirements into functional specifications. We can use tools like Microsoft Visio, Draw.io, Lucid Chart, and many more to draw these diagrams. Let your creativity shine!

The primary components of use case modelling in a UML diagram are:

- **System**—The outline of the diagram is represented as the system. The above diagram depicts the rectangular box as the Lead Management system.
- **Actors**—The human-like shape in the diagram represents the user/department/ team associated with the use case or functionality.

We represent them outside the rectangular box. In the above example, the Salesperson/Sales team creates the Lead in the system.

- **Use Case**—In a UML diagram, an oval shape represents a UML case, and an individual use case represents a single functionality. In the above example, Create Lead, Qualify Lead, Close Lead & Create Order, etc., are separate functionalities executed as part of the Lead management process. Per the convention, every action in the use case is represented using an active verb.

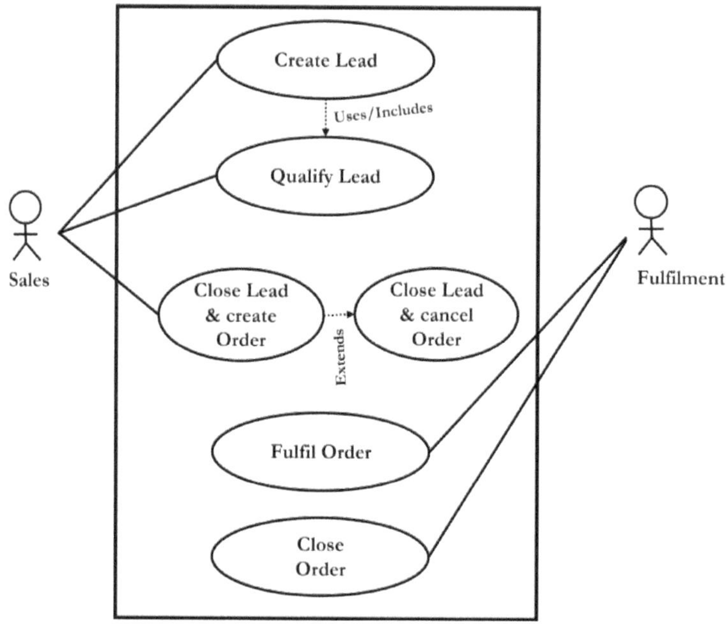

- **Association**—An actor's interaction with the system via use cases is an association. The above diagram shows that the Sales Person/Sales Team and Fulfilment Person/Fulfilment Team are the key actors interacting with the system through different use cases.
- **Stereotypes**—The relationships between the use cases are known as Stereotypes. There are two types of Stereotypes –

<<Includes>> OR <<uses>>
<<extends>>

- "Uses" or an "Include Relationship" refers to a connection where one-use case (the foundational use case) encompasses the features of another use case (the included use case). (Example: In the above diagram, creation of Lead & Qualification of Lead)

- "Extends" depicts an optional or alternative behaviour in a use case diagram. It signifies that one use case can extend another by adding additional steps or variations under certain conditions. The extended use case is not always required to be executed but provides an optional or alternative flow in the main use case. (Example: In the above diagram, Close Lead could be "Create Order" or "Cancel Order")

The beauty of this technique lies in its user-centric approach. As we analyze the requirements from the users' perspective, the outcome is both user-focused and highly effective. It's all about putting the users at the heart of the process and creating solutions that truly cater to their needs.

Exercise For You—
Create a Use Case diagram which should depict all the above elements for a process of your choice.

Brainstorming: One of the most common techniques is Brainstorming! It is mainly used for generating fresh ideas, uncovering the root causes of problems, and cracking the code to complex business challenges. Brainstorming is the go-to group activity that BAs adore. It's all about unleashing our imaginations, diving deep into the root causes, and dishing out mind-blowing solutions. And guess what? Brainstorming sets the stage for other epic business analysis methods like SWOT sensation and PESTLE power-up.

The strength of brainstorming lies in its capacity to unlock our creative potential. The key objective here is to generate a substantial volume of fresh and innovative ideas while uncovering captivating themes for further exploration.

- What options do we have to tackle the pesky problem at hand?
- What's holding us back from chasing a dazzling approach or option?
- Who's the culprit causing a delay in activity 'A'?
- How can we join forces to conquer problem 'B'?

The magic of Brainstorming comes alive and is best enjoyed in a group, where everyone can bring their unique experiences to the table and unleash their creativity. But don't fret if you're a lone ranger—saddle up and embark on a solo brainstorming to ignite those ingenious ideas. The secret

sauce? Embrace fresh perspectives and let your thoughts roam free in every direction.
Now, let's break down our quest into three exhilarating phases:

Phase 1: Preparation

- Clarify the area we're diving into with crystal clarity.
- Set a time limit for idea generation, considering the group's size.
- Assemble a diverse crew of facilitators and participants representing a range of backgrounds and experiences.
- Rally the troops and establish the ground rules for this epic session.
- Craft the criteria for evaluating and rating our mind-blowing ideas.

Phase 2: Sessions

- Unleash a flurry of fresh ideas without any debates, critiques, or judgments.
- Capture all ideas visually for everyone to feast their eyes upon.
- Encourage everyone to unleash their wildest creativity, share over-the-top concepts, and build upon each other's brilliance.
- Note, there are no limits to the number of ideas we can generate. The more, the merrier!

Phase 3: Present Findings

- When the time's up, it's showtime! Discuss and evaluate our ideas using the predetermined criteria.
- Create a condensed list of the most electrifying ideas, merging them when they complement each other and eliminating duplicates.
- Give our ideas the star treatment by rating them like the rock stars they are.
- Finally, distribute the ultimate list of ideas to the party that needs them most.

Now, let's take a moment to weigh the pros and cons of this legendary technique:

Pros:

- **Enhanced Idea Generation:** The brainstorming process facilitates the rapid generation of numerous ideas within a short timeframe, allowing many creative possibilities to be explored.
- **Non-judgmental Environment:** Brainstorming creates a safe and inclusive space where all ideas are welcomed without criticism or

judgment. This fosters a climate that encourages participants to think creatively and share their thoughts freely.

- **Improved Collaboration:** Brainstorming sessions can alleviate tension and foster better collaboration among team members. By engaging in open discussions and idea sharing, individuals can build upon each other's concepts, leading to innovative solutions and stronger teamwork.

Cons:

- **Individual Engagement:** The success of Brainstorming relies on the creativity and willingness of each individual to actively participate. If some team members are less engaged or hesitant to contribute, it may limit the overall effectiveness of the session.
- **Organizational and Interpersonal Politics:** In some cases, organizational or interpersonal politics can hinder participation and open expression of ideas. Power dynamics or personal biases may suppress certain voices or lead to favouritism, potentially inhibiting the full potential of the brainstorming process.
- **Debating Ideas:** Group members must agree to postpone debates and discussions during the idea-generation phase to ensure a productive brainstorming session.
- If participants get caught up in debating ideas rather than generating them, it can impede the free flow of creativity.

Ishikawa Cause and Effect: The Fishbone diagram is a well-known tool that helps us uncover the reasons behind a problem. This diagram comes to our rescue whenever we want to dig deep and analyze the root causes. It's a fantastic blend of Brainstorming and mind mapping, incredibly powerful in figuring out what's happening.

We can use the fishbone diagram while developing a product or striving to fix a problem. It assists us in honing our focus and engaging in fruitful discussions about the issue at hand.
The mastermind behind this genius tool is Dr. Kaoru Ishikawa, an expert in quality control. He aimed to help people find real solutions to issues, not just treat symptoms. Some call this diagram as cause-and-effect diagrams or Ishikawa diagrams.

Creating a fishbone diagram is an exciting team endeavour. Typically, when you want to present a problem with a process and present a solution for the same, you can draw such diagrams to make your conversations more meaningful with your customer.

Here's how it works: The BA & the team gather around a big sheet of paper or a whiteboard when the team stumble upon a problem that demands further examination, exploring all the possible causes of the problem. Then, a leader takes charge and helps us rank the causes based on their importance. We bring these causes to life on the diagram, arranging them in a hierarchy. Picture it like a fish skeleton, where we start with the big causes and gradually branch out into finer details.

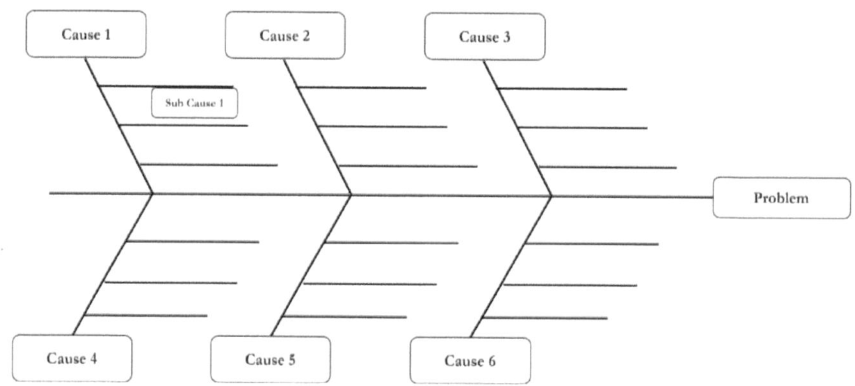

Here are the steps to conduct an analysis session leveraging the Fishbone diagram:

- **Step 1:** Jot down the problem in a box and draw a mighty horizontal arrow that points right at it. Think of it as the backbone of the fish.
- **Step 2:** Identify at least four major causes that could contribute to the problem. It's like playing detective, exploring different categories such as methods, skills, equipment, people, materials, environment, or measurements. Draw these causes, branching off from the backbone, forming the initial bones of our fish.
- **Step 3:** For each cause, delve deeper and brainstorm any related information. Ask yourselves/within the team the questions like "Why?" or consider factors such as policies, procedures, people, and the physical setup. Meticulously note these contributing factors, connecting them to their respective cause with branches.
- **Step 4:** Keep the ball rolling, breaking down each cause further until we unearth the root causes of the problem. Once the diagram is complete, analyze it as a team and agree on the following steps to tackle the issue head-on.

Using a fishbone diagram is like embarking on an exciting adventure to uncover the real culprits behind a problem. Did you ever try this technique?

SWOT Analysis: SWOT analysis is a popular technique for identifying a company's strengths and weaknesses. By perceiving these aspects as opportunities and threats, BAs/Consultants/Analysts are empowered to make informed decisions regarding resource allocation and organizational improvement.

SWOT analysis is instrumental in various decision-making scenarios. Established organizations use it to evaluate and adapt to changing cultures or environments. For new businesses, SWOT analysis is valuable during the planning process as it prompts decision-makers to consider both internal and external factors, determining the most suitable course of action. The core elements of SWOT encompass:

- **Strengths (S):** These encompass the unique qualities or advantages that differentiate a project or business from its competitors.
- **Weaknesses (W):** These highlight the characteristics that place the business at a disadvantage relative to competitors or other projects.
- **Opportunities (O)** involve external factors in the business environment that the project or organization can leverage.
- **Threats (T):** These refer to external environmental elements that may present challenges or obstacles to the business.

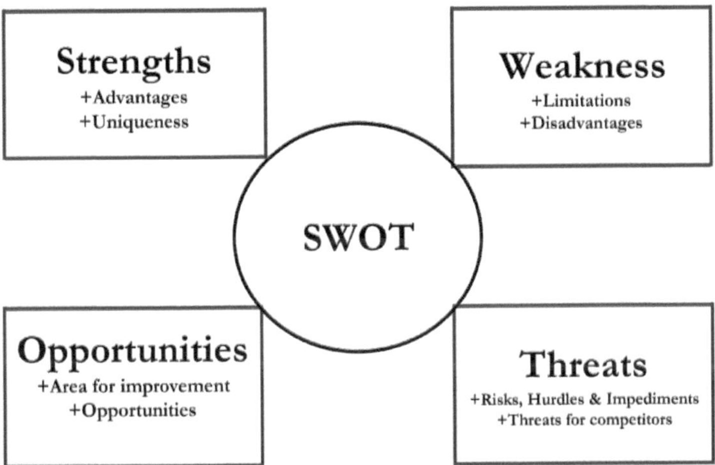

SWOT analysis is a versatile and straightforward technique suitable for quick or comprehensive analyses of organizations, processes, and more, regardless of size. It can also be applied to evaluate groups, functions, or individuals. This technique can be used easily at any stage of a project, not just limited to business analysis. Professionals across various domains are familiar with and utilize this technique.

To conduct a comprehensive SWOT analysis, BAs evaluate internal factors (strengths and weaknesses) and external factors (opportunities and threats). They then categorize the data into four quadrants and provide detailed responses.

During the SWOT analysis process, businesses and teams can explore a range of questions:

- **Strengths:** What areas do we excel in? What internal resources do we possess? What advantages do we hold over our competitors?
- **Weaknesses:** What are the limitations or shortcomings of our business, team, or organization? In what areas do we lag behind our competitors?
- **Opportunities:** Are there any external opportunities or environmental changes that our organization can benefit from?
- **Threats:** Are there upcoming changes from competitors that could impact our viability? Are supplier costs increasing? Have there been any shifts in consumer behaviour or the economy?

It is advisable to involve multiple stakeholders to ensure diverse perspectives are considered. While SWOT analysis generates numerous valuable ideas, it is crucial to prioritize and convert them into actionable strategies. By aligning opportunities with strengths, businesses can maximize their chances of success. Similarly, evaluating threats in light of forces helps minimize their impact.

CATWOE: CATWOE is an innovative approach that brings together the perspectives of different stakeholders on a single platform, allowing BAs to assess the impact of proposed actions thoroughly. The acronym represents the following elements:

- **Customers (C):** Who are the beneficiaries of the business?
- **Actors (A):** Who are the key players involved?
- **Transformation (T):** What is the main thing that drives the change in the system?
- **World View (W):** What is the broader picture, and how does it impact the situation?
- **Owner (O):** Who owns the affected system, and what is their relationship to it?

- **Environmental Constraints (E):** What are the environmental limitations, and how do they influence the solution?

The CATWOE technique is valuable for BAs to gain insights into stakeholder perspectives and effectively manage the change. By investigating each stakeholder's viewpoint individually, BAs can capture crucial information. This information, gathered from face-to-face meetings separately, aids in building a clearer picture of stakeholders' perspectives.

The outcome of each CATWOE analysis is tailored to the unique stakeholder, contributing to improved decision-making within the project. CATWOE empowers BAs to navigate project challenges while considering every angle. Let's explore the elements considered in this approach:

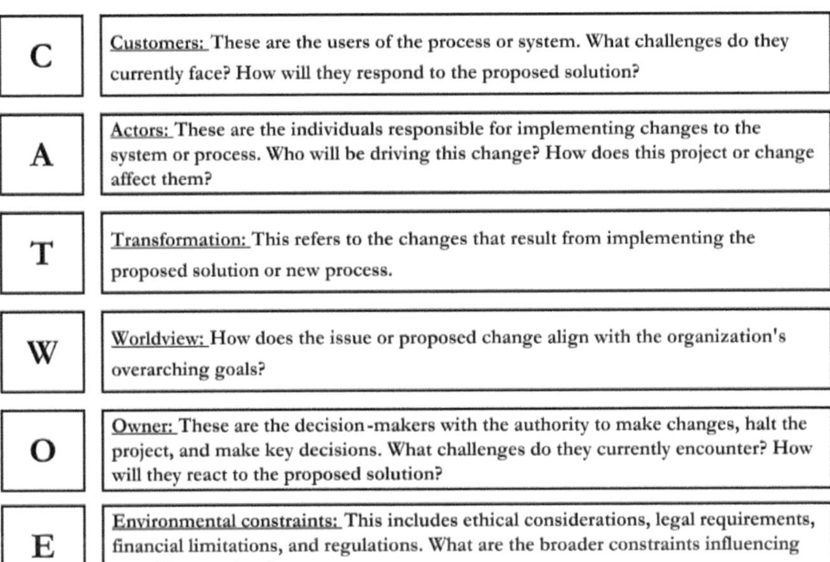

C	Customers: These are the users of the process or system. What challenges do they currently face? How will they respond to the proposed solution?
A	Actors: These are the individuals responsible for implementing changes to the system or process. Who will be driving this change? How does this project or change affect them?
T	Transformation: This refers to the changes that result from implementing the proposed solution or new process.
W	Worldview: How does the issue or proposed change align with the organization's overarching goals?
O	Owner: These are the decision-makers with the authority to make changes, halt the project, and make key decisions. What challenges do they currently encounter? How will they react to the proposed solution?
E	Environmental constraints: This includes ethical considerations, legal requirements, financial limitations, and regulations. What are the broader constraints influencing your ideas or plans?

CATWOE is most effective when utilised at the initial stages of a project or brainstorming process. Developed by Peter Checkland as part of the Soft Systems Methodology, this approach thoroughly considers problems, goals, or strategies and their impact on the business and stakeholders. It provides direction and helps stakeholders and actors avoid future complications.

MoSCoW (Must or Should, Could or Would): The main virtue of a BA is decision-making. A bad decision can always become a costly affair in life or a project. An ability to logically prioritise and decide what to/what not to do now and what can be done later is extremely essential for a BA. This requires good critical thinking skills—a skill to analyse the available facts, observations, data, arguments, and business needs to come up with a decision.

In a Project, let's say to prioritise a set of requirements for a Sprint/Phase, a BA and PM must perform detailed analysis and have conversations with stakeholders and team members. This will clarify why a set of requirements should/should not be a part of the next Sprint/Phase. Prioritisation or decision-making must happen based on the facts, cost-benefit analysis, and value analysis, and in collaboration and agreement with all stakeholders and team members. Can one perform "prioritisation" just by looking at a set of requirements? How does one perform this methodically?

There are various techniques in practice, but **"MoSCoW"** is widely used. It is simple yet effective. Though this technique can be used in various other scenarios/purposes, I am considering the scenario of Requirements prioritisation for this post.

MoSCoW stands for—**Must have, Should have, Could have, and Won't have**. That is which items/ requirements one "must consider", "should consider (but not so mandatory)", "can consider (if time permits)", and lastly, "will not consider".

Must-Have:

- Without these sets of Requirements, the delivery/output won't serve the intended purpose. During analysis, ask yourself:
    - Is this Requirement essential? Why?
    - What could be the outcome without this Requirement?
    - What is the vision/purpose of this sprint/release? Can that be achieved w/o this?

Should Have:

- Requirements that are not so critical but users need it. The output will still be good, but better with these. During analysis, ask yourself:
    - Can this be a Must-have? What will happen if we don't deliver this?
    - Can users wait for some more time without these?

Could Have:

- These are kind of nice to have features that won't impact the core functionality and intended purpose. The key benefit would be a well-defined scope agreed upon by all stakeholders and team members. During analysis, ask yourself:

- How will this Requirement add value to the current release/ Sprint/Phase?
- Is this a Wishlist item?

Won't Have:

- This section is critical because when you say something like "Won't have," you will get many questions from everywhere. Be prepared. During analysis, ask yourself:
  - Why are these items intentionally not included? Why should this item be postponed?
  - Why does this set of Requirements impact the current release in any way?

Key Benefits of this Technique:

- Critical resources can be deployed accordingly because there is a clear distinction between Musts, Shoulds, and could Haves.
- One can clearly define what is not included (Won't Have). So, the scope is well-defined and agreed upon among all stakeholders and team members.

The FIVE WHYS: The "Five Whys" technique revolves solely around the "Why" question. By posing a series of sequential "why" questions, this approach enables BAs to trace the root cause of a problem. This approach helps solve a problem and clarify and finalise a requirement. This technique can be used in a workshop as well. Let's take a look at an example:

Problem: Customer complaints about delayed response in case resolution.

1. Why? Because the support team is not allocating tasks efficiently.
2. Why? Because there's no clear tracking system for case assignments.
3. Why? Because the current software lacks task management features.
4. Why? Because management prioritised other projects.
5. Why? Because there was no awareness of the impact on response times.

Solution: Enhance/Upgrade the software. Prioritise this project and allocate budgetary funds for modernising the software.
The BAs utilise this technique for projects involving technology solutions, whether replacing, changing, or building from scratch. This analysis identifies and captures the essential characteristics required for a new or modified

system. It primarily addresses non-functional requirements related to data storage, performance, and other implicit technical aspects.

The scope of non-functional requirement analysis encompasses various factors, including logging, performance, reliability, security, and more. Non-functional requirement analysis is crucially conducted during the Analysis phase of a project, with its findings put into action during the subsequent Design phase. This technique proves highly valuable when modifying or upgrading a technology solution. For instance, it can be used during migration, where shifting from one technology to another necessitates building the system anew.

BAs primarily focus on assessing system performance and data storage requirements during this analysis. They aim to gauge the performance factors of the proposed system, especially when handling real-time data. This ensures that the system meets the necessary performance benchmarks and can handle data storage efficiently.

Let's explore how you can use the **"Five Whys"** method for non-functional requirements:

- **Step 1:** Choose a non-functional requirement you want to analyse. Let's take an example of the Requirement: "The system should respond in under 2 seconds."
- **Step 2:** Ask "Why?" for the Requirement. For instance, "Why is it necessary for the system to respond in under 2 seconds?"
- **Step 3:** Analyse the initial answer and ask "Why?" again to dig deeper. If the answer is "To ensure a satisfying user experience."
- **Step 4:** Continue asking "Why?". Ask, "Why is it crucial to provide a satisfying user experience?"
- **Step 5:** Repeat the process by asking "Why?" for each answer received. Keep going until you reach the root cause or underlying factor. Each "Why?" will help unveil deeper insights and comprehension of the Requirement.
- **Step 6:** Identify the root cause: The objective is to pinpoint the root cause that drives the non-functional Requirement. This cause reveals the fundamental reason behind the Requirement, which can relate to business goals, user expectations, technical limitations, or regulatory compliance.

Here is a simplified version of the above example:

Requirement: The system should respond in under 2 seconds.

1. Why is it necessary for the system to respond in under 2 seconds? Answer: To provide a satisfying user experience.
2. Why is it crucial to provide a satisfying user experience? Answer: This is the industry standard, and users expect a quick and responsive system.
3. Why do users expect a quick and responsive system? Answer: Users have limited time and high expectations for smooth system interactions.
4. Why do users have limited time and high expectations? Answer: Users need to complete tasks within tight deadlines and want to avoid frustration (user experience) caused by slow system performance.

What did You Learn in this Chapter?

- Why Non-functional (NFRs) are important and how they can be gathered?
- What are the benefits of SWOT analysis?
- In which scenario you can use Fish-bone diagram technique?
- What are the Benefits of MOSCOW technique?
- Why flow diagrams are important?
- Do you know about 5 Whys Technique?

CHAPTER 7

TECHNIQUES OF REQUIREMENTS GATHERING

- *What Exactly Is Requirements Gathering?*
- *Process Diagrams, Wireframes and Much More*
- *Effective Requirements Gathering Techniques*

If you are in this chapter after finishing all the previous chapters, that's indeed an outstanding achievement. You are off to a terrific start!

So, do you think a BA job is a cool one? Here are some facts that I have realized:

- A BA does not just do requirement gathering. They must manage and work with stakeholders, understand true business needs, think of solutions, assist the Project Manager, and answer not-so-easy questions from developers, testers, and customers.
- Requirements don't come; a BA must extract them.
- Gathering requirements is not the only job; rejecting some requirements is also part of the BA's job.
- Developers cannot develop business requirements. A BA must help developers by thinking from a developer's mindset and applying system rules/logic to derive functional requirements.

What Is Requirement Gathering, actually?

Requirements gathering (People also call it Requirements elicitation or Capture) is the process of identifying (by collaborating with the various stakeholders, customers, users, vendors, IT staff, and more.) and documenting (set of requirements – functional, system, technical, etc.) clear specifications of what needs to be developed/implemented (Development of features within a software/Apps etc.) as part of the project you are in.

Usually, this process occurs during the project initiation phase (In waterfall methodology and intermittently each cycle/sprint in Agile based methodologies). Still, as a BA, you are responsible for gathering requirements (or eliciting requirements) and continuing to manage them throughout the project timeline—until its realization or delivery.

Make it very firm in your mind. Requirements aren't given to a BA or created in isolation. The BA involves extracting or uncovering them from the relevant project stakeholders. Therefore, to be an efficient BA, knowing the right requirements-gathering techniques is extremely important (Assuming you have identified the right stakeholders to work with—we will learn about this in subsequent chapters).

The below picture depicts key activities performed during gathering requirements. You can consider this as a "Requirement Gathering Framework". Three key stages of analysis are important for fully understanding a business need/problem, converting them into clearly written and visually depicted requirements, further supported by deep data level information.

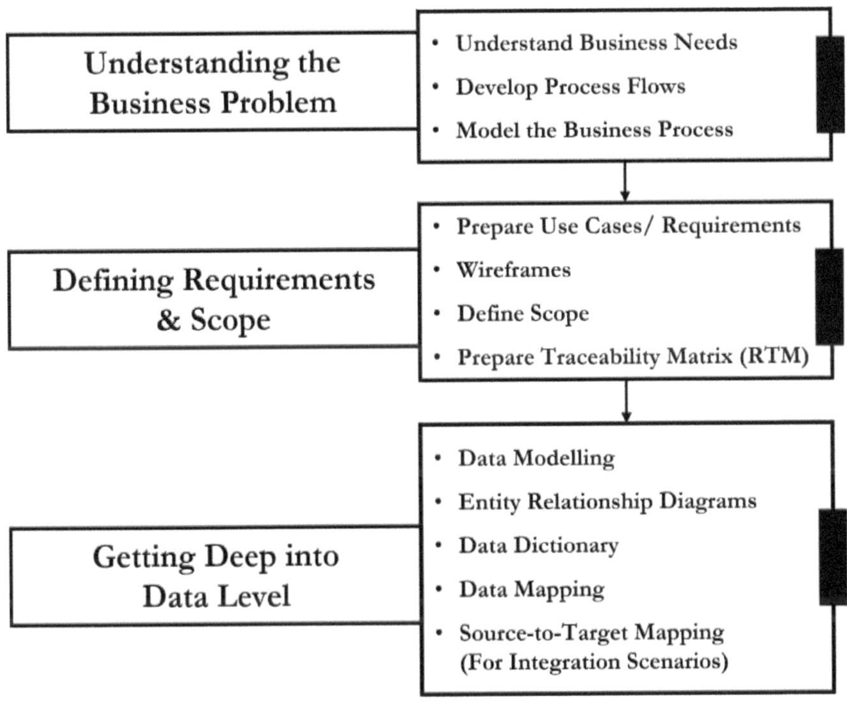

Let's understand the components of requirements gathering within the three stages quickly. The components mentioned above are only indicative lists. Several other components or techniques may fall into these stages, which we will understand in subsequent chapters. However, generally, these are the key components/techniques sufficient for a BA to perform his/her job efficiently.

Understand Business Needs: Before you gather requirements, it's essential to understand the business needs—business needs are driven by the organisation's Vision, Mission, and Goals. Though, as a BA, it is not mandatory to capture and document business needs, basic documentation would be ideal. Before getting into requirements, it should articulate the organisation's strategic vision and any key concerns about its success, challenges, risks, or issues.

While understanding business needs, leaders of the organisation may not be able to give information about what they need. Still, they will tell you what they want, express current issues and concerns, and capabilities they want in their systems and more. Hence, as a BA, you should be making a lot of interpretations—and should be able to differentiate between "What is needed Vs. What customers want." As an outcome of this exercise, a brief document of 'business needs' highlighting current issues or problems that are getting in the way and a broad solution will be suggested/considered. This document should serve as a kind of Vision document – which will revalidate the BA's or implementation team's understanding of the organisation's overall vision and the project's objective aligned with that vision.

As a BA, you may document the above as below:

#	Vision & Mission	Issues/Problem	Opportunity
1	Digital Transformation	Manually update customer data which is consuming time	Digital Automaton—Integrate relevant systems to automate the updating of customer data
2			
3			

Sometimes, Customers themselves give such documentation or information. In such cases, a BA must study the document thoroughly and normally BAs utilize discovery sessions to clarify and revalidate the business needs before the actual requirements session begins.

Develop Process Flows: As a BA, during the requirements phase, one should identify and draw the business process that needs to be implemented. The BA creates a graphical representation of business processes and process flows called a Business Process Flow diagram. Such diagrams are one of the core tools of business analysis and process re-engineering. They let us identify and easily understand process flows within an organization, the parts that form the flow, and visually represent who interacts with what.

Model the Business Process: As described earlier, Business process modelling (Also called process modelling) is the analytical representation or, simply put, an illustration of an organization's business processes. Creating models of processes is an essential aspect of successful business process management. In subsequent chapters, we will learn about the basics of drawing process flows. Here is a simple pictorial example:

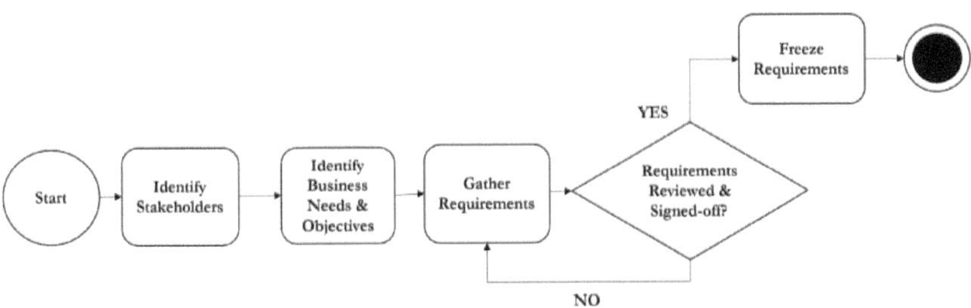

Requirements and Use Cases: A Requirement is a clearly defined statement that describes how a system or software tool should behave for a particular business or technical scenario when the system receives input from its users. A requirement is generally a broad statement, while a "use case" is usually a more specific statement implied or derived from the requirement. It's possible for a requirement to correspond to multiple use cases. A scenario can be a collection of background assumptions that provide context for a use case or a grouping of use cases. Hence, developing teams can comprehensively understand specific functionalities and interactions by breaking down requirements into well-defined use cases or user stories.

These are just basics. We will learn more about various formats and writing requirements in subsequent chapters.

Visual Elements (Wireframes or Mock-ups): First and foremost, wireframes act as a visual representation that helps bridge the gap between conceptual ideas and concrete design. They are grayscale mock-ups that emphasize the structure and layout of a page, clarifying how the information will be presented.

Think of wireframes as the blueprint of user experience. They provide a visual representation of the data elements to be displayed on the page and guide the development team on the placement of controls and functionalities. They allow project stakeholders to envision a digital product or website's overall layout, structure, and functionality before moving into the development phase. By presenting each key page's look, feel, and purpose, wireframes facilitate productive discussions and decision-making among team members and stakeholders.

Moreover, wireframes play a pivotal role in defining user interactions. They outline the navigation flow, placement of key elements, and interactions between different components within a page. This enables designers and developers to understand how users engage with the interface and ensures a seamless user experience. By providing a development blueprint, wireframes guide the implementation phase and assist developers in accurately translating the design concepts into functional code. A typical wireframe (Mobile App) will look like as below:

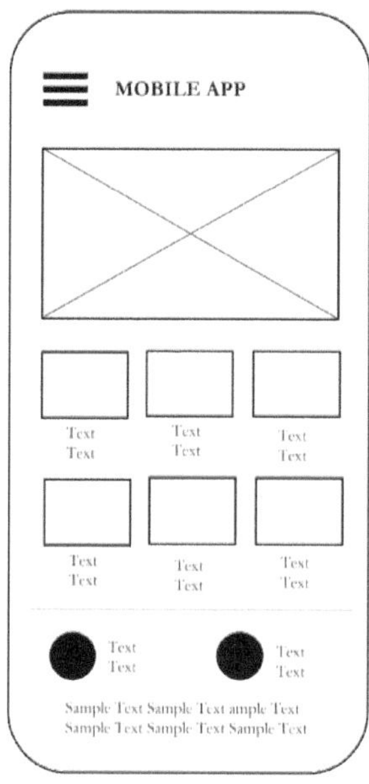

Visual Elements (Prototypes): Prototypes take the design process a step further and give a little life to the concepts. Prototypes evolve from wireframes into functional models. Unlike wireframes, prototypes introduce colour, animation, and actual content, giving stakeholders a tangible representation of the final product. In essence, they are interactive. These "working models" showcase the application or webpage's features and functionalities in action, providing a near-real experience of the end product. Prototyping allows users to test their ideas for the next solution. Prototypes allow BAs or designers to gather valuable user insights by observing how users interact with the functionality. This Feedback helps inform decision-making and ensures the creation of user-centric experiences.

One of the significant advantages of prototypes lies in usability testing. Business users can interact with the prototype, offering valuable insights into the user interface's effectiveness and usability. This stage is crucial for refining the product before its actual development, resulting in a more user-centric end product.

With modern wireframes and prototyping tools, developers can easily modify prototypes to quickly discover what satisfies users. After establishing a working model, the requirements describing the accepted functionality can be reverse-engineered. So, a typical iterative process of Prototyping involves the following steps:

- Trial of the prototype by users
- Feedback from users
- Modification of the prototype

Another benefit of prototypes is their ability to identify design flaws early on. By enabling users to interact with the prototype, potential issues, usability challenges, or inconsistencies can be uncovered and addressed promptly. This early detection saves time and resources that would otherwise be spent on rectifying such flaws during later stages of development.

Creating Wireframes & Prototyping: Both wireframes and prototypes can be created using a variety of tools available. For wireframes, popular tools include Visual Paradigm, Visio, Figma, Balsamiq and many more. Even the Excel can be used. These tools empower BAs to transform abstract concepts into visual representations with ease.

When it comes to prototypes, the options are equally diverse. Tools like Framer, Envision, Figma, Axure and Adobe XD offer functionalities for creating interactive and engaging prototypes. Developers can use rapid prototyping tools to create interactive mock-ups in no time. For instance, Figma's Prototype feature facilitates the creation of interactive prototypes, enabling BAs or designers to define actions and simulate behaviours like transitions, overlays, navigation, and linking.

The best part is that you don't need extensive training to use these tools effectively. A little practice and experimentation can go a long way in mastering them. However, when UI/UX is involved heavily, a BA can create basic functional Prototypes unless he/she is also a UI/UX expert. Usually,

BAs work with designers or UI/UX experts to develop mock-ups or Prototypes.

Should A BA Be Responsible for Creating Wireframes or Prototypes?

The BA owns the product/system being built as part of the Project. No further questions on that. However, if you are building a custom App/System/product (Not implementing any COTS product or SaaS product), a UI/UX person plays a major role along with the BA.

Though the UI/UX person does not own the product, he/she owns how it should look and interact with users (UI) and the experience (UX) that the App/ System/ product will provide.

Often, as the BA is the product owner, naturally, he/she develops the tendency to control the UI/UX aspects of the product/App/System as well. This creates a clash between two individuals about how they should look and behave, mostly due to a lack of awareness about their responsibilities.

The fact is that both are equally responsible roles and hence, the collaboration between a BA & the UI/UX person is the absolute must. Hence, a clear responsibility matrix must be developed to prevent friction during the Project between these two individuals.

As we know already, the primary goal of a BA is to deliver a Product/System/App that meets business requirements. Suppose the BA is also a product manager. In that case, he/she has other responsibilities like building a vision for the product and sharing it with stakeholders, getting market feedback, working with marketing teams and more.

The mindset of a UI/UX person is different. He/she thinks about how requirements can be delivered in a user-friendly way. Hence, a BA & UI/UX person must be present during requirements workshops. While the BA documents Requirements, the UI/UX gathers information about UI/UX, current problems w.r.t UI/UX and more.

Generally, the BA is responsible for drafting the requirements and a relevant wireframe. The Wireframe may not fully depict how a final product looks, but it visually references the stakeholders by bringing everyone to a common page. The BA must keep the diagram simple but easy to understand, and he/she should pay attention to the details first.

A BA's main responsibility is to ensure he/she captures the requirement via the Wireframe. Also, the wireframe design should be simple and easy to communicate the requirements to the project team/developers. However, in this scenario, the BA should collaborate with a UI/UX person to take up the ownership of wireframes, especially interface design-heavy projects.
In addition, wherever the prototype or comps (short for comprehensive layouts) are needed, the BA should collaborate with the UI/UX person. Ultimately, the BA and the UI/UX person will present the requirements (With UI/UX) to the customer and get the sign-off.

The typical rule is how you can visually represent a requirement, along with your textual documentation. A simple visual would be helpful for quick decision-making. With visuals, users can see what it could be, whereas relying on textual documentation can delay decision-making as people need to read through it. Also, this will avoid misunderstandings of a requirement from person to person.

You must have the below info with you before you start wireframing:

- Who are the users?
- How is the current system designed; what's the current pain point?
- Details about functionalities and features
- Data Model
- Type of data in the UI

As a BA, you may not be able to design a Wireframe or Prototype like a graphic artist (UI/UX expert). That is not expected either. However, the initial Wireframe is expected to be created by the BA in a simple, easy-to-follow and understandable way, focussing on the system screens, behaviour and more because 1 picture speaks 100 words.

When they see the visual in front of everyone, the possibility of conflict of understanding is minimal. To begin with, MS PowerPoint & Excel can be used to create Wireframes. By the way, all the diagrams in this book are created using MS PowerPoint only!

Microsoft PowerPoint & Excel provide all the required basic shapes and flows (Shapes & Smart Arts). In Excel, too, you can create the required Wireframe by merging/unmerging columns and Rows. The below Wireframe (of a Web Blog layout) is created using an Excel sheet.

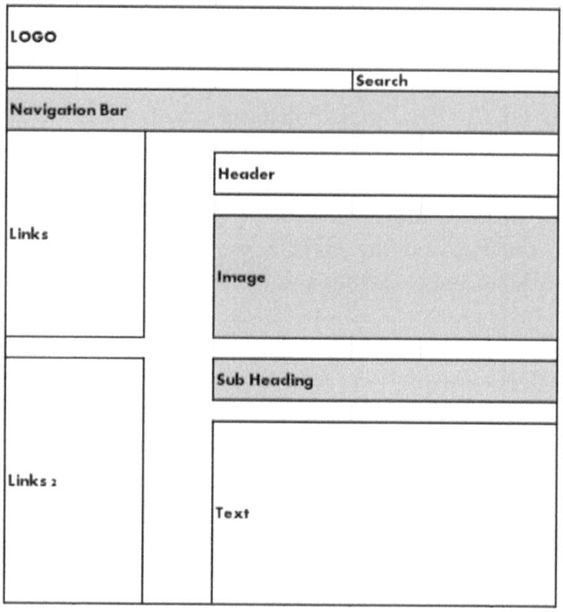

POCs & Prototypes: What is a Proof of Concept (POC)? What is its relationship with Prototype? Are they the same or different? Many newcomers often get confused by the two terms—POCs and Prototypes. Let me make it very clear to you.

One must understand that both concepts are driven by their purposes. A POC is one of the tactics organizations employ to validate the viability of a novel idea. Its core mission is to test the foundational assumptions embedded within an idea and validate its technical execution.

Let me provide a use case. An organization has a process to capture Leads and convert those leads into a sale, which will involve some complex processes in between, including integration. Someone suggested that the Microsoft Dynamics 365 Sales App (or Salesforce Sales Cloud) can help easily achieve the functionality.

However, they wanted to see how it actually would work. So, the BA, in collaboration with the technical team/dev team (by connecting with their vendor partners), will configure the requirements quickly to show how it can be done. It will not be a full-fledged configuration, but it will be helpful for the team to show a flavour of how the requirements can be configured to fulfil the business need. So, in essence, this acts as a demonstration that the software can effectively tackle a particular business challenge.

Hence, a successful POC offers assurance that the chosen technology is suitable and that constructing the complete product is attainable. POCs are potent instruments for probing key hypotheses and confirming core assumptions about intended users and software concepts.

As we already read above, a prototype is a simulated iteration of a product designed to evaluate its UX/UI design and functionality. It embodies the visual essence of the end product and incorporates chosen features. Prototyping aims to detect user pain points and ensure favourable user experiences. In comparison, a POC zeroes in on technical feasibility, and a prototype zeroes in on user interaction and design evaluation.

POCs are relevant in software, app development, cybersecurity, healthcare, and beyond. For example, in software development, a POC might encompass scrutinizing the viability of a novel mobile payment mechanism.

Though POCs and Prototypes have different purposes, they share common goals. Simply put, as we have seen above, a POC targets technical viability, whereas a prototype scrutinizes user interaction and design. They are complementary facets, not interchangeable substitutes.
Scope: The scope is simply all the work or deliverables needed to achieve a project's objectives within a predefined timeline. We have a dedicated chapter on Scope Management later on.

Requirement Traceability Matrix: Requirement Traceability Matrix (RTM) is a mapping of your Business Requirements (With an ID) to the corresponding functional requirement document (FRD) > Technical Requirement Document (TRD) > Technical Design Document (TDD) > Functional or User testing Documentation with test cases, results, and bugs pertaining to the Business Requirement. The Matrix also contains the statuses of each requirement and its corresponding stages. Generally, BAs use an Excel sheet with the above columns to prepare RTM. Tools like AzureDevOps (Earlier called as TFS), JIRA and other such tools automatically provide such traceability.

The Titanic tragedy is well-known, and the aftermath of the sinking involved rescue ships from Halifax, Nova Scotia, venturing out to recover victims and return them to the city. Each victim was assigned a unique number upon recovery, and their information was documented along with a description in a ledger book. Personal belongings found with the victims were also tagged with the same identification number. If a victim was laid to rest in one of the three cemeteries in Halifax, their grave marker would bear the engraved victim number. This systematic traceability approach enabled researchers and others to establish connections between victim descriptions, property details, and cemetery locations, facilitating a comprehensive understanding of the events and individuals involved in the tragedy.

Now that you know what traceability is, let's understand why traceability is essential in Requirements and project management. From a Project management perspective, there is a logical connection between the requirements of a project and its strategic objectives. By establishing traceability between project requirements and objectives, you can determine the relevance and necessity of each requirement. If a requirement does not align with the project's strategic objectives, it prompts a critical evaluation of whether it should be included in the system. This approach prevents unnecessary scope creep and keeps the project focused on what truly matters.

Similarly, from a requirements management standpoint, traceability must extend beyond requirements and encompass other artefacts throughout the requirements lifecycle. This includes design documents, test cases, implementation details, and more. Ensuring traceability between these artefacts ensures consistency and transparency, making it easier to identify the impact of changes, track progress, and verify that the final deliverables meet the initial objectives.

Data Modelling: Data modelling (e.g., Entity relationship diagram) involves simplifying a software system and its data elements into a diagram using symbols and text.

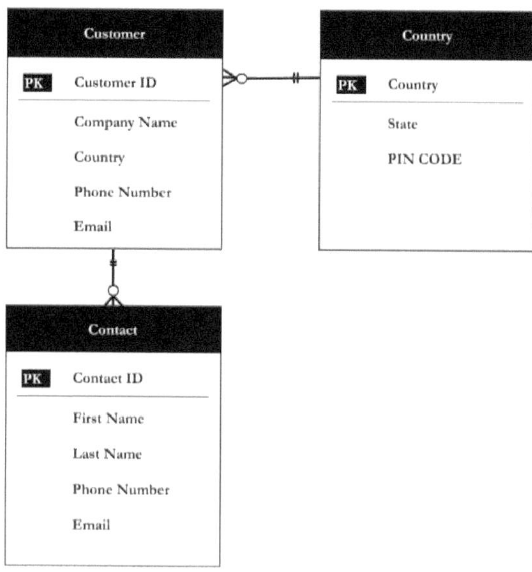

This diagram illustrates how data flows between tables, their relationships and other important details. There are different types of data modelling diagrams depending on their purpose. If there are any integration scenarios, then how the data flow between the two systems can be represented in a sequence diagram. For example, the following can be represented below to show how several tables are connected via a relationship.

Data Dictionary: A data dictionary is a centralised metadata repository (data about the data). The data dictionary is essential as it contains information such as what is in the database, who can access it, where it is physically stored, unique names of fields/columns in all the organisation's databases and other information.

Data Mapping: Data mapping involves matching fields/columns between databases (Let's say, source and target system databases) for data migration and management. Before data can be analysed for business insights, it must be homogenised to make it accessible to decision-makers.

Source to Target Mapping Document: Source to Target Mapping (STM) document is generally used to map the data fields and tables during Integration and Data Migration. This is the mapping (Just like Data Mapping) of fields/columns between two systems (Fields or columns of Database tables) that need to be integrated or when data needs to be migrated.

Effective Requirements Gathering Techniques

There isn't a fixed approach or technique for gathering requirements. Yet, from the inception of Business Analysis, diverse interaction methods have been employed to comprehend business needs, customer pain points, and requirements.

To ensure a comprehensive and robust set of requirements, adopting a multi-faceted approach to requirements gathering is recommended. While no single technique can capture all the necessary information, employing various methods throughout the process is considered best practice in requirements engineering.

BAs should avoid the pressure of using every elicitation technique available and instead focus on achieving simplicity and uncovering the true project needs. Combining interviews, requirements workshops, and brainstorming sessions often yields the best results. Continuous improvement of elicitation skills is essential, even for experienced BAs.

There are over ten practical requirements-gathering techniques available. These techniques can be tailored to the specific needs of each project, improving requirements coverage and minimising issues during software development and beyond. While not every technique must be utilised for every project, selecting a suitable mix of techniques is critical to achieving successful outcomes. Let's explore various types of Requirements-gathering techniques.

- **User Interviews**
- **Requirements Workshops**
  - *Interface Analysis*
  - *Root Cause Analysis*
  - *Process Analysis and Assessments*
- **User Observation or Job Shadowing**
- **Customer Document Analysis**
- **Collective Brainstorming**
- **Focus Groups**
- **Situational Role-Plays**
- **Questionnaires and Surveys**

User Interviews are invaluable for gathering background information, understanding business needs, and addressing stakeholders' concerns. They provide an opportunity to gather detailed info and can be conducted one-on-one, making them practical for sensitive or confidential matters. It is crucial to include diverse stakeholders to gain a comprehensive perspective and avoid bias in system requirements.

When conducting interviews, using open-ended questions is essential. These questions elicit specific information and encourage interviewees to provide explanations and reasons, providing valuable context for evaluating and validating requirements. Follow-up questions play a crucial role in interviews, either delving into details or zooming out for a broader understanding. Here is an example:

- **BA (Open-ended Question):** "Could you describe the current challenges you face while managing the customer feedback process?"
- **Stakeholder:** "We often struggle to organise and prioritise the feedback we receive, leading to delays in addressing important concerns."
- **BA (Follow-up):** "Can you give me an example of a specific instance where this delay had a significant impact on the customer experience?"

During interviews, it is common to encounter individuals with different communication styles. Some may focus on specific details and exceptions, requiring you to broaden the discussion and explore the bigger picture. On the other hand, some individuals may provide a broader context without delving into specifics, necessitating the need to probe deeper and obtain more detailed information. Adapting your approach based on the interviewee's communication style allows for a more effective and comprehensive understanding of the requirements.

Requirements Workshops: When gathering requirements from diverse stakeholders, conflicting opinions are bound to arise, requiring resolution before implementation. Requirements workshops serve as an effective method for addressing such conflicts. By convening stakeholders and collectively discussing and refining candidate requirements, workshops facilitate the resolution of discrepancies, the attainment of consensus, and the validation of requirements. These activities are essential for ensuring that the system caters to the needs of all users and stakeholders rather than just the most vocal groups.

While interviews and workshops serve different purposes in data gathering, workshops offer a forum for discussion, collaboration, and idea generation. They bring together representatives from various departments, promoting creativity and cooperation among participants. Workshops provide an inclusive setting where everyone's opinions are heard, and participants can build upon each other's ideas. This inclusive approach facilitates the resolution of issues with all relevant parties present.

Generally, workshops are a popular and effective means of gathering requirements, as they foster a collaborative environment and encourage the involvement of all stakeholders.

We will discuss "Requirements Workshops" in detail later in this chapter.

Interface Analysis will generally be part of the Requirements workshop or User interviews (Interviewing customer IT team). Understanding the integration requirements of a system is essential for ensuring a comprehensive and usable system. A crucial aspect of this is analysing the system's interfaces, which include integrations with system components (e.g., Scanners/Sensors, etc.) and external systems.

Conducting a thorough interface analysis often reveals requirements that may not be immediately apparent to users. These hidden requirements can significantly impact the system's functionality and performance. In simple terms, these requirements show how different systems must work together smoothly.

It's important to talk to people using these systems and understand their needs. Simple questions like "What information should move between systems?" help gather the needed details. Also, it's wise to consider how fast the information needs to move and how often. All these details help ensure the integration works well, making the whole project more substantial and compelling.

Root Cause Analysis: "If I had an hour to solve a problem, I'd spend 55 minutes thinking about the problem and 5 minutes thinking about solutions," said Albert Einstein famously.

His argument was valid. To conduct a thorough analysis, it is crucial to differentiate between cause and effect, pain points and root causes. Uncovering these factors begins by identifying stakeholders' pain points, annoyances, delays, inconveniences, and customer complaints. Root cause analysis of a problem can be part of the Requirements workshop or User interviews.

Assessment: Sometimes, customers might ask you to check and assess their current ways of doing things and suggest how to improve them. This happens when they have lots of technology, but things are messy.

As a BA, you'll look into this and suggest ways to make it digital and smoother—Digital transformation. This is not always about getting requirements. It is about analysing the AS-IS state and proposing the TO-BE state. Sometimes, just looking and suggesting solutions is enough. Occasionally, such assessments will be a mini-paid project for your organisation.

Essential Considerations for Conducting Assessments:

- Begin by identifying and labelling processes, and remember to inquire about the availability of a business process catalogue that can provide valuable insights.
- Gain a comprehensive understanding of how the processes operate through various means such as process documentation, conducting interviews/workshops, and asking pertinent questions.
- Develop process flow models that accurately capture the sequences and activities involved and the roles played by individuals.
- Analyse to identify inefficiencies within the processes, such as redundant steps, duplicated sub-flows, and unnecessary hand-offs.
- Pinpoint areas that require improvement, focusing on enhancing efficiency, reducing complexity, increasing speed, and improving reliability.

- Determine the necessary changes to the processes, which will subsequently serve as business requirements.
- And always remember the importance of enhancing and optimising the processes, if required, before proposing an automation approach.

User Observation or Job Shadowing: Observing users performing their daily tasks effectively uncovers their genuine needs. User observation can be passive or active, with active observation involving asking questions while observing. BAs gain insights into workflows, pain points, and concerns by working closely with users.

During this process, document users' actions, activities, and challenges. Ask open-ended questions to elicit valuable information:

- What is a typical day like for you?
- How do you determine your tasks for the day?
- Can you demonstrate your usual approach?
- What challenges or issues do you face?
- What are the outcomes in different scenarios?
- Which tasks are time-consuming or difficult?

Maintain a non-judgmental stance during observation and questioning. Focus on understanding rather than evaluation. Understanding deviations from procedures reveals underlying issues. Observe users' actions rather than relying solely on self-reports or managerial perceptions.

By observing users within their work contexts, BAs can grasp challenges and identify areas for improvement. This enables the specification of a system that can improve processes, delivering substantial benefits.

Document Analysis: Document analysis is a highly effective but often overlooked technique for gathering requirements. The BA can gain valuable insights when provided with documentation of the current system, such as during the RFP or discovery workshops. Studying these documents allows for analysing the current system's functionality, performing AS-IS process analysis and identifying gaps. This analysis helps identify areas where improvements can be made to the user's process and highlights where the existing system fails to meet business needs discovered through interviews, questionnaires, and user observations.

While analysing the system's requirements documents is essential, reviewing other system-level documentation, such as user manuals and problem reports, is also beneficial. These sources often contain valuable information about the system's design, specifications, and the reasoning behind its current functionality.

By conducting document analysis, the BA can gather essential insights, formulate additional questions, and evaluate the completeness of the requirement set. Existing artefacts, such as process flows, data dictionaries, Reports, Design documents, SOPs, KT documents, and training manuals, provide a wealth of helpful information that can streamline the requirement-gathering process.

Performing due diligence in document analysis helps the BA acquire a foundational understanding of the current state, identify existing problems and issues, and familiarise themselves with relevant business terminology. It also uncovers vital information that may have been taken for granted or assumed to be already known.

Collective Brainstorming: Brainstorming can be done as part of your workshop or on its own, with a large or small group. You focus on different system parts during the session and develop new ideas. The goal is to think outside the box and develop innovative concepts. To help with Brainstorming, you can use tools like whiteboards and mind-mapping software. These tools make it easier to share ideas and organise your thoughts.

Using Mind Maps as part of Brainstorming: I start with a caution. Even to use Mind Maps effectively, one needs practice. This is how a typical Mind map looks like.

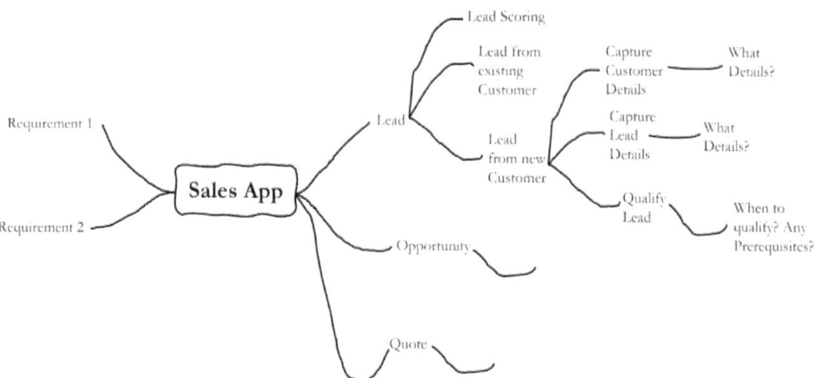

Don't get into a workshop with customers without the required practice if you are still figuring it out. Because without practice, it will take more time initially, even though Mind maps are faster to put together and explain.

Hence, use this technique during your calls with internal team members for Brainstorming. You can try this in a customer workshop once you are comfortable and confident using the tool efficiently.

A mind map provides an easy way to brainstorm without worrying about the structure because you are building the structure. Mind maps help you break down requirements hierarchically, with an 'n' number of lower nodes as required. A Mind map allows you to "actively listen" to your stakeholders and ask proper questions by visually structuring your ideas during the conversation.

The essential advantage is that the requirements can often be covered on a single page, which can be projected live to your stakeholders during the workshop. This gives a visual output to your stakeholders about your understanding of the topic in conversation. As a result, stakeholders can quickly correct your understanding, if needed, and also, you can clarify many things right there by asking deep questions, "Is this part of A, or is it a separate functionality?" etc.

Also, you can choose one requirement and expand it and further drill down till you have those minute details covered, as you can see in the above example Mind map; for example, during the workshop itself, you can validate the set of fields that should be part of a Table or entity (Ex: What fields you will have when you capture a Lead record).

The use of Mind Maps does not mean that there is no need to prepare other artefacts. They are required as a deliverable. With Mind maps, as a BA, you can organize the thoughts quickly, and after the workshop, you can elaborate those thoughts/requirements easily for documentation.
Though you have a Mind map, some of our BAs think that preparation before a customer workshop is not essential. Mind Map is just a tool, so you should know the topic of the conversation beforehand to drive the workshop; hence, preparation is a must.

Note: Miro is one of the good mind map tools you can use.

Focussed Group Discussions: These structured discussions bring together individuals with similar backgrounds or experiences to provide feedback, express needs, and guide development.
The focus group technique serves three primary purposes:

1. Gathering feedback
2. Understanding user needs

3. Offer guidance for project implementation or software development

A focused group discussion is a structured conversation among individuals with similar backgrounds or experiences to gather insights and perspectives on a specific topic of interest. You are discussing with key people within a department who can make or influence a decision and know the process well. When you bring together people within a group, you can hear wide perspectives, which will help you understand what is needed for the business rather than individual preferences.

Focus groups play a dual role in requirements gathering by engaging participants in focused conversations. They can gather information for requirements development by involving participants in open discussions. Additionally, focus groups validate previously elicited requirements by seeking feedback on design prototypes or proposed solutions. This iterative process ensures the final requirements align with user expectations.

Focus groups differ from brainstorming as they predominantly involve external stakeholders while brainstorming primarily includes internal stakeholders. This external input enriches the requirements-gathering process, leading to improved product outcomes.

A few BAs may hesitate about this technique due to challenges like dominant individuals with narrow agendas. However, the benefits of diverse perspectives outweigh these concerns. When executed thoughtfully, focus groups offer an invaluable tool for effective requirements gathering.

Situational Role-plays: By acting out different user roles and facilitating interactions, these sessions allow for a comprehensive exploration of system requirements from various perspectives, sparking discussions and generating fresh ideas. Role-play is another brainstorming technique that helps understand how different system parts should function to support the overall process.

As a BA, scriptwriting and workshop planning proficiency is crucial for successful role-play sessions. All pertinent issues can be uncovered by identifying the situation, gathering participants, introducing the problem, and encouraging open discussions. Though this technique is effective, it is rarely used in Business software implementation projects.

Questionnaires/Surveys: Conducting individual interviews can present difficulties due to scheduling limitations and the time required for interviewers. Furthermore, these interviews may only provide surface-level insights into requirements, as not all interviewers possess strong real-time follow-up questioning skills.

To tackle these obstacles, questionnaires or surveys offer an efficient alternative that enables simultaneous follow-up with multiple stakeholders.

A thoughtfully crafted questionnaire with inquisitive inquiries serves as a valuable instrument to unearth underlying requirements that stakeholders may not fully recognize but are vital for successful design. It is crucial, however, to supplement the questionnaire findings with a Q&A session involving users. This allows BAs to ask focused questions, gather additional insights, and clarify aspects that may have been overlooked in the questionnaires.

Asking questions is integral to business analysis and should be ingrained as an expected practice. Whether you are a consultant or a newly appointed BA seeking to comprehend the business at hand, keep the following guidelines in mind:

- Explore unfamiliar aspects by posing exploratory questions.
- Ask open-ended questions rather than asking just YES/NO questions.
- Avoid Leading questions* that sway responses in a particular direction.
- Ask one question at a time to ensure accurate and dependable answers.
- Obtain diverse perspectives by directing key questions to multiple individuals.
- Embrace curiosity and approach questions without hesitation. Please note that no question is STUPID. If you don't ask questions, you are STUPID.

*[*Leading Questions: A leading question is a type of question that is phrased in a way that suggests or encourages a specific answer or a particular response from the person being asked.]*

"He who asks a question is a fool for five minutes; he who does not ask a question remains a fool forever"— Confucius

Requirements Workshop That Works

If you are clueless about planning and organizing, you are unfit to be a BA. Planning, Organizing, and hosting skills are critical for a BA—along with an organized mind.

✪ **Remember –** No one will come to you. You need to go to them (customers) to get what you want.

Have you ever been involved in a workshop that didn't go smoothly or didn't achieve its desired outcome? If that's the case, it's likely due to inadequate preparation, unclear objectives, or a lack of alignment among participants. Now, let's discuss the essential principles to avoid disappointing workshop outcomes and ensure the success of your upcoming workshop.

So, what is a Requirement Workshop? As mentioned earlier in this chapter, a workshop can be defined as a concentrated gathering of relevant stakeholders to accomplish a specific objective within a defined timeframe. Requirement workshops are extensively utilized in business analysis and requirements elicitation, making them one of the most popular techniques in these domains.

Key steps of a Requirements Gathering process are:

We will learn about all the four steps in subsequent sections.

Key Roles involved in the workshop are:

- **Workshop Facilitator:** The individual responsible for organizing the workshop, determining its objectives, creating the agenda, and defining the expected outcomes. Typically, the BA assumes the role of the facilitator. However, it is beneficial for the BA to have a team member assist in note-taking and timekeeping during the workshop.

- **Workshop Participants:** This refers to the group of stakeholders and Subject Matter Experts (SMEs) invited to participate in the workshop based on the topic or agenda to be discussed. Depending on the subject matter, the BA should identify and invite the most appropriate stakeholders, such as Process owners or End users, to ensure their involvement and contribution to the workshop.

How to Plan a Requirements Workshop Schedule?

Where to start? How to start? BAs usually struggle when working on a medium/ large project, as interactions need to happen with multiple stakeholders representing different departments within the organization. So, how can one plan to meet all of them? How do I get all the requirements?
The situation might be overwhelming for a BA. However, if he/she patiently thinks and plans, he can meet all the requirements in a structured way within a scheduled period. If you are planning an elicitation workshop, you need to plan the entire Event (A series of workshops) very well. Here are the tips for planning the workshops/interviews:

- Identify modules. There might be several Requirements you might have already that now need to be elicited. Group them based on the topic/modules – like Lead Management, Case Management, etc.)
- Identify and confirm the key stakeholders related to that module from the customer side, who can give us more info and later sign off.
- Prepare a Timetable. See the image – an example timetable. In Excel, you can simply prepare a great timetable. You can also add the Stakeholder name/email as an additional column.

Weeks	Day/Date		Sessions	Time	Topic	Session Objectives	Business Unit	Customer Stakeholders	
Weeks	Day	Date		(2-3 Hrs)		(Agenda)		Functional	Technical
WK 1	Day1	1-Jun	Session1	10:00 AM	Kick-off				
	Day2		Session2	12:00 PM	Lead Mgmt.				
WK 2	Day1	3-Jun	Session1	10:00 AM	Oppty Mgmt.				
	Day2		Session2	12:00 PM					

- Keep the Agenda for each session crystal clear. You should know what requirements detail to be discussed. Aim to freeze the requirements by getting all the required information. There will be unforeseen delays. They are part & parcel of any project.

- Once ready with details, share the Timetable with the key Customer point of contact to assign stakeholders (Business or IT team) for each module and to confirm the stakeholder availability.

- Once you get all the required inputs for your Timetable, schedule the meetings – online /offline workshops if you are onsite.

Typically, it's recommended to have a session lasting 1.5 to 2.5 hours, including a break. You shouldn't schedule more than two sessions daily because you'll need time to write down all the discussed points as precise requirements. You should finish this on the same day to ensure you don't forget important details. It is ideal to get the interim review of your draft documents before the actual sign-off. Schedule a follow-up session to discuss and clarify any significant changes/edits to the written document.

With this approach, by the end of the Requirements Phase, you will have your Requirements document with requirements captured from all ready for review and sign-off.

As a BA, you should be clear about what to discuss and how to drive each workshop. Before each workshop, prepare well. Email a list of questions so that stakeholders are prepared well.

How to Prepare for a Requirement Workshop?

After getting some experience, many BAs take the best practices for granted. They will realize how dangerous it is within no time.

BAs, including myself, often feel too lazy to prepare for tomorrow. Just like you need to invest for better financial stability tomorrow, one needs to invest time to prepare for the next day's workshop—Requirements Workshops.

Effective planning and preparation are crucial for ensuring a productive workshop. When preparing for a workshop, a BA will take into account various activities, including:

- It is essential to define the objectives and desired outcomes for the workshop clearly.
- Identifying the stakeholders who will participate in the workshop.
- Striving to balance comprehensive coverage and enabling active contributions from all participants.
- Identifying any concerns or issues that stakeholders may have based on existing knowledge.
- Determining which team members, such as Architects or Tech Leads, should be present during the workshop and identifying individuals who can assist with timekeeping and note-taking.
- Choosing appropriate techniques to facilitate the workshop, such as whiteboarding, creating flow charts, or reviewing requirements.

- Developing a well-structured agenda that includes the allotted duration for each agenda item.
- Conducting preliminary research or pre-workshop interviews to gather relevant information and insights.
- Distribute the Agenda and any necessary instructions to attendees at least 24 hours in advance to allow them to prepare.
- Be prepared with a set of thought-provoking questions, and if possible, share them with participants beforehand.

By carefully considering these aspects and engaging in thorough planning and preparation, the BA can lay the foundation for a successful workshop experience.

If we already have a set of questions to ask often, we think that this is enough, we will manage the show. Please note – tomorrow, you are not only managing the show but also running and leading the show. Hence, your preps should be at that level. Before going to bed, Ask yourself below questions:

Do I have sufficient background information about the topics to be discussed tomorrow? — Whether you are an experienced BA or not, a BA must gather as much background information on the requirements as possible. Suppose you can quickly read relevant info about the industry/business area in which you are a customer.

In that case, you will be able to talk in their language, which will help you engage actively with the stakeholders and ask the relevant questions as the workshop facilitator. Do you have mentally prepared how to run and lead the show tomorrow? —Please note, leading something is internalizing the stuff yourself first. It's training your mind on acting so you won't fumble.

While conducting the workshop, you may take the help of a PPT/Requirement list/Mind Map (a lot of free mind map tools available online) projected on a screen to present your topics and facilitate the discussion – this will help the participants to focus. As you get more and more info, you build the mind map/Running notes in front of the participants; that way, you involve them in all steps.

- **Bonus Tip:** Don't have any bias towards any requirement, like "it has to be tackled this way only..." etc. Have an open mind. Give a proper rest to your mind the previous day. Have a good sleep for a fruitful tomorrow.

How to Manage the Workshop?

You should think about these always. Am I clear about what output I expect from the upcoming or tomorrow's workshop? —Because once the objectives are clear to you, first you have clarity and confidence to run the show.

Have I made my participants clear about the agenda tomorrow? —To align your participants with you, send them the detailed Agenda so they are well informed and prepared. As you may know, an agenda is a list of critical topics to be discussed during the workshop.

When commencing the workshop, it can be beneficial to incorporate icebreakers to initiate engagement. A simple approach involves introducing yourself and sharing your experiences while encouraging participants to introduce themselves, mainly if they are new and unfamiliar with one another and your team. Key requirements for conducting a successful workshop encompass the following:

- Ensuring both the facilitator and participants are adequately prepared for the session.
- Maintaining a steadfast focus on the workshop's objective throughout its duration.
- Adhering to the predetermined Agenda and diligently staying on track.
- Enforcing the agreed-upon ground rules may include fostering respect, encouraging contributions from all participants, and refraining from personal biases or emotions.
- Temporarily setting aside irrelevant topics for future discussions and recording them for future reference.
- Establishing a mutually agreed-upon approach to address conflicts that may arise during the workshop.
- Establishing a consensus on the decision-making process to be employed.
- Summarizing the key points, takeaways, and action items discussed during the workshop.
- Ensuring that specific action items are assigned to the relevant participants, ensuring their resolution.

The workshop can proceed effectively by adhering to these requirements and guidelines, enabling meaningful discussions, constructive outcomes, and implementing necessary actions.

Framework for a BA to Ask Questions During a Workshop

Are you struggling to prepare/ask questions to your customer during a Requirement Elicitation process/workshop?

I was also struggling with the same—I was more worried about whether my questions were relevant or sufficient to cover a problem's angles. What if my probing proves insufficient, leading to the Requirement gap?

I often get questions from my colleagues in this regard, too.

A couple of years back, one of my mentors suggested a simple process – a framework to overcome this problem. This is not a 100% foolproof method or framework. But does its job without making you break your head.

This is not my innovation or framework – inspired by a book titled "The Quest for Software Requirements" by Roxanne E. Miller. Indeed, it is very powerful. This framework uses six interrogative pronouns—"How, why, who, where, when, what". Now, look at the framework in the below diagrams.

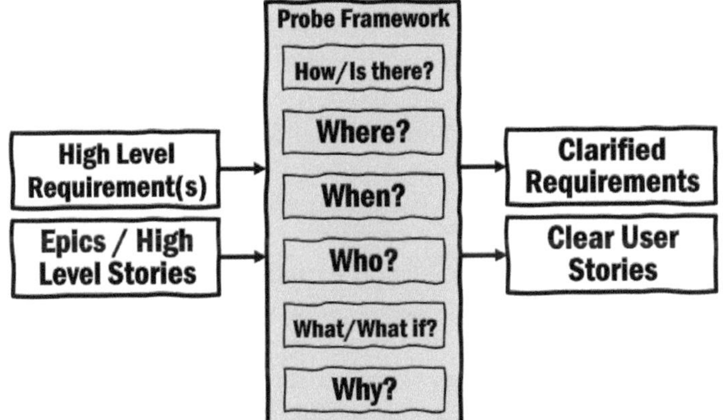

I have provided example questions for an example requirement as well. You must remember this framework to ask questions from the best possible angles to understand the problem and, hence, the Requirement.

Here are set of sample questions that may be asked based on the framework.

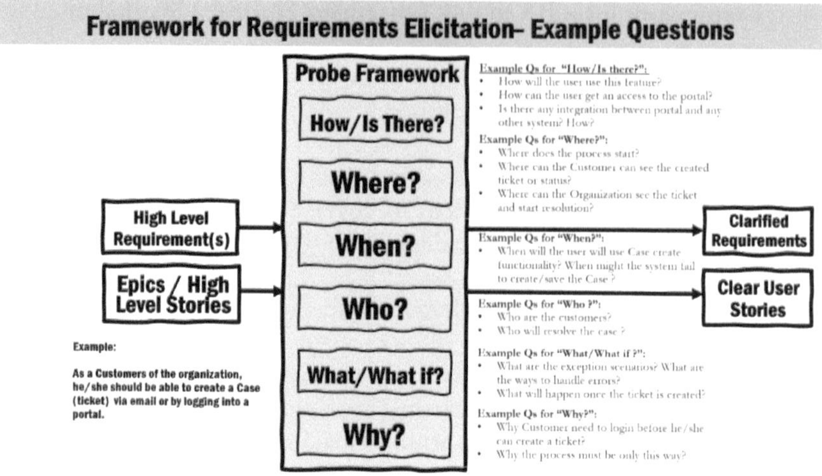

You can use this framework to generate as many questions as you want to understand a requirement completely.

Whatever question you ask a customer will fall under one or the other bucket (framework). When you go blank during a workshop, do not get enough questions to ask, or if you feel some more information is needed but are unable to ask, just remember this framework. This will help you.

More importantly, these questions should be logically ordered, and you should use your conversational skills with customers to ask questions.

Caution: It requires a practice to entirely depend on this framework.

How to do Post Workshop Follow-up

The BA should prioritize the completion of follow-up activities promptly. Finalizing these tasks on the same day as the workshop is advisable to prevent essential details from being forgotten. By delivering the agreed-upon items on time, you and the participants can ensure the effectiveness of post-workshop activities. This approach is powerful because participants tend to pay more attention to your actions than just your words, leading them to reciprocate accordingly.

Before sharing the workshop output (Document or any artefact) with participants, seeking a peer review with any of your team members is recommended. Provide the reviewer with sufficient time and set a deadline for their feedback. Conducting a peer review at this stage allows you to identify and rectify any errors or gaps before participants have the chance to notice them. While a peer review is typically an informal process, it presents an opportunity to discover areas for improvement.

Contact all participants and provide them with a link to access the workshop output. Additionally, ensure that stakeholders who could not attend or send representatives receive the outcome. When communicating post-workshop, being clear and concise about the next steps and the associated deadlines is crucial. If participants need to review and provide feedback, offer them a mechanism, such as a comments log.

To facilitate feedback collection, store the comments log (could be comments within the document or a separate Excel sheet) alongside the workshop output in a centralized location. This approach makes it easier for participants to provide their input and enables them to view comments made by others.

It is important to outline any risks associated with not giving feedback on time, helping participants understand the potential consequences of their inaction. The workshop output is valuable for keeping other interested parties informed.

As part of the post-workshop follow-up, consider the following activities:

- Distributing notes and minutes of the meeting (MOM)
- Following up on recorded action items
- Requesting feedback on the workshop's effectiveness

Ensure that any action items identified during the workshop are tracked until completion. Remember to include items assigned to the Parking Lot (Requirement item on hold) during the workshop.

When distributing the workshop output, share the actions log (Could be via email or a separate Excel sheet) to reinforce specific tasks and target dates agreed upon. Seeing that others have already completed their actions may motivate participants to fulfil their commitments.

Lastly, if scheduling another workshop with the same group, seize the opportunity to evaluate what worked well and what could have been improved.

Reflecting on past workshops will help enhance future sessions and ensure continuous improvement in your facilitation skills.

Types of Workshops Typically Led by A BA

Let's explore various workshop types led by a BA that play pivotal roles in different project phases:

Project Vision and Planning: At the outset of a project, a vision and planning workshop is the guiding compass for the team's journey. Initially, the team's primary objective is to grasp the organization's business vision and establish a clear alignment between the current project and that vision. This collaborative session sets the parameters for the project, defining its scope, objectives, stakeholders, priorities, and timelines. In an Agile environment, planning workshops are held at the project's initiation and at the commencement of each iteration, where release and iteration plans are charted out.

Discovery: In the initial stages of a project, the discovery workshop evolves to delve deeper into comprehending the business issue, goals, and potential remedies. BAs conduct stakeholder interviews, gather preliminary data, pinpoint business objectives, evaluate potential risks and limitations, and sketch out a well-defined project vision.

Requirements Elicitation: This workshop encompasses the documentation of extraction, analysis, and comprehensive project requirements. By leveraging various methods, including brainstorming, use case analysis, process walkthroughs, prototyping, and more, the BA constructs a well-organized documentation of the project's requirements.

User Story Mapping: Within the Agile development framework, this workshop serves as a means to visualize user stories, enhancing the process of prioritization and planning. Guided by the BA or Product Owner, the workshop arranges user stories into a coherent sequence and visually depicts the user journey. This, in turn, fosters productive conversations regarding feature interdependencies.

Idea Storming: Idea-storming sessions are concentrated working sessions that promote the collaborative design and development of software applications, effectively bridging the communication divide between business stakeholders and technical experts. During these sessions, participants collectively outline functional and non-functional requirements, generate wireframes or prototypes, construct use cases, and render pivotal design choices encompassing functional and technical aspects.

Document Review: These workshops serve as critical evaluation points in which finished and in-progress documentation and deliverables are thoroughly examined to ensure they align with stakeholders' expectations. Essentially, these are document review sessions, and during these sessions, stakeholders offer their input/review on requirement documents, design elements, or any work output, pinpointing any discrepancies, flaws, or required modifications.

RTM Workshops: Requirements Traceability Matrix (RTM) workshops serve as collaborative sessions where all project stakeholders (Customers and project teams) come together to discuss and agree on various project requirements, their respective sources, progress, current state and more. These workshops facilitate clear communication and alignment among customer stakeholders and project team members, helping to ensure that each requirement can be traced back to its origin, whether it's a business need, a customer request, or a regulatory requirement. RTM workshops enhance project transparency and accountability and play a important role in mitigating risks by enabling a systematic approach to managing changes and ensuring that all requirements are addressed throughout the project lifecycle.

Backlog Refinement: Frequently linked with Agile methodologies like SCRUM, this workshop readies and enhances items within the product backlog for future iterations. The BA works closely with the team (and the Product Owner) to examine and clarify backlog items, improve acceptance criteria, gauge effort (using story points), decompose large tasks, and prioritize stories. This process sets the foundation for the subsequent planning workshop.

What did You Learn in this Chapter?

- How do you plan for a customer workshop?
- What activities will you perform as a BA while planning for a Workshop?
- How will you prepare the right questions to your stakeholders?
- How do you ensure that you have enough info to draft a requirement clearly?
- Explain the different techniques of Business analysis Explain your favourite one.
- What is the difference between Wireframe & Prototype?
- What is the difference between Prototype & POC?
- Explain how to do post workshop follow-up?

CHAPTER 8

HOW TO GET THE REQUIREMEMNTS RIGHT?

- *Fundamentals Of Requirements*
- *How Write Correct Requirements?*
- *Manage & Validate Requirements*

There's no definitive right or wrong approach for anything. However, whichever path you choose, it's essential to ensure you achieve the desired outcome. Similarly, there is never a "right" or "wrong" way to get the requirements right. Requirements must align with their corresponding goals to be considered correct. A correct requirement is one that not only supports its goal but also contributes to its achievement. To determine the correctness, assessing whether a requirement effectively helps achieve the intended goal and is essential for its attainment is necessary.

Unfortunately, the process of requirements gathering is not as straightforward as asking customers and stakeholders what they want the system to do. This is because stakeholders often have limited awareness of alternative development approaches and are influenced by the current status quo. It can be challenging for users to detach themselves from their current practices and envision possibilities beyond their existing methods. As a result, their input may overlook innovative solutions or fail to consider significant departures from the present system. Therefore, additional measures are needed to overcome these limitations and ensure comprehensive and forward-thinking requirements gathering.

When multiple people are involved, Requirements are always subjective. People give requirements based on their needs and their perceptions. Hence, it's the BA's responsibility to figure out the real need, write the requirements that meet business needs and find the ideal solution that will suit the users in an organization.

Improper management of requirements is a significant cause of project failure. Bad management can make the project go over budget or take longer than expected.

To make sure a product or project is successful, it is important to manage requirements well. This means collecting and organizing requirements, keeping track of changes, and talking to everyone involved. Each step helps make sure the project meets its goals.

To write better requirements, it is crucial to understand what the users need and what the problem is by repeatedly asking questions like below can help understand the users' problems and find ways to solve them:

- What are we doing?
- Why are we doing it?
- Who will benefit from it?

> ➲ **Pro Tip**
>
> - As a BA, before you start your analysis or anything in a Project, first off, you need to know why you're doing it. Once you get an answer for "why", the next steps will be very clearly visible. Also, whenever you are 'stuck' in the middle, go back and refer to that answer. Your next path will be very clearly visible.
>
> - Every project must have well-planned Requirements Elicitation sessions (More details will follow in subsequent chapters). No requirements should be written based on already provided documents or based on assumptions. User interaction is a must for Requirements gathering and finalization.

Types of Requirements

As we know, a requirement can be a service, software functionality or feature that a user or customer needs to perform as part of his/her tasks. While a Requirement can be called a user need expressed clearly and concisely, one cannot use those requirements only for solution design and development. One Requirement can have multiple facets expressed as various types of requirements; for instance, a single functional requirement may encompass several non-functional requirements.

Imagine you have a rule or need with different sides to it. For example, if you're building something, like a website, there could be a main rule about how it should work (functional Requirement). But then there might be other details about how it should look or how fast it should be (non-functional requirements). Hence, one significant rule can have many more minor rules that go with it as a BA; one must understand them which helps to build a fool-proof system.

Here are the key types of Requirements:

1. Business Requirements
2. User/Stakeholder Requirements
3. System/Solution Requirements
4. Functional Requirements
5. Non-functional Requirements
6. Technical Requirements (Sometimes called as Non-functional Requirements)
7. Transient (Transition) Requirements

Business Requirements: Business requirements outline a project's purpose and success criteria. Usually, they also depict the need for a Project, its benefits, who will benefit, when & where and more. Business Requirements are something that the business should do to be in business. Just look at the below example. If you observe clearly, the statement does not state how this can be implemented or what is required but states the objectives.

Example: A salesperson must communicate product benefits to his/her customers every time customers purchase a product.

User/Stakeholder Requirements: User requirements capture the needs and expectations of the end-users or stakeholders who will interact with the system. They describe the system from the users' perspective and are often expressed in natural language. User requirements help ensure the system meets the users' goals and provides a satisfactory user experience.

Example: The sales team requires the CRM system to have an interface to easily track and manage customer interactions, view sales pipelines, and generate reports for sales performance analysis. They also need the CRM to integrate with their existing email platform for seamless communication tracking.

System/Solution Requirements: System requirements state functionalities that a system needs to satisfy the customer's requirements.
Example: Hardware Requirements, Operating Systems etc.

Functional Requirements: Usually, this is a type of System Requirements itself. These specify the functional behaviours or capabilities of the system. Look at the functional aspects of the proposed solution/system, i.e., what it does, what it should contain, how it should behave, etc.

Example: As an X User, I should be able to create a Lead Record to use that lead information for future follow-ups.

Non-Functional Requirements: Usually, this is a type of System Requirements itself. Depicts how well a Requirement should perform against a pre-defined parameter. Non-functional Requirements describe technical and solution attributes such as performance, response time, efficiency, security, availability, etc.

Example: As an X user, I should be able to open the Lead page within 2 seconds so that I can start filling in the lead information quickly

Technical Requirements: A technical requirement involves the technical aspects your system must meet, encompassing performance, reliability, and availability concerns. They are also sometimes called as Non-functional Requirements.

Example: The system must maintain a 99.99% availability within 24 hours.

Transient (Transition) Requirements: PMI.Org provides the most succinct definition for this type of Requirement. These are the requirements that the project has to implement to facilitate the transition from the current state of the Organization to a desired future state. These are temporary requirements that must be in place for a certain period. They hinge on the Organization's readiness for the new solution; higher readiness means fewer Transition Requirements are needed.

Example: Before the UAT/production deployment/go-live, conduct training sessions for select/all users to ensure proficient use of the new CRM system.

Requirements, Use Cases & User Stories

You might have heard or used terms like Use Cases & User stories more often in addition to "Requirements". However, often people get confused about those terms. Are they different or the same?
We will learn about this topic in the "Chapter: Techniques of Documentation". Hence, we will discuss this topic here very briefly.

Requirements and Use Cases are vital components in software development, ensuring that the end product meets the expectations and needs of users. A Requirement is a statement that describes a need, constraint, or desired functionality that a system or software must satisfy or possess (Mostly written at a level). A Use Case describes how a user or actor interacts with a system to achieve a specific goal.

A Use Case is derived from the Requirement. By breaking down Requirements into well-defined Use Cases, development teams can comprehensively understand specific functionalities and interactions. This approach facilitates collaboration, enhances development efficiency, and ultimately delivers a high-quality software solution.

Transforming Requirements into Use Cases: To transform requirements into use cases, the focus shifts from high-level objectives (Requirements) to specific scenarios or interactions between the system and its users.

Use Cases provide a detailed understanding of how users will interact with the system and the expected system behaviour in response. Each Use Case represents a specific user goal or task the system must support.

What are "User Stories" then? The term "User Stories" comes from the Agile world.

What are Epic, Feature and User Stories?

Epics, Features, and User Stories are essential components of the Agile setup, aiding in successfully planning, developing, and delivering software projects. An epic is a large and high-level user requirement that encapsulates significant functionality. It represents a substantial business objective or customer need that cannot be accomplished within a single iteration. Epics are usually defined broadly without delving into granular details, allowing teams to focus on the overarching goals and deliverables.

To transform an epic into a feature, the epic needs to be broken down into smaller, more manageable units. A feature represents a cohesive set of functionalities that fulfil a part of the epic. It provides a more specific focus and scope for development, allowing for more straightforward estimation, prioritisation, and implementation. Features are still relatively high-level and provide a clear path towards achieving the epic's goal.

Once the features have been defined, they can be further divided into User Stories. User stories are concise, independent units of functionality that can be implemented within a single iteration. A user story is a customer's perspective on a software feature.

By splitting the features into User Stories, the development team can focus on building and delivering small, testable units of functionality. Each User Story can be estimated, prioritised, and worked on independently, enhancing the flexibility and efficiency of the development process.

What Is a Correct Requirement?

[NOTE: I will use "Requirement" as a general term here. It Could be a Use Case or User Story as well.]

An essential aspect of a software development lifecycle (SDLC) is understanding the customer problem. Whether it is a BA or a Product Owner, whoever is responsible for implementing or building a product/project first should facilitate the discussion on the 'customer problem'. Because a Product or a Project must solve the 'customer problem'; otherwise, the entire endeavour will fail.

Once the problem is understood, the next step is to understand what needs to be done to solve those problems—product/project to implement a system.

- Mark these facts: **Business needs arise out of problems. Requirements arise out of Business needs.** We must understand problems/Business needs first. Requirements next. Solution later.

Converting user or business "needs" into clear, concise, and verifiable requirements is an essential skill for a BA. In essence, every Requirement must have a solid foundation on which it is written. Well-written requirements, whether they are in the form of requirements, use cases, or user stories, are the ones that are necessary, verifiable, attainable, and aligned with the business goals. Even if a requirement is verifiable, achievable, and eloquently written, if it is not necessary, it cannot be considered a good requirement.

For a requirement to be verifiable, it must state something that can be examined, analysed, tested, or demonstrated. Statements that are subjective or contain subjective words, such as "easy," cannot be verified. Writing an unattainable requirement serves little purpose. A good requirement should be clearly and unambiguously stated.

To Summarise, A "Correct Requirement" Is:

- A requirement that is needed (which is a Business Need)
- Verifiable (You know it can be tested)
- Technically feasible (Anything can be feasible technically. But it should fit within the plan, budget, schedule, and other constraints.)
- Clear & Concise (Simple Sentence – A statement which should talk about a single idea without any ambiguity)
- Unambiguous (The statement should be black & white. There is no room for other thoughts.)

Effective User Stories, agile way!

Anyone can write a user story with the help of a template or with some experience. However, writing an effective and clear user story that does not create confusion and ambiguity in the minds of readers requires real practice.

Here is a well-known framework to write a great user story, normally used in an agile world. One cannot write an effective user story overnight if he/she follows this framework, but it will help considerably improve the quality of a user story.

INVEST: Invest is the framework (people can call them just as an acronym or principle) as I see it. This framework has helped me improve the quality of user stories I write.

I – Independent: One should be able to develop each user story independently. There should not be any dependencies a user story should have. However, this does not mean the user story should not have dependencies. As a BA, one should be able to write/break down a feature into a user story so that a user story can be individually developed. Though this is one of the main conditions for writing an effective user story, this situation always cannot be achieved.

N – Negotiable: A user story should encourage conversations between developers and customers. Agile is based on conversations and is "always ready for change" to deliver real value. When the conversations are allowed, better requirements will emerge, leading to better implementations/output.

V – Value: Let's imagine any product or app you are using. It has several functionalities. But how many of them deliver real value for users? A value should be perceivable. The crux here is how one can make a user's life easy with a certain functionality. A user story should capture that essence. Users should be happy with what is delivered – that's value.

E – Must be able to Estimate: A written user story can be estimated easily because every aspect of the user story—who/ how/what, etc. is clear. Prioritisation can be effective only if there are well-estimated stories are present.

S – Small: Every user story that is part of a Sprint/iteration should be completed within the Sprint/iteration timeline. Hence, one should write/break down the stories so they are small enough to be accommodated within a sprint.

T –Testable: If one can write the acceptance criteria quickly by reading the user story, then it means that the user story is testable. Once the acceptance criteria are met, the user story can be closed as complete.

Why Do People Write Bad Requirements Sometimes?

The most common reason is Insufficient information. Either the BA could not obtain the required information, or the stakeholders could not provide it. Sometimes, to complete the requirements phase, he/she will assume few things—which may eventually can go wrong.

As a BA, above all, understanding a project's vision, mission & purpose is important. Without these and other information like constraints of the customer business, Budget, Schedule, and Organization, a BA will not be able to write requirements aligned to all these (Mission, Vision Budget, etc., as stated above), resulting in bad requirements.

There are situations when no one has the required information. In such cases, the BA can write requirements based on certain assumptions. When reviewing the requirements, it's important to review the assumptions to quickly identify any problems. However, designing and building a solution based on assumptions is always dangerous. The BA, as well as Stakeholders, must understand this simple fact.

[**Note:** *Wherever required, the BAs must include the assumptions based on which the solution will be built. These assumptions have to be explicitly called out in Requirements documents. Assumptions are BA's (Or Projects) Saviour. It will avoid surprises later.*]

A BA's job is first to capture requirements. Though the BA is equally participating in solution design and implementation activities while gathering requirements, he/she should focus on writing "What is required" rather than "How it can be implemented."

For example, Let's assume there is a need for storing certain information on the cloud. As a BA, how should he/she write the Requirement?

1. As a user, I should be able to upload and store my documents in a database.
2. As a user, I should be able to upload and store my documents in a system from which I can download them whenever I want.

Which one do you prefer?

The answer is #2. Because it states what is needed (I have just provided this one line as an example). Statement #1 states the solution, not the Requirement (Providing a database is the solution for the problem/need)—and this is not the only solution option.

Hence, Requirements should state *WHAT* is needed, not *HOW* it will be provided.

To prevent such errors during the requirement writing process, it is important to inquire about the purpose behind each Requirement. In the provided example, by asking the question "WHY," the author (or the BA) can identify all the necessary functionalities (such as document storage, download, and editing capabilities) that the system must possess.

This enables the author to articulate the requirements, focusing on the "WHAT" rather than the "HOW" of achieving them. The reason for emphasising the "WHAT" is to ensure that the BA does not inadvertently impose a specific design. It is worth considering that the Requirement may be fulfilled without a database.

Furthermore, an additional risk is associated with specifying the "HOW" in requirements. The requirement writer may mistakenly believe that all the requirements have been addressed when, in reality, some are overlooked.

Taking the same example into account, simply providing a database would not be sufficient for those who require a comprehensive document management tool. It is crucial to explicitly state the capabilities of the tool as requirements.

The quality assurance or testing team must be able to validate whether a requirement has been implemented correctly or not. The testing should result in either a pass or a failed outcome.

While writing the requirements, it is essential to determine how the Requirement will be verified and establish the acceptance criteria to ensure this. Well-defined requirements typically include clearly stated acceptance criteria.

General Rules to Write Requirements Clearly & Correctly

While writing Requirements, Use Cases, or User Stories, a BA should know clearly when to use certain words. Based on worldwide practice, the most used words in the requirements world are "shall, will, and should".

Here is a formula:

- If you are writing Requirements, then use "SHALL."
- If you are writing statements or facts, use "WILL."
- If you are writing Goals to be achieved, then use "SHOULD."

It is very important to understand that Terms like "are, is, was, and must" should not be part of a requirement statement. However, you can use them while describing the Requirement further as an additional note (elaborating context) or description. These practices are followed to achieve that ultimate clarity and unambiguity in the written Requirement.

In addition to the above, avoid using terms or words such as "Support, but not limited to, etc, And/Or, much more, Let's say, Minimise, Maximise, User-friendly, Easily, Sufficiently, quickly," in requirements. The inclusion of such terms introduces ambiguity in the Requirement. Since all requirements should be verifiable, verifying terms like "Easily" becomes challenging. Testers face difficulties in testing the same, as there is no clear definition or measure for what constitutes "Easily".

Note, unclear requirements can lead to misunderstandings, potentially causing significant financial and resource expenditures without effectively fulfilling your customers' requirements. Let me give you an example:

- WRONG: As a user, I shall need A, B, C, etc.
- RIGHT: As a User, I shall need A, B, C.

As stated earlier, the requirements should be crisp and easy to read and understand. Hence, the best practice is to write the Requirement in an industry-accepted format so that your requirement document can speak the universal language. The simple and universally accepted format is:

- *The XYZ System shall be capable of ...*
- *The XYZ System shall provide ...*
- *The XYZ System shall integrate with ...*

Such simple statements describing 'one idea' at a time avoid the risk of the reader misinterpreting the statement. Also, if the above patterns are followed, you don't need to worry much about grammatical issues.

It is better to use positive requirements that outline what should be done. Instead, rephrase them to specify what should be done. For instance, rather than writing a requirement as "The application should not allow all employees to access internal sales leads," it is better to phrase it as "The application should only allow sales team to access internal sales leads."

Pictorial Representations: We discussed this briefly in previous chapters. They say one picture is better than 1,000 words. It is highly advisable to have a pictorial representation of certain things if needed.

For example, if you are capturing the requirements for a Lead Management functionality, it would be good if you, as a BA, included a process flow diagram in the beginning so that readers can understand the process first before dwelling on a set of requirements.

In addition, wherever needed, a sample wireframe that showcases a high-level visualisation of what is to be required. Detailed and accurate Wireframes will generally be prepared during the design phase. However, from a requirements perspective, the BA should use these pictures should be used to keep everyone on the same page. A 'picture' creates a common visual/impression in the minds of different users/people, whereas the 'words' create different visuals/impressions in the minds of different users/people.

Writing clear and correct requirements takes time and practice. Here is an easy mental trick. Imagine you are a developer who develops the system. Then ask yourself, is the information clear enough for me to develop the system as stated in the Requirement?

Ask yourself.

How to Manage Requirements Effectively?

Once you capture the requirements, managing requirements effectively is crucial for project success till its closure (implemented). Here are some ways to manage the Requirements based on various needs and factors:

Categorisation: As mentioned previously, it is important to classify requirements into suitable categories such as Business Requirements, Functional Requirements, Non-Functional Requirements, System Requirements, etc., tailored to the specific requirements of your company. This categorisation aids stakeholders in identifying and focusing on the requirements that are pertinent to their roles and responsibilities.

Prioritisation: Prioritising requirements involves arranging them in order of significance to stakeholders, serving two main purposes: defining the project scope and scheduling implementation. This ensures the team focuses on essential requirements before addressing "nice to have" ones.

Various techniques can be used for prioritisation, such as grouping or ranking requirements using indicators like high/medium/low or numerical values, timeboxing/ budgeting based on fixed timelines and budgets, or negotiation/voting to establish stakeholder consensus. Prioritisation is always driven by the value a requirement adds to a user.

Techniques like MOSCOW are generally used to prioritise the requirements—more about this technique is discussed in the chapter: "Techniques of Business Analysis".

Requirement prioritisation is critical to leverage the resources effectively, to enable stakeholders to focus on their real needs, to minimise the risk of scope creep, and to increase the chances of project success by addressing critical requirements first.

Traceability: As we discussed earlier, the RTM or Requirement traceability matrix, is a tool or method that maps requirements to project components

like design documents, test cases, and system features, is typically presented as a grid or table (in an Excel sheet).
RTM involves documenting and monitoring a requirement's entire lifecycle, encompassing its origins, design, implementation, and more. This practice ensures that requirements and their associated elements remain aligned and facilitates effective change management.

Key Takeaways—

- Requirements should be gathered through user interaction to ensure accuracy and understanding
- Requirements should be comprehensive, unambiguous, and testable
- Make sure you have proper wireframes or diagrams so that readers, including stakeholders and users, understand the requirements correctly
- Utilize visual representations to enhance clarity and comprehension for all stakeholders
- Break down requirements into concise, one-line statements, avoiding jargon or buzzwords
- Make requirements easily readable and understandable for developers, testers, and customers
- Work with the testing team and collaboratively test scenarios based on the requirements. Note, if you can't test a requirement, it is a badly written requirement
- Organize requirements based on modules or related components for structured analysis
- Prioritize requirements in collaboration with users, identifying the Minimum Viable Product (MVP) and immediate needs using techniques like MOSCOW
- Maintain a clear distinction between requirements and solution details in the document, allowing for effective traceability using a RTM

Don't Forget to—

- Involve the right stakeholders
- Validate a requirement from different perspectives
- Adapt documentation type appropriately
- Structure and format requirements documents
- Adhere to organizational knowledge and standards

How To Conclude That Requirements Gathering Is Complete?

Is there any way in reality? This could be your tricky interview question. As a BA, ensuring that all requirements have been adequately gathered is crucial for the successful execution of any project.

Several key indicators help in determining whether all the requirements have been effectively collected:

- **Validation and Approval:** The most crucial aspect is obtaining validation and approval from the business users, who are the primary stakeholders. Their acceptance confirms that the requirements meet their needs and expectations, eliminating ambiguity or misinterpretations.
- **Clear Acceptance Criteria:** Can you define a clear Acceptance criterion for each requirement? If yes, it proves that you have clearly written requirements without ambiguity and are complete.
- **Alignment with Business Requirements:** All the functional or other requirements must be mapped with relevant business requirements. When you do that, the gathered requirements must align seamlessly with the project's business requirements or objectives. This alignment ensures that the project's outcomes directly fulfil the organization's strategic goals.

Throughout the project, it's crucial to keep communication open with stakeholders to accommodate changes or additional requirements due to evolving business needs.

Always remember complete requirements are not a one-time accomplishment; they evolve throughout the project's lifecycle. Stay in constant communication with stakeholders and remain receptive to feedback to meet their evolving needs.

Bonus Section: Expectations from a BA in a Modernization Project

Here is a scenario. As a BA, I plan the analysis for a project where customers expect to modernize their existing processes. This requires a systematic and comprehensive approach. Here are the key steps to consider:

- **Understanding Current Processes:** Begin by thoroughly understanding the customer's existing processes. Conduct stakeholder interviews, observe workflow, and gather documentation to understand how things operate.

- **Identify Pain Points and Goals:** Work closely with the customer to identify pain points, inefficiencies, and areas that require improvement. Simultaneously, understand the customer's modernization goals, whether improving efficiency, reducing costs, enhancing customer experience, or embracing new technology.

- **Define Scope and Objectives:** Clearly define the scope of the modernization effort and set specific, measurable, achievable, relevant, and time-bound (SMART) objectives. This will help manage expectations and ensure alignment between the customer's goals and the project's outcomes.

- **Research Modern Solutions:** As a BA, research modern technologies, tools, and best practices relevant to the customer's industry and processes. Identify potential solutions that align with the customer's goals and requirements. Sometimes, the customer might have already would have identified the solution.

- **Gap Analysis:** Compare the current processes with the desired future state to identify the gaps. This analysis will help determine what needs to be changed, improved, or replaced to achieve the modernization objectives.

- **Engage Stakeholders:** Involve all key stakeholders, including end-users, management, IT teams, and any other relevant parties, in the analysis process. Their input and feedback are essential for understanding diverse perspectives and ensuring successful adoption.

- **Prioritize Requirements:** Prioritize the identified requirements based on their impact, feasibility, and alignment with the customer's goals. Create a requirements roadmap that outlines the order in which modernization initiatives will be undertaken.

- **Create User Stories and Use Cases:** Translate the requirements into user stories and use cases that depict how users will interact with the modernized processes. This helps in visualizing the expected outcomes and validating the solutions with stakeholders.

- **Validate and Iterate:** Continuously validate the proposed modernization solutions with stakeholders and be open to feedback. Iterate on the analysis and requirements as necessary to ensure alignment and stakeholder satisfaction.

- **Document and Communicate:** Thoroughly document the analysis process, requirements, and proposed solutions. Regularly communicate progress and findings to all stakeholders to maintain transparency and foster a collaborative environment.

What did You Learn in this Chapter?

- Why Requirements Validation is important?
- How you will make sure you are writing the correct Requirements?
- What are the characteristics of a Correct Requirement?
- What is Epic, Feature & User Stories?
- What are the types (categories) of Requirements?
- How to conclude that Requirements Gathering is complete?

CHAPTER 9

TECHNIQUES OF DOCUMENTATION

- *Importance of Documentation*
- *What Is a Good Documentation Mean?*

The first essential step is acquiring a ticket when embarking on a journey, whether by bus, train, or flight. But have you ever wondered what this seemingly ordinary piece of paper or digital document truly represents? Beyond its physical or electronic form, a ticket encapsulates a wealth of information related to your travel and acts as proof (receipt) of payment to your travel provider.

Similar to how a ticket for transportation details your travel itinerary, price, and seating information, documentation in the realm of business analysis serves a comparable purpose. Just as a ticket records your financial transaction with the transportation operator, documentation in business analysis serves as documentary proof of mutual agreement between stakeholders.

More importantly, by documenting a project's objectives, expectations, and requirements, a BA creates a tangible representation of the collective understanding and consensus between all parties involved. This comprehensive documentation is a guiding light, ensuring the project progresses in the desired direction.

Much like holding onto your ticket throughout your journey until completion, a BA carries the weight of the documentation until the project reaches fruition. The documentation becomes an invaluable resource during challenging times, providing the BA with a solid foundation and a point of reference to navigate any obstacles encountered while interacting with the customer.

Just as a ticket provides vital travel information and proof of payment, comprehensive documentation in business analysis plays a crucial role in facilitating effective communication, reducing ambiguity, and fostering and enabling shared understanding among stakeholders and serves as the backbone that supports the BA's decision-making process, enhancing collaboration, and ultimately leading to project success.

Importance of Documentation

Documentation is often met with disdain by individuals who prefer focusing on their core tasks rather than putting their knowledge on paper. Moreover, some theorists argue against documentation, further fuelling the aversion. This, coupled with the misconception that Agile
methodologies discourage documentation and contribute to the unpopularity of generating and maintaining documentation.

In reality, Agile values documentation while prioritizing working software. The key is ensuring documentation efforts align with the "Deliver Value" philosophy, focusing on customer needs.

Traditionally, Waterfall documentation can be very detailed and exhaustive, while Agile recommends minimal, crisp, clear documentation. But, honestly, in today's world, every person and every methodology prefer crisp documentation!

Clear and crisp documentation helps to communicate the project-related information to all required stakeholders easily. For a BA, written documentation helps aggressive customers who occasionally change the scope.

A requirements document is a crucial guide for all stakeholders, enabling effective communication and understanding. From product and sales managers to software architects, designers, programmers, and QA, the Requirements Document ensures everyone is on the same page. Without it, stakeholders form interpretations, leading to misunderstandings, feature discrepancies, and frustrated users.

While generating comprehensive documentation can be challenging, there are strategies to ease the process by prioritizing substance over form ensuring the necessary information is captured before refining its appearance. Always the BA should begin with a basic version and iteratively improve it over time.

Undoubtedly, accuracy is paramount. The document must be meticulously scrutinized and "regularly updated" to avoid errors and prevent potential harm. One wrongly written requirement can derail the entire project.

Hence, for a BA, being skilled in documentation is very important, and he/she should embrace documentation, follow effective practices, and reap the benefits of clarity and collaboration. There is no fixed rule on how documentation should look. But there are some clear practices, which we will discuss in subsequent sections.

✪ **Remember**: Documentation is not outdated. Clear, crisp, and updated documentation is always a must.

➲ **Pro Tip**

Though templates are helpful, there is no need to worry much about documentation templates or following a specific structure. This will add further complexity. Just use your common sense. Your primary focus should be on documenting things clearly and straightforwardly. Avoid ambiguity, and make sure your paragraphs, sections, and chapters are coherent. Please keep it simple and easy to understand for all stakeholders. Trust your instincts and document with confidence!

Characteristics of "Good Documentation"

There are thousands of free templates, and template sellers are available online. As a BA, your only job is to make the documentation as perfect as possible (Documentation can include anything from requirements to designs and should be approved by stakeholders). It must provide clarity, convey a single meaning (without any ambiguity), be simple enough to understand, and have all necessary artefacts that contribute to improving understanding of people/stakeholders who consume it.

Aim For Clarity and Unambiguity: There was an incident in a Project that happened long back. I was still learning the tricks of the trade then. The customer asked: "Where is it written like that?"

The BA showed: "Here you see..."

Customer: "Okay, I read this line earlier, but the way I understood what you have written and what you have implemented are totally different. The way it is developed now, is not acceptable and it's not useful for users."

The BA is in shock now! As per BA, the project team has developed a feature as per the agreed requirement, written in the document. The customer even gave the sign-off. The customer's expectations were different when the team did a demo. The BA cannot defend himself other than by showing the customer a couple of lines written about that requirement.

So, what might have gone wrong?

It is Simple. Inaccurate and ambiguously written requirements. As a BA, the first thing he/she should learn is to write a requirement clearly – which should be understood by both BA (& Project Team) and customers in the same way. There should not be any room for a different understanding by any party. Even though the customer says, "Oh, I thought it's like that", later, the BA should be able to defend why it is not so.

That's why a BA should document requirements comprehensively—with all possible supporting artefacts, where he/she can use graphical depictions, such as process flows, wireframes, etc.—wherever possible, and have a supporting visual element, detailed description of a requirement.

However, whether you are an experienced BA or not, when writing a Requirement, BAs often fail to figure out whether the written content is perfect, that is, free from ambiguity and lack of clarity. I call it "Cloudy Mind Syndrome"—people find their content perfect, but when reviewed with a third party, they discover glaring imperfections.

Here are some quick tips to get over such situations:

- Before any review, read the content aloud yourself. You should hear what you are reading. You'll start hearing a lot of imperfections. This is the best approach to self-edit written content.
- As the following action, have a colleague review it to eliminate any potential occurrence of the "cloudy mind syndrome." Compare and validate that their content comprehension matches your understanding and what you've written.
- Every line within a requirement statement must be clear of ambiguity. It should express a single meaning, be verifiable through testing, and come with an acceptance criterion. This criterion represents the conditions under which the customer will consider the requirement "successfully implemented" upon its realization.
- Always remember the standard formula to write a Requirement: "The System shall provide <designated user>the ability to <describe the action>."
- Always remember the standard formula to write a User Story: "As a <User Profile or Role > I want <functionality within the system > so that <benefit statement>"

Note: In subsequent sections, we will learn about the subtle difference between a Requirement and a User Story. We have covered this topic briefly in the previous chapter as well.

> ➲ **Pro Tip**
>
> Before you "Keep it simple and stupid", "Keep it crisp and clear". That is the goal a BA should have in his/her mind when doing documentation.

Characteristics of "Good documentation" encompass diverse mediums and methods of communication, aiming to discover the most effective means of conveying ideas. To enhance your proficiency in documentation, here are five essential skills you must master:

Be Clear, Concise, & Precise: Effective writing employs appropriate vocabulary to ensure clarity. It is concise, conveying information succinctly. Precision involves providing the necessary level of detail. Communication and collaboration within the organisation are enhanced when writing with clarity, conciseness, and accuracy. Mastering this skill requires practice, and as a result, your documentation will receive a commendation. Here are a few examples of clear-unclear, concise-not very concise, and precise-not-so-precise sentences.

- **Unclear Sentence:** The button should be placed at the bottom.
- **Clear Sentence:** The developer should position the "Submit" button at the bottom of the contact form, aligned to the right side.
- **Not very concise:** The hero image should span the entire page width and have a parallax effect.
- **Concise:** The developer should implement a full-width hero image with a parallax effect for an engaging visual experience.
- **Not so Precise:** Use a large font for the page headings.
- **Precise:** Apply a font size of 36 pixels for the titles in the main content area of the web page to enhance readability and visual hierarchy.

Speak the Universal BA Language: When you travel to a foreign country, you don't expect the locals to understand you automatically. Most people try to learn a few words before arriving to communicate with natives. Sometimes, you get lucky and come across people who will understand you speaking in English, but it's undoubtedly less enjoyable for them. The message here is simple: learn to speak the "business analysis" language.

To write clearly, it's essential to understand the meanings of universally used business analysis terms. A crucial skill in effective communication as a BA is distinguishing between similar terms.
The nuances between these words can significantly alter the meaning of a message. In the Chapter 1 we have already discussed about a set of universally used BA terms, that you may already know—Top 25 Terms a Every BA Must Know!

Reading Between and Beyond the Lines: Let me narrate a real event that happened during a project I was part of long back. Many BAs would have faced this situation. Let me describe it for you. I was a BA with minimal experience then. In a Show & Tell demo, the customer shouted at the BA (That was me!), "What is this, Mr. BA? This is so simple and implicit. You should have common sense. Everything we cannot specify in a document."

We documented the requirements for designing and implementing a Sales Lead page for an application we are building as part of the project. The page had around 20 fields. As part of the requirement, we even asked the customer what the data types are (Drop-down, whole number, free text, etc.) for each field.

When we showed the phone number field to the customer, he/she got annoyed because we just designed the field as a whole number field—as documented in the requirement document signed off earlier by the customer. However, now the customer wants a field for the phone number that should demand ten digits automatically so that the user does not make an error while entering the information.

So, whose responsibility does it lie with now? The BA or the Customer?

BA says: "I have captured the requirement as stated by the customer – as per their needs. Why can't they tell it earlier"?

The customer says: "BA should have common sense. Capturing a Phone number is important process. Users make mistakes when entering numbers. Hence, a proper check should be provided. This is implicit; we don't need to specify every aspect of a requirement."
So, what is an implicit Requirement?

Implicit requirements are features and characteristics of a product or service that customers expect, but they may not explicitly express these expectations.

To be a good BA, he must ask the right questions during customer interaction. He/She should always question every statement. If the BA has answers to all the "Whys", then he/she can write a clear requirement. Always, a well-written requirement should be verifiable, testable or can be demonstrated. However, in the above example, the requirement was to meet all of them (verifiable, testable). Still, the BA failed to ask or follow industry standards when capturing requirements. Hence, as a BA, he must know the best practices and industry standards used while designing such systems. This knowledge will help BA in reading between and beyond the lines.

This could be a very simple or very basic scenario. There could be several such instances where the customer did not give the specific requirements to describe the requirements clearly and without any ambiguity, covering all the angles. I have seen customers who use this "implicit" blame to cover up their mistakes or ignorance. There could be several instances where the customer must explicitly give the exact requirements, and the BA might miss those unless otherwise stated – as they may be innovative features or key. Unless the customer specifies those, the BA may not be able to grasp them, as sometimes those little nuances go beyond what users expect in a system.

We all should agree that we cannot document 100% accurate requirements. However, incomplete requirements always pose a risk that the developed requirements differ from what the customer expects.

Use of Pictures/Flow Diagrams & Wireframes: We discussed this already. Always have a clear wireframe; you can build a wireframe using a simple Excel sheet if you do not have access to any tools.

Once you capture the requirement, as a BA, prepare a visual representation with all the details. When all can see the same picture, the possibility of missing out or understanding differences is less. Note that if you cannot represent it visually, your requirement is incomplete. Have a mock screen for every field's behaviour in different scenarios, if possible.

Lastly, as a BA, he/she should study the documented requirements once again before it is developed to identify any "implicit" or "assumed" situations. He/she should go deep and think deeply by asking questions. Break down a high-level requirement into multiple small pieces. If required, go and speak to customers again. For instance, the requirements (or user story) for the above example can be captured below, along with a wireframe and additional details:

"In a Sales form, as a user, I should be able to enter the customer's 10-digit mobile phone number and the area code and automatically save it in the 'Mobile Number' field.
Further Details:

- The "Mobile Number" field should be mandatory, and the user must fill in the data.
- The Mobile Number field should request ten digits and automatically show the area code
- The phone number format should be shown to users for validation ([+XX]: (XXX) XXX-XXXX)
- The field should automatically verify if ten numbers are entered; if not, it should not allow the user to move forward
- As soon as the correct "Mobile Number" is entered, the form should save automatically
- Even after saving, the Mobile number should be editable

Please note that the above "Requirement/use case (or User Story)" is still not 100% complete. You might already be getting several questions in your mind!

Azure DevOps/JIRA/Confluence Expertise: Documentation is tough and time-consuming. That's why organisations leverage collaboration tools (for planning, tracking and managing issues, features, requirements and more) such as JIRA, Microsoft Azure DevOps (Earlier called as Team Foundation Server (TFS)) and many more.

Various other ALM (Application Lifecycle Management) tools are available in the market. Depending on the organisation/ customer you work for, you should be flexible enough to work on any tool. These technologies are a world unto themselves. It can take months to fully master them, but it's worth it. Tools like JIRA or Microsoft Azure DevOps can assist every team member and stakeholder in better organising themselves. These tools ensure that individuals have consistent project updates, avoiding disruptive follow-ups.

Learning SDLC and documentation by leveraging such tools will greatly enhance your ability to deliver quality documentation and do so quickly. (Please note that documentation doesn't mean creating numerous documents.

Using tools like the above is also called as documentation.) Various other ALM tools are available in the market, such as IBM Rational Team Concert,

GitLab and Micro Focus ALM (formerly HP ALM) other such ALM tools. Depending on the organisation/customer you work for, you should be flexible enough to work on any tool.

Requirements, Use Cases & Epics, Features, User Stories

Let's understand some basics before we get into further details about writing requirements.

Requirements and use cases are vital components in software development, ensuring that the end product meets the expectations and needs of users. By breaking down requirements into well-defined use cases, development teams can comprehensively understand specific functionalities and interactions. This approach facilitates collaboration, enhances development efficiency, and ultimately delivers a high-quality software solution.

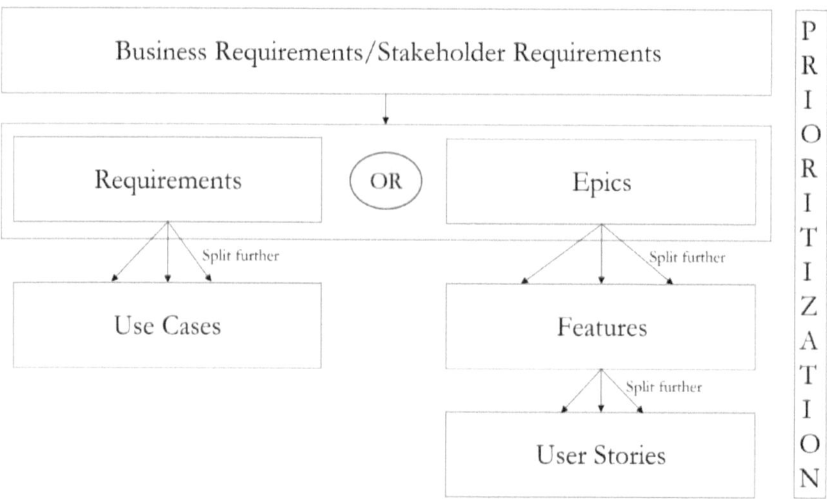

Transforming Requirements into Use Cases: To transform requirements into use cases, the focus shifts from high-level objectives to specific scenarios or interactions between the system and its users. Use cases provide a detailed understanding of how users interact with the software and the expected system behaviour. Each use case represents a specific user goal or task the system must support.

Let me give an example. Let's consider an example of a fictional e-commerce platform called ShopNOWExpress, an e-commerce platform. We'll consider the "Product Search and Filtering" requirement and demonstrate how it can be split into numerous use cases.

Requirement Name: "Product Search and Filtering"

Enable users to search for products and apply filters to refine search results on the ShopNOWExpress platform. Users should be able to sort search results based on different parameters. The system should also support saving and accessing frequently performed searches for user convenience.

Use Case 1: "Basic Product Search"

Description: Allows users to perform a basic search for products based on keywords.
Actors: ShopNOWExpress User
Main Flow:

- The user enters search keywords in the search bar.
- The system validates and processes the search query.
- The system retrieves relevant products matching the search query.
- The system displays the search results to the user.

Use Case 2: "Advanced Product Filtering"

Description: Provides users with advanced filtering options to narrow down search results.
Actors: ShopNOWExpress User
Main Flow:

- The user selects the filtering criteria (e.g., price range, brand, category).
- The system updates the search results based on the selected filters.
- Users can further refine the filters or remove them.
- The system dynamically updates the search results as filters are modified.

Use Case 3: "Sorting Products"

Description: Enables users to sort search results based on different parameters.
Actors: ShopNOWExpress User
Main Flow:

- The user selects a sorting parameter (e.g., price, popularity, rating).

- The system reorders the search results based on the selected parameter.
- Users can change the sorting parameter or reverse the sorting order.
- The system updates the displayed products accordingly.

Use Case 4: "Saved Searches"

Description: Allows users to save their frequently performed searches for future use.
Actors: ShopNOWExpress User
Main Flow:

- The user performs a search with specific criteria.
- The system offers an option to save the search with a custom name.
- The user chooses to save the search for future reference.
- The system stores the saved search for the user's account.
- Users can access and reuse the saved search at any time.

The development team can get more clarity and specificity by splitting the requirement of "Product Search and Filtering" into the above use cases (Use Case 1 – Use Case 4). Each use case focuses on functionality and user interaction, enabling efficient implementation, testing, and validation.

Epics, features, and user stories are essential components of the Agile setup, aiding in successfully planning, developing, and delivering software projects. Epics provide a high-level perspective, while features and user stories break the work into manageable increments. By understanding the relationship between these components and effectively transforming epics into features and user stories, development teams can foster collaboration, prioritize work, and deliver value to end-users more efficiently.

What is an Epic & Feature?

An epic is a large and high-level user requirement that encapsulates significant functionality. It represents a substantial business objective or customer need that cannot be accomplished within a single iteration. Epics are usually defined broadly without delving into granular details, allowing teams to focus on the overarching goals and deliverables

To transform an epic into a feature, the epic needs to be broken down into smaller, more manageable units (features). A feature represents a cohesive set of functionalities that fulfil a part of the epic. It provides a more specific focus and scope for development, allowing for easier estimation, prioritization, and implementation. Features are still relatively high-level and provide a clear path towards achieving the epic's goal. Hence, features can be split into user stories if required.

Let's continue with the example of "ShopNOWExpress". One of the epics for this platform could be "Enhanced Payment Options." This epic aims to improve the payment system to offer customers a wider range of payment methods.

To transform the epic into a feature, it can be divided into two distinct features:

1. **Integration of PayPal Payment Gateway:** This feature focuses on integrating PayPal payment gateway into the ShopNOWExpress platform, providing customers with an additional payment option. It involves leveraging/integrating with the PayPal API, implementing secure payment transactions, and updating the user interface to accommodate payments.

2. **Support for Mobile Wallets:** This feature aims to enhance the payment system by supporting popular mobile wallet services such as Apple Pay, G-pay, and Samsung Pay. It involves integrating with the corresponding APIs, ensuring secure transactions, and adapting the platform's user interface to handle mobile wallet payments seamlessly.

How to Split Features into User Stories?

Once the features have been defined, they can be further divided into user stories. User stories are concise, independent units of functionality that can be implemented within a single iteration. They are expressed/written from the user's point of view. They provide specific details about what needs to be built and what value it will deliver to the end-users. Let's continue with our example; let's split each of the above features into user stories:

User Stories for "Integration of PayPal Payment Gateway":

- As a customer, I want to see the PayPal payment option on the checkout page.

- As a customer, I want to process payments using my PayPal account securely.
- I want to view and manage PayPal transactions in the backend system as an administrator.

User Stories for "Support for Mobile Wallets":

- I want to use Apple Pay to make **quick and secure payments** as a customer.
  - *[**Note:** 'Quick' & 'Secure' words add ambiguity. So, we need to define the meaning of Quick—is it within 5 seconds? This becomes a Non-functional or technical requirement. Similarly, for Security—define what is the meaning of secure.]*
- As a customer, I want to have the option to pay using G-pay on the payment page.
- As a customer, I should be presented with an option to pay with Samsung Pay.

By splitting the features into user stories, the development team can focus on building and delivering small, testable units of functionality (feature). Each user story can be tackled individually, making it easier to estimate, develop, test, and prioritize, thus enhancing the flexibility and efficiency of the development process. The same technique can be leveraged to split the complex user stories further as well, if needed.

Elements of "Effective Documentation"

Regarding documentation skills, we often think about writing – grammar, spelling, and sentence structure. But should documentation be like a story? Should it be fiction or non-fiction? What should we keep in mind while documenting?

Whether you are doing documentation for a Waterfall or Agile project, your first job as a BA is to agree with customers on key deliverables in terms of documentation. Some customers want very detailed documentation on Requirements, Design, and many other documents. They may supply a specific template as well. However, some customers want documents to be minimal and online. By "Online", I mean using ALM/SDLC tools like JIRA or Microsoft Azure DevOps.

The key advantages of such ALM tools are that the entire lifecycle of a Requirement (From Requirement > Design > Development > Test Cases > Test Executions > Closure) can be maintained, tracked, and traced via Stages/State/Status of a Requirement item.

Which Approach? Requirements or User Stories?

When documenting, based on the project's need and stage, the project team can choose what approach to take. The team can choose the Requirements (Use Cases) Approach or User Stories Approach. Requirements articulate the value and purpose of a functionality/feature from the product's perspective. On the other hand, user stories capture the value and purpose of a feature from the user's perspective. You can select an approach according to your present requirements and customer expectations of the project.

Requirements (Use Cases) Approach: As you may know, A requirement is generally a broad statement, while a "use case" is usually a more specific statement implied or derived from the Requirement. It's possible for a requirement to correspond to multiple use cases. A scenario can be a collection of background assumptions that provide context for a use case or a grouping of use cases, as described in the previous section. Now, let's investigate how, as a BA, one can write Requirements (and then Use Cases).

REQUIREMENT	
Related Process Flow Diagram	Place/have a link to Process Flow diagram related to this requirement
Requirement Name (Or Epic/Feature)	Give Meaningful Headline to call this Requirement
Requirement ID (Or Epic/Feature)	Give a Unique number to your Requirement. Example: If the name of the Project is "Sales Automation" and the Module within the Project is Lead Management, then you can give a unique ID as SA-LEAD-REQ01
Use Case/User Story Name	Give Meaningful Headline to call this Use Case/User Story
Use Case/User Story ID/Number	Give a Unique number to your Use Case/User Story. You can use one or two letters from your Project Name + Two letters from the module (Sub area) within the Project + Unique Number. Example: If The name of the Project is "Sales Automation" and the Module within the Project is Lead Management, then you can give a unique ID as SA-LEAD-0001
Priority	Have any of the 4 priorities listed below as a Priority of this requirements & assign anyone post your discussion with stakeholders/PO etc. ▪ must-have ▪ should-have ▪ could-have ▪ won't-have
USE CASE/USER STORY DETAILS	
Use case or User Story	The System shall provide <designated user>the ability to <describe the action> OR As a <User Profile/Role> I want <functionality within the system > so that <benefit statement>
Documents Reference:	Write the Documents you Referred while writing this requirement
Stakeholders Consulted	Write the name of stakeholders you consulted to understand this requirement during the Workshop/Or people who've contributed to this requirement

I will explain the basic components of a Requirement understandably. The above structure/ table can be used to write a Requirement in detail on a Word document.

Note: The format/template can be helpful to document your Use Case/User Story about a Requirement (Or Epic/Feature). You may use the entire format or simplify the format/template as required. Remember that this is not only the best way to Write Requirements. You can use your creativity to write Requirements in a much simpler way.

Primary Actor	A primary actor initiates an interaction with the system
Secondary Actor(s)	The system initiates interactions with secondary actors **Example:** A user clicks on a button in a website to initiate some action. As a response, the website sends query to Database and the Database responds with data. In this scenario the user is a primary actor because he initiates the interaction with the website. The database system is a secondary actor because the website initiates the interaction with Database. Secondary Actors can be Systems or Users too.
Trigger(s)	Triggers are the events or actions that gets the use case to be initiated – beginning of use case. **Note:** This detail may not be available for you initially. This is optional. You can update this once the design is complete.
Pre-Conditions	A state of the system that the system must comply for the use case to be able to begin. **Note:** This detail may not be available for you initially. This is optional. You can update this once the design is complete.
Post-Conditions – Success	Write the outcome of the use case **Note:** This detail may not be available for you initially. This is optional. You can update this once the design is complete.
Post-Conditions – Failure / Exceptions / Alternative paths	Write about what if the Success Precondition did not meet, what are the exceptions/what should happen next. **Note:** This detail may not be available for you initially. This is optional. You can update this once the design is complete.
Acceptance Criteria	Conditions where the system is behaving as expected when a use case is executed. Simply put, conditions that the system must meet to be accepted by the system user, customer, or other systems and based on this the customer will pass the requirement as "successfully implemented", when it is implemented.
Requirements Description/Wireframes/Screenshots: 1. Write Additional details 2. Add Wireframes if any 3. Include Flow diagrams/Sequence diagrams, if required 4. Add any reference material which will be helpful for a user to understand the user story better. You can include details about context of the requirements in detail. You need to keep all the above columns crisp and clear. However, you can keep this section detailed. This section should be used to write details for the benefit of readers for their additional understanding. Hence you should make sure not to make any conflicting statements here.	

An Example Requirement (with Use Case or User Story): Here's an illustrative requirement (accompanied by a use case or user story) demonstrating the recommended documentation format.

This example is intended to serve as a model or template for how requirements should be typically documented, helping others understand and follow the recommended documentation format. This is for your guidance only. In practice, or in actual projects, you may have a properly defined templates which you may be asked to make use of.

REQUIREMENT	
Related Process Flow Diagram	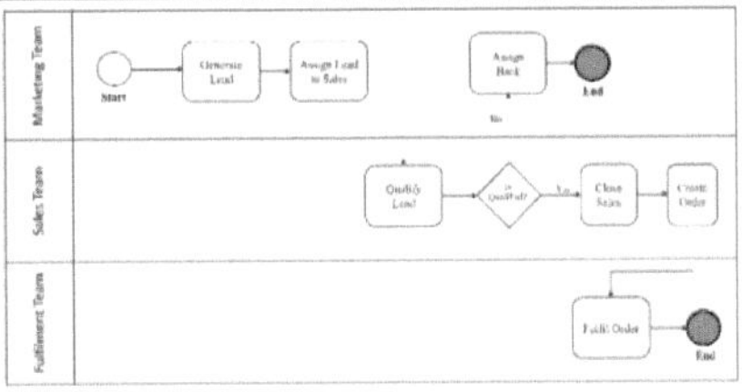
Requirement Name (Epic/Feature)	Lead Management
Requirement ID (Or Epic/Feature)	SA-LEAD-REQ01
Use Case Name	Convert Lead to Opportunity
Use Case ID/Number	LEAD123
Priority	Must-Have
USECASE /USER STORY DETAILS	
Use Case/User Story	The System shall provide the Salesperson user an ability to qualify a Lead to an Opportunity by clicking a button OR As a Salesperson I should be able to qualify a lead to an Opportunity by clicking a button
Documents Reference	NA
Stakeholders Consulted	Mr. X, Mr. Y
Primary Actor	Salesperson
Secondary Actor(s)	System
Trigger(s)	[This section will be updated post design finalization] The user shall select the Lead record in the list view and click the "Qualify" button to qualify the lead into an Opportunity. User can also open the Lead record and shall click the "Qualify" button in the Lead Page to convert the lead into an Opportunity.

Here is the continued part of the above Requirement Sample:

Pre-Conditions	[This section will be updated post design finalization] User has permission to use the system.
Post-Conditions – Success	[This section will be updated post design finalization] The Lead is qualified into an Opportunity.
Post-Conditions – Failure / Exceptions / Alternative paths	The Lead is not qualified into an Opportunity.
Acceptance Criteria	The functionality should meet all the pre-conditions, Post conditions (success & Failure).

Here is the continued part of the above Requirement Sample: (See next page)

Additional Details, Context & Description:

- Write Additional details
- Add Wireframes if any (Lead Page Wireframe & fields)

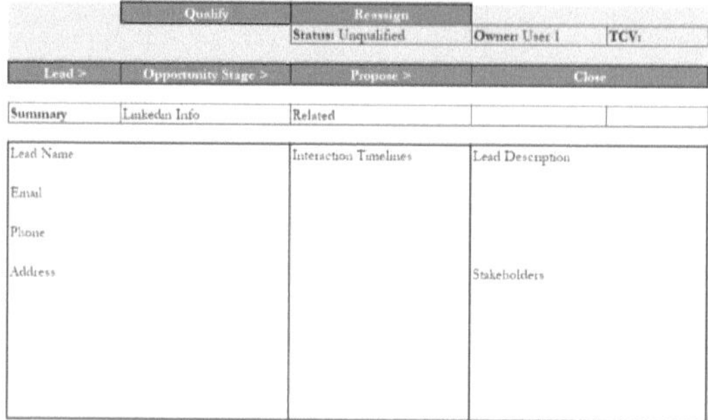

- Add any reference material which will be helpful for a user to understand the user story better

Example:

- The fields in the sections "Contact" and "Company" will be pre-filled with the relevant information retrieved from the database and will be read-only
- An additional tab including the all the information already entered for the existing Lead will be accessible/carried forward to Opportunity screen.
- When the Lead is qualified into an Opportunity, corresponding "Account (Customer)" & "Contact" information shall be created. This shall be the Primary contact for that Account. The contact record will get associated with the account.
- Etc.

User Stories Approach: As you already know, User stories are concise, high-level descriptions of a feature or functionality expressed from an end-user's perspective. Though there is no harm in using the "User Stories" approach in Waterfall projects, User Stories are commonly used in Agile methodologies, such as Scrum. They are part of an iterative, incremental approach to software development and serve as placeholders for conversations between the development team and stakeholders. As described in the previous section, User stories will be a part of a feature and a corresponding Epic.

ALM tools such as JIRA or Microsoft Azure DevOps provide an interface that looks more or less like the one below (You can configure them as per your process needs).

One can track the current State/Stage/Status of a Requirement/User Story within a single page. As a BA, once you agree with the customer on documentation deliverables, you should adapt your documentation skills to the agreed-upon format.

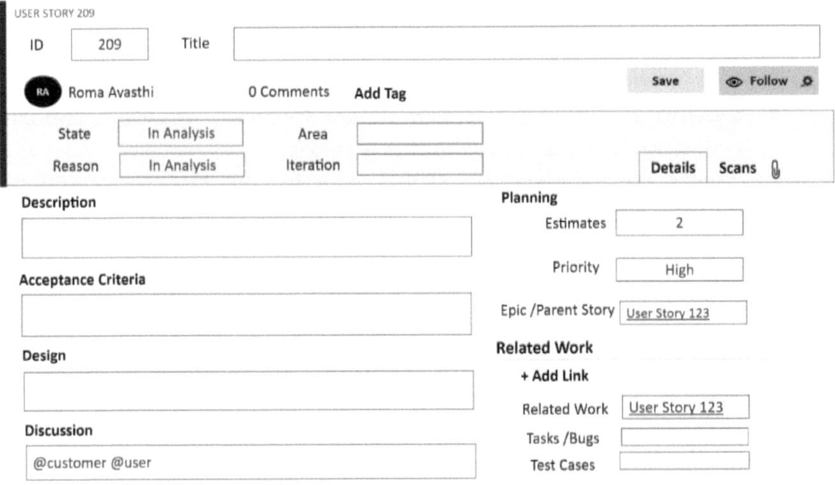

Let's understand the typical terms used during capturing a 'User Story' in tools like JIRA or AzureDevOps (Within the tool, you can tag or connect a User Story to a corresponding feature and Epic as well):

- **Title:** Give Meaningful Title to a User Story
- **ID:** Give a Unique number to identify a User Story
- **State:** This would be a dropdown. You can configure it in the Tool [Ex: In Analysis/In-Design/In-Dev/ In-Testing/UAT/Ready to be deployed/Deployed/Closed]
    - **User Story Description:** Always remember the standard formula [*This format is created by Rachel Davies [as mentioned in Scrumalliance.org]*] to write a User Sory—As a <User Profile/Role> I want <functionality within the system > so that <benefit statement>
- **Estimates:** This could be any number (Man Days, Man Hours, etc.)
- **Acceptance Criteria:** Conditions where the system behaves as expected when executing a use case. Simply put, conditions that the system must meet must be accepted by the system user, customer, or other systems. Based on this, the customer will pass the requirement as "successfully implemented" when it is implemented.
- **Parent Epic/Feature:** Tag any parent Epic or Feature; the tool provides this functionality. Sometimes, you will have only a Feature associated with a User Story if you have started your hierarchy with a Feature.
- **The usual hierarchy is:** Epic → Feature → User Story [Also, there are Tasks & bugs]

- **Additional Documents**: Upload any relevant documents
- **Related Stories**: Tag any related User Story/Epic or Feature; the tool provides this functionality
- **Design**: Describe the detailed design approach. Typically, you can even copy-paste an image in this text box.
- **Test Cases:** Create several test cases for this User Story and tag those to the User Story. Like the User story, you can track the test cases until the closure.
- **Discussion:** You can include details about the context of the requirements in detail. You need to keep all the above columns crisp and clear. However, you can keep this section detailed. This section should be used to write details for the benefit of readers for their additional understanding. Hence, you should make sure not to make any conflicting statements here. Include Requirements description/ Wireframes/ Screenshots etc.
    - Write Additional details
    - Add Wireframes, Include Flow diagrams, if any
    - Add any reference material related to the user story
- **Tasks:** Add any tasks against a User Story and tag those to the User Story. Like a user story, you can also track tasks till the closure.
- **Bugs:** Raise any Bugs against a User Story and tag those to the User Story. Like a user story, you can also track bugs till the closure.

Pro Tip

When to Write What: When writing a user story or a use case, the key focus should be describing the customer's desired outcome and equipping the development team with the essential details to ensure successful dev/implementation. It can be challenging to determine what to write, so here's a straightforward approach to help you make that decision:

- If the requested feature directly impacts the end-users; if your audience is end-users, write a user story. Otherwise, go ahead with the Use Case approach.
- Simply put, use cases articulate the value and purpose of a Requirement from the product's perspective. On the other hand, user stories capture the value and purpose of a feature (or Requirement) from the user's perspective.
- Ultimately, documentation should happen as per customer needs. Hence, clearly agree on documentation expectations—approach, format, structure, etc.

Documenting Integration Requirements

Understanding the business objectives driving the need for integrating two systems is crucial as this will shape the requirements-gathering process and help prioritize the integration features and functionalities.

Here are the key steps you must remember when capturing Integration Requirements.

Identify Systems and Stakeholders → Define Integration Scenarios → Data Mapping & Transformation → Error Handling and Exception Scenarios → Security and Compliance

Identify Systems and Stakeholders:

1. Identify the systems that require integration and the stakeholders involved in the process.
2. Engage with representatives from each system and understand their unique requirements, constraints, and dependencies.
3. Consider each system's technical capabilities, data formats, security protocols, and any existing APIs or integration points.

Define Integration Scenarios: Work closely with stakeholders to define integration scenarios that outline the desired data flows, triggers, and actions between the systems. Identify the specific data elements and attributes that must be exchanged and transformed during integration. Document the expected data formats, frequency of data updates, and any validation or transformation rules. When capturing this data, kindly use various diagrams we have discussed in the earlier chapters—sequence diagrams, data flow diagrams, etc.

Data Mapping and Transformation: Data mapping and transformation are critical in ensuring seamless integration. Analyze the data structures and formats of the systems involved and identify any discrepancies or mismatches. Define clear mapping rules to reconcile these differences and ensure data consistency and accuracy throughout the integration process.

Consider Error Handling and Exception Scenarios:

1. Anticipate and document error handling mechanisms and exception scenarios that may occur during data transmission or integration failures.
2. Define how errors will be logged, monitored, and resolved.
3. Consider data reconciliation processes, rollback mechanisms, and notifications to stakeholders in case of integration failures or discrepancies.

Ensure Security and Compliance: Security and compliance are paramount when integrating systems that handle sensitive data. Identify and address security requirements, such as authentication, authorization, encryption, and data privacy regulations. Collaborate with security and compliance teams to ensure the integration solution meets the necessary standards and safeguards.

In the next chapter, we will look into a typical documentation template (which is usually a part of your main requirements document. However, if there are several integrations, a BA can maintain a separate document as well) that can be used to capture any Integration requirements.

✪ **Remember**—all these activities should happen in collaboration with Technical Leads, development teams, customer business users and IT teams, and ideally, the entire activity should be led by a BA.

Steps to Capture Requirements for Data Migration

Capturing requirements for data migration to a newly implemented system is essential for a successful and error-free migration process. By assessing the current data landscape, defining migration objectives, establishing data mapping and transformation, planning for data extraction and load, addressing security and privacy, and documenting the requirements, organizations can ensure a seamless transition of data to the new system. Effective requirement capture for data migration minimizes risks, ensures data integrity, and enables a smooth migration process, ultimately contributing to the success of the new system implementation.

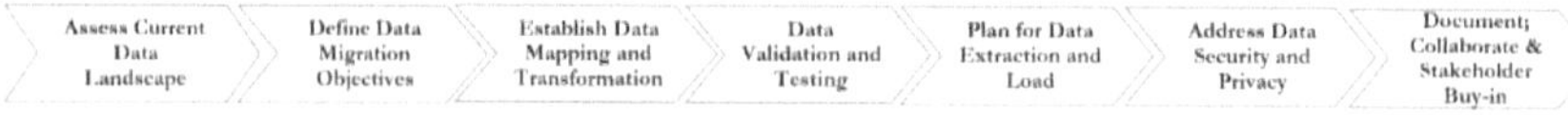

Assess Current Data Landscape: Begin by thoroughly assessing the current data landscape within the organization. Identify the data sources, formats, structures, and quality. Understand the dependencies, relationships, and data dependencies across different systems and databases. This assessment will provide insights into the complexity and scope of the data migration process.

Define Data Migration Objectives: Clearly define the objectives of the data migration project. Determine what specific data elements, records, or entities must be migrated to the new system. Consider the data cleansing, transformation, enrichment requirements, and data consolidation or restructuring needs.

Establish Data Mapping and Transformation: Data mapping is a crucial step in data migration, where the data from the source system is mapped to the corresponding fields in the target system. Collaborate with stakeholders to define mapping rules handling discrepancies or data format differences between the source and target systems. Determine if any data transformation or cleansing is required during migration.

Consider Data Validation and Testing:

1. Develop a comprehensive data validation strategy to ensure the accuracy and integrity of the migrated data.
2. Define validation rules and conduct thorough testing to identify and rectify data anomalies or inconsistencies.
3. Consider the use of data profiling techniques and sample data sets for validation.

Plan for Data Extraction and Load:

1. Define the strategies and mechanisms for data extraction from the source systems and loading them into the new system.
2. Determine the extraction methods, data transfer protocols, and scheduling of data loads to minimize disruption to the business operations.
3. Consider the sequencing of data loads to maintain data relationships and dependencies.

Address Data Security and Privacy: Data security and privacy should be a top priority during the data migration. Identify and address any sensitive or confidential data that needs to be protected. Work with appropriate teams during data migration to ensure data security with encryption, access controls, and anonymization techniques.

Document Data Migration Requirements: Thoroughly document the data migration requirements, including data mapping rules, transformation logic, validation procedures, and any specific business rules or constraints. Make sure all stakeholders can easily understand comprehensive and clear documentation for the migration process.

Collaborate and Stakeholder Buy-in: Regularly engage with stakeholders, including business users, IT teams, and data owners, to ensure their involvement and buy-in throughout the data migration project. Seek feedback, address concerns, and obtain sign-off on the captured requirements to ensure alignment and ownership.

✪ **Remember**—all these activities should happen in collaboration with Technical Leads, development teams, customer business users, and the customer IT teams. Ideally, the entire activity should be led by a BA.

Misuse Cases

Sometimes, you will have to write some misuse cases, especially if you are working on security-related Projects or projects in industries with zero tolerance for any security or data breach. Ex: Banking. A Misuse Case, a derivative of a Use Case, serves as a concept for requirements and process modelling, illustrating the steps and scenarios when a user engages in malicious actions against a system or business process.

Despite the negative intent, misuse cases share similarities with regular use cases, defining the user's steps towards achieving a goal. This approach enables an early focus on security aspects that businesses and systems must address.

Consequently, creating misuse cases often leads to new use cases being developed as protective measures against such malicious actions, unveiling diverse design options to mitigate the issue and placing significant emphasis on security considerations during the analysis process. This emphasis will likely uncover additional use case scenarios to handle potential countermeasures.

Example: Let's consider a situation in which an unethical hacker attempts to exploit vulnerabilities in the login process of an online banking system to gain unauthorized access. The misuse case would outline the steps and scenarios involved in the hacker's attempts to compromise the system's security, prompting the bank's analysts to create new use cases to strengthen security measures and protect against such unauthorized access attempts.

Visual Diagrams in Business Analysis

I would advise that before you learn a range of techniques, master a select few techniques that BAs widely use. Initially, start with simple visual models like Process Flowcharts, Workflow charts/ Diagrams, Swimlane Diagrams, Data Flowchart, Sequence diagrams and Use case diagrams. Once you master these, you can start learning and using advanced UML and BPMN diagrams (if required) in your project. By leveraging the appropriate visual tools, BAs must effectively convey information to different stakeholders. Hence, learning and mastering widely used visual techniques is very important.

Basic Shapes & notations of Common Flowcharts and diagrams are as below. If you further research, you will find many more symbols or notations. You don't have to be overwhelmed by the wide variety of notations that are available out there.

While it is good to have good knowledge about them, it is unnecessary to understand every notation. If you are overwhelmed or confused, it's ok. Just remember some common notations as listed below, which are commonly used:

Common Notations:

Notation	Notation	Description
	Process	This Shape/notation shape represents a process, a function or action.
	Start/End	This notation symbol represents the start points, end points in a flow chart
	Document	This notation represents document input/output. Ex: Receive/generate report/email etc.
	Decision	This notation used to indicate decision making – YES/NO or True/False.
	On Page Connector	Connects multiple parts of a flowchart on the same page.
	Off-Page Connector	Connects multiple parts of a flowchart on the different page.
	Data Input/Output	Denotes inputting/outputting of external data
{	Annotation	Used to indicate any additional info regarding a step

Processes & Operations Notations: In this book, we will only learn basic Flowcharting and diagramming techniques. The idea is to provide you with a fundamental understanding, and hence, only basic information about advanced charting techniques like BPMN, UML, etc. are included in this book. However, the information in this book about the diagrams is sufficient for any new or aspiring or practising BA to read and understand.

Notation	Notation	Description
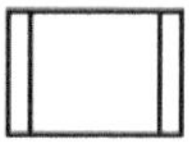	Process	Denotes named process
	Delay	Any delay period within a process
	Alternate Process	An alternate process to the existing normal process
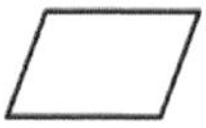	Data	Data input or output
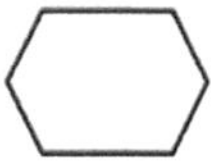	Preparation	Preparation Stage
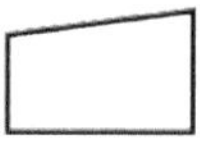	Manual Input	Denotes Manual Input
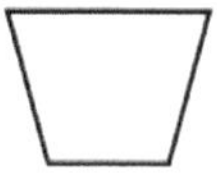	Manual Operation	Denotes a Manual Process
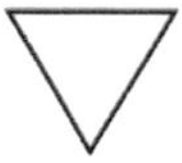	Merge	Denotes a point where multiple processes Merge

Tools like Lucid Chart Visio can draw BPMN and UML diagrams. You may use those websites to learn more about them.

Common Types of Flowcharts and Diagrams

A **Process Flow Chart** is the most commonly used diagram or chart to represent a process simply and understandably. In general, it represents a process with a clear depiction of individual steps in sequential order.

A flowchart is a visual representation of the steps in a workflow. They are commonly used to illustrate various concepts, including workflows.

Here Is an Example:

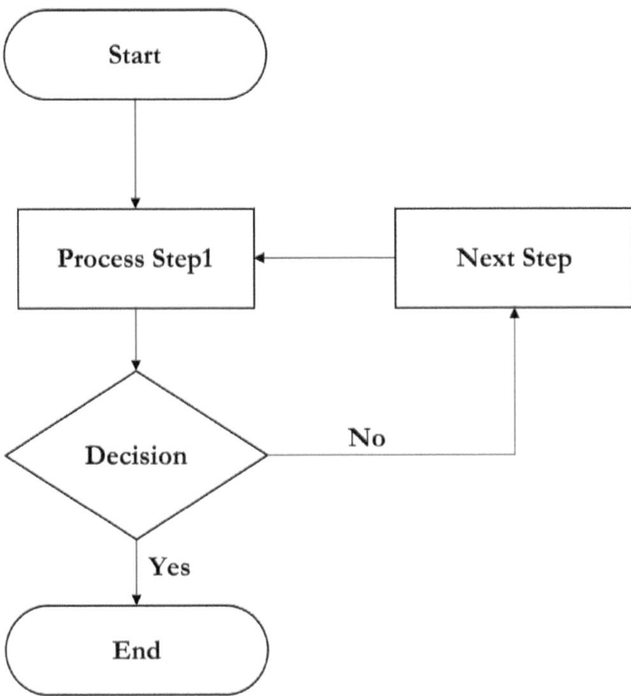

Workflow Diagrams: Workflow is the sequence of processes that a piece of work passes through from initiation to completion, as defined by the Oxford Dictionary.

So, what is a Workflow diagram? A workflow diagram visually depicts any business process by leveraging flowcharts. As described earlier, Flowcharts (Flowchart diagrams) illustrate many concepts and ideas, including workflows. Refer to the above diagram as an example of a workflow.

We will also discuss BPMN later. Within these BPMNs, Workflow is just one part. Within a BPMN, there might be several workflows.

Swimlane Diagrams: This flowchart diagram depicts who does what within a Business Process. For example, if three teams or people are involved in a process, three lanes can represent that, and the process tasks performed by each of these teams/ people can be depicted inside the lane about that individual team/person. A swim lane diagram clearly shows connections between teams/people involved, their communications and handoffs.

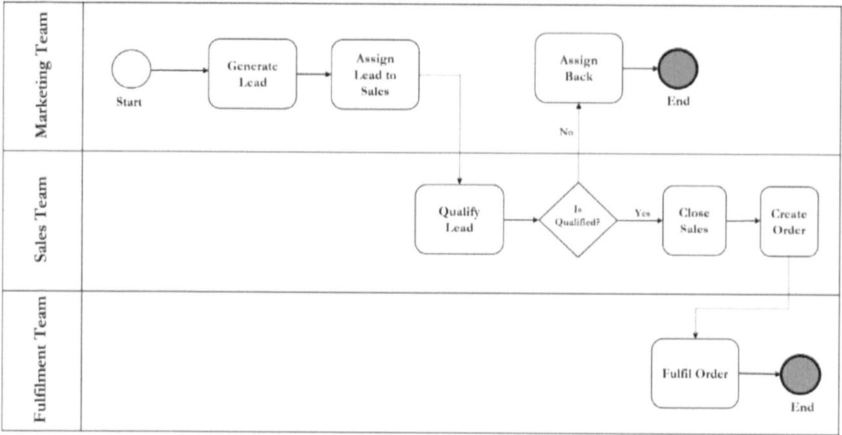

Dataflow Charts or diagrams: They are also called as DFD. As the name indicates, a dataflow diagram indicates a flow of data through a process or a set of systems. DFD has its notations. I have provided only the important ones below.

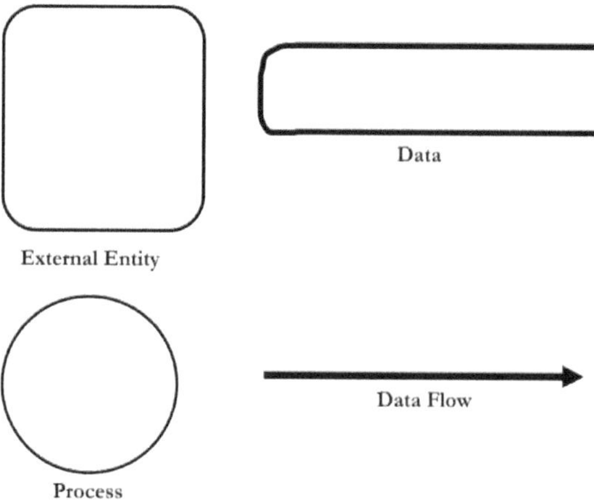

An example of DFD is as below:

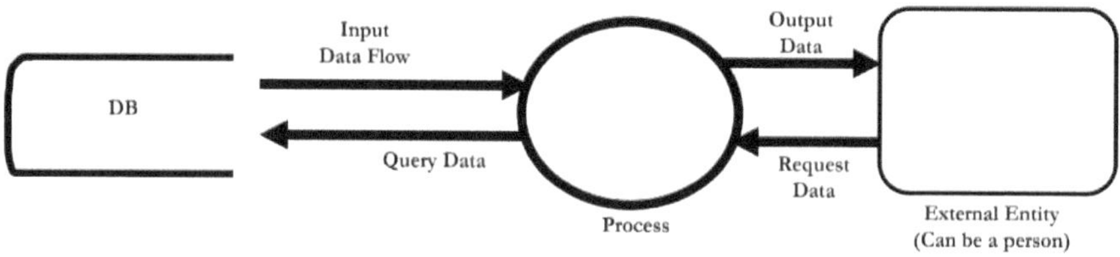

Common UML diagrams Used in Projects:

Use case Diagrams: A Use case diagram is part of the Unified Modelling Language called UML. The UML is a modelling tool or language used to visualize the design of a system.

A use case diagram depicts how users/actors interact with the system. Generally, a use case diagram represents a scenario involving a use case, users/actors, & systems in a single picture at a high level.

Common components of a use case diagram are use cases, Users/Actors, Systems, and End goals. Additional notations a UML based diagrams are:

- A person-like notation used to represent a user and an oval shape to represent a use case
- A a square shape representing a system and lines or arrows connecting them.

An example of a use case diagram is as below. The diagram is self-explanatory; hence, I will not delve much into the details.

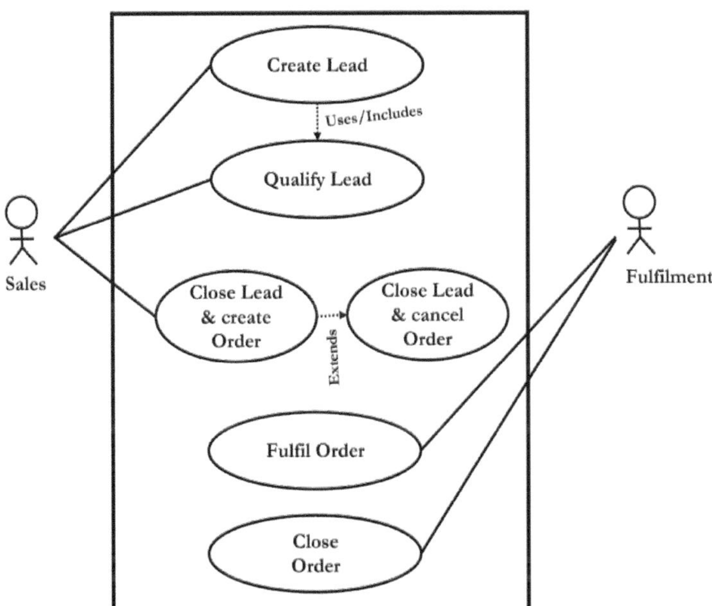

Sequence Diagrams: A sequence diagram is also a part of the UML typically used to depict the sequence of data exchange or message exchange between the tables/objects or between the systems. Key notations and an example of a Sequence Diagram are as follows:

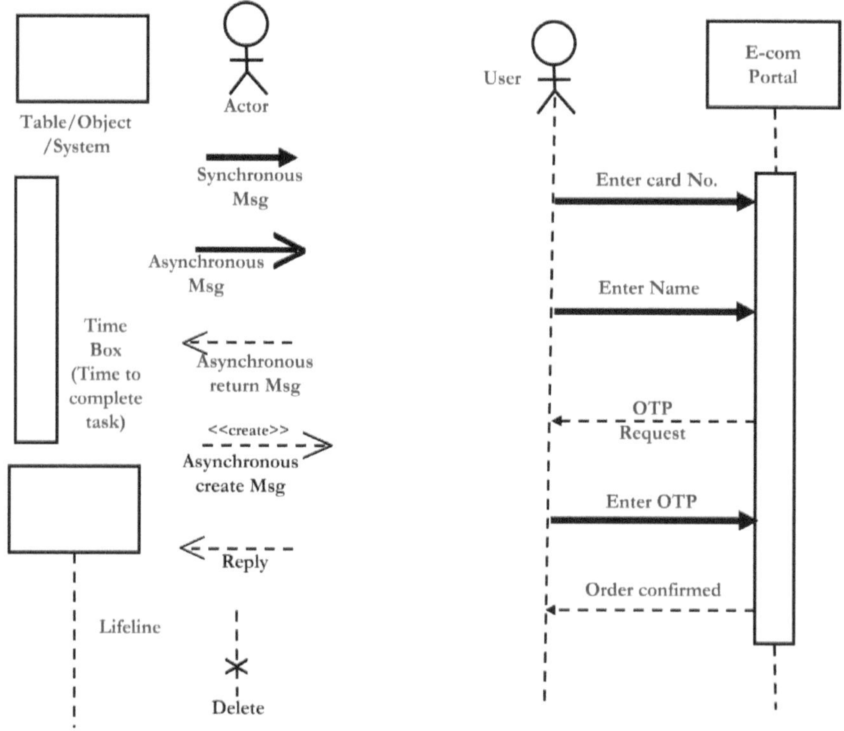

In a nutshell, Sequence diagrams:

- Shine as a potent tool for BAs to convey technical intricacies to non-technical stakeholders in meetings, presentations, or discussions
- Showcases the system's behaviour under diverse scenarios - showing how systems interact with each other, error handling, exceptions, alternative paths, etc.
- Become a valuable asset in the process of validating requirements and scenarios with stakeholders, as these diagrams offer greater clarity and precision
- Offer a crystal-clear window into the system's inner workings—helpful for developers to understand.
- Facilitates technical discussions as these diagrams offer a clear blueprint that outlines how various components should interact

- Effective in coming up with accurate test cases to ensure that the system behaves as intended under a spectrum of scenarios

Class Diagrams: If you are into technical analysis and technical design, then understanding Class diagrams is important. The class diagram is a technical diagram that describes the data structure of a system containing classes, attributes, data operations, and relationships among objects or tables

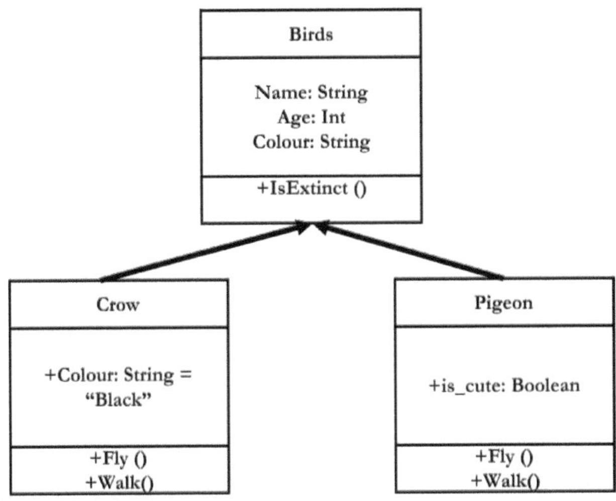

A typical class diagram consists of a rectangle with three rows. The top row contains the class, the second row has the class's attributes, and the third row depicts the related methods/ operations, etc. Generally, class diagrams are used to showcase the data model and technical schematics of a system. A Typical Class diagram looks like below. This is just for your visualization. There are a lot of concepts that need to be understood in a class diagram that I have not covered in this book.

If you think Class diagrams are similar to Entity relationship diagrams, no, it is not. Class diagrams and Entity relationship Diagrams have some differences. Class diagrams represent both the structural and behavioural features. Entity relationship Diagrams depict only data structure and hence offer only a static view of an application/system.

As this book is intended for functional BAs, I have not included detailed information about class diagrams. You may study about them online. However, please note that sometimes, the BA may need to create a class diagram if he/she is involved in the technical design. However, a general understanding of the class diagram is sufficient for a typical BA role.

Common BPMN diagrams Used in Projects

Business Process Modelling Notation (BPMN) is a widely used flow chart method for modelling end-to-end business processes. It plays a key role in Business Process Management by visually representing the sequence of business activities and information flows required to complete a process.

BPMN's primary goal is to visually represent a business procedure that is easily understandable to all stakeholders. It allows different business units to comprehend the collaboration and transactions occurring within an organization.

With standardized symbols and notations, BPMN simplifies process maps for various parties involved, including management, employees, and consultants. It establishes a common language and notation that is universally recognized, enabling easy analysis of both public and private business processes. Here are the commonly used BPMN Symbols and notations:

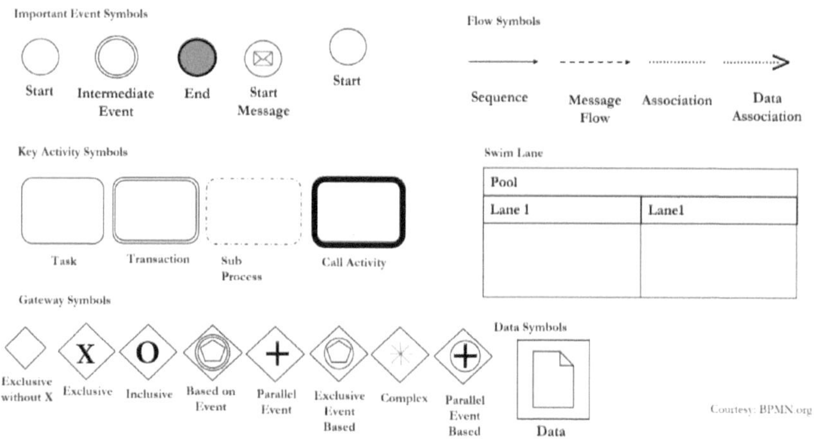

BPMN serves two primary purposes. Firstly, at a high level, it aims to enhance understanding among participants and stakeholders involved in a business process. Secondly, at a more detailed level, it provides the necessary information for precise process implementation. BPMN bridges the gap between process intention and implementation by offering a standard, common language. It caters to technical and non-technical stakeholders, such as business analysts, process participants, managers, technical developers, external teams, and consultants.

It brings clarity and detail to the sequence of business activities, fostering effective communication and collaboration.

Here is a sample BPMN Diagram that will look like this (With Swimlane):

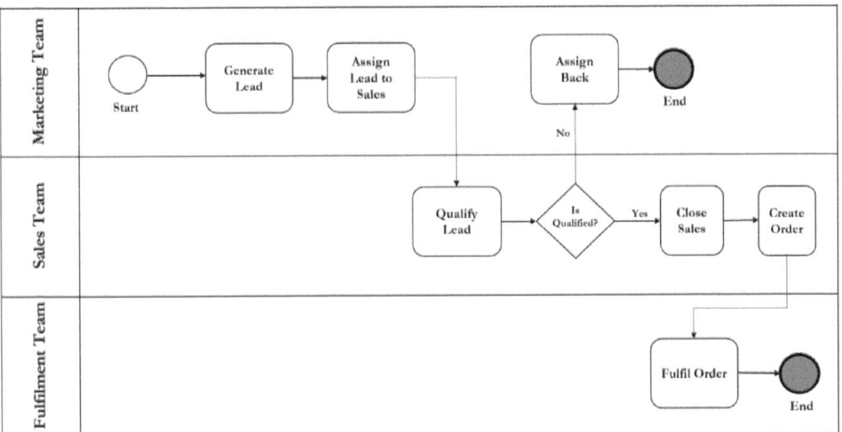

BPMN helps companies and organizations to:

- Visualize business processes
- Document processes
- Analyse business processes
- Discuss the processes using a common language

Free Tools a BA can Leverage

Some of the popular Free/Paid Tools that can be used for your practice.

Wireframing:

- Basic wireframing can be done using **Excel Sheet.**
- **Balsamiq:** User-friendly wireframing tool with a drag-and-drop interface.
- **Figma:** Versatile design tool for collaborative wireframing and prototyping.
- **Adobe XD:** Comprehensive tool for wireframing, prototyping, and design.

Flowcharts and Flow Diagrams:

- **Lucid Chart:** Web-based platform for creating flowcharts, process maps, and diagrams.
- **draw.io:** Free online tool for creating various diagram types, including flowcharts.
- **Microsoft Visio Online:** Web-based application for professional flowcharts and diagrams.

Requirements Management Tools:

- **Trello:** Flexible project management tool that can be adapted for requirements management.
- **JIRA:** Comprehensive project management and issue tracking tool with features for requirements management and traceability.
- **Req. View:** Specialized requirements management tool for capturing, organizing, and tracking requirements.

Mind Mapping Tools:

- **Mind Meister:** Web-based tool for collaborative mind mapping with real-time editing and sharing capabilities.
- **Xmind:** Popular open-source software for visualizing ideas and concepts through mind maps.
- **Coggle:** Easy-to-use online tool for creating interactive and collaborative mind maps.

Note: While the mentioned tools offer free/trial options, they may also offer premium plans with additional features. Refer to each tool's website for more information on pricing and plans.

What did You Learn in this Chapter?

- What are the key factors to consider while writing Requirements?
- What are Requirements, Use Cases & Epics, Features, User Stories?
- What is an implicit Requirement?
- Do you think Documentation is outdated?
- How will you Document the Integration Requirements?
- How will you Document the Data Migration Requirements?
- How will decide whether you need a Use case or User Story?
- What are Misuse cases?
- What are the Common Types of Flowcharts and Diagrams?

CHAPTER 10

SAMPLE DOCUMENT TEMPLATES

- *8 Important Templates a BA Should Know*
- *Sample Requirements Templates*
- *Effective Requirements Gathering Techniques*

Document preparation is a critical responsibility for all diligent BAs. This chapter could be a valuable resource for newcomers to the field or those aspiring to become successful BAs. Throughout the project, BAs fulfil various project needs by creating documents tailored to different audiences within the project. These documents are an integral part of a BA's job function.

It is important to note that customers often prefer to avoid lengthy documentation in Agile Principles-inspired projects. Instead, they use tools like Jira or Azure DevOps to document project requirements. Sometimes, customers may expect minimal documentation and sometimes detailed documentation. As a BA, agreeing with the customers on the documents they expect from the BA and their team is essential.

In this chapter, I will provide you with basic structures (document templates) of key documents used in the business analysis process. However, before we get into structures (document templates), let's understand which are key types of documents a BA prepares or involves himself/herself in preparing such documentation. I have provided abbreviated names of various important Business Analysis and Project Management documents with a short description.

- **BRD:** This is a business requirements document (BRD), a formally used document that details the business needs and objectives (perhaps Requirements).
- **FRD/FRS:** Functional requirement specification (FRS) or Functional Specification Document (FSD) is a formally used document to describe requirements, functionalities and system behaviours so that developers understand the intended functionalities of a proposed system clearly.

- **SRD/SRS:** System Requirement Document (SRD) or System Requirement Specifications (SRS) define system-level functional and Non-functional Requirements, including system performance requirements.
- **TDD:** The dev team writes a Technical Design Document (TDD) to describe the design aspects of requirements in detail.
- **HLD:** High-level Design (HLD) is a high-level technical design document generally used for the consumption of non-technical people
- **LLD:** Low-Level Design (LLD) describes the minutest details of design, including logic, code snippets, etc.
- **STM:** Source to Target Mapping (STM) documents the mapping of fields between two systems to be integrated
- **RTM:** Requirements traceability matrix (RTM) is a document that connects requirements to their respective design, development, testing artefacts
- **CRD/CCR:** Change Request Document (CRD) /Change Control Request (CCR) is a document which contains a request for changes to already developed requirements
- **SOW:** Statement of work (SOW) is a legally binding document that contains information about the agreed Project Scope, plan, timeline and management, Various legal and financial clauses w.r.t delivery.
- **RAID:** Keeping a RAID log is crucial for effective project management as it helps to track risks, actions, issues, and decisions.
- **RACI:** The RACI (Responsible, Accountable, Consulted, Informed) matrix documents the distribution of various responsibilities among the team and individuals within the team.
- **WBS:** Work breakdown structure (WBS) is a visual/ diagram for PMs to break down the Project activities into tasks and plan the deliverables accordingly by assigning those tasks to relevant team members.
- **PCP:** Project communication plan (PCP) is the document that describes the communication process and hierarchy among the Project team & stakeholders, including management.
- **LLR:** Lessons Learned Register (LLR) document is aimed to document any learnings from the project
- **PC:** A Project Charter (PC) is typically a document containing information about the project scope, objectives, and project team.
- **PSR:** A Project Status Report (PSR)is document to present/share the current project status with the management

In the next section, I will provide basic structures of only the top 8 documents generally used in a project. These documents are output/deliverable from a business analysis activity.

Please note that I won't provide readymade digital templates as digital downloads with this Book. However, I have included them as a wireframe/table/image in the Book. When you study the Book in detail, you can easily understand the contents of those template images, and you can create your templates by keeping the wireframe/table/images provided in this Book as a reference.

For you, this will not only help you understand the subject better, but also you will remember them better and easily get a hold of the subject, and you can create several such templates easily. Note, as a BA, you will create such templates and documents as required. As a BA, you should be creative enough to build and solve your issues, and you should be able to create your arsenal on your own.

8 Important Documents Every BA Should Be Able to Create

#1 – Business Requirement Document (BRD)

If you are a customer-side BA or a Product Owner, then you are the person who will be creating this document. If you are a vendor-side BA (BA from the Project team), you will primarily collaborate with the customer to develop this document.

A Business Requirement Document (BRD) outlines the specific business requirements and expected results when developing a product or process. The BRD is a widely accepted project requirement document referenced throughout the development life cycle.

A BRD addresses 'what is Required (Requirements)' rather than 'Solution or how to achieve the solution.' The BRD is developed with the assistance of the project team, including the BA, customers, SMEs, and any other critical and relevant project team members. It serves as a communication tool for other stakeholders and external service providers.

BRD Template: The Business Requirements Document contains the following Sections:

- Project Name & Confidentiality Clause
- Version History
    - A table of complete version history of the document with date and more.

Version No.	*Date*	*Version Changes*	*Name (Who did/ why)*
Document Name_V0.0	*23-11-2022*	*NA*	*NA*
Document Name_V0.1	*25-11-2022*	*Changed the Lead flow*	*Customer feedback*

- Project Background
  - A high-level info about Project Background, why the project started, what is the vision, and purpose etc.
- Executive Summary
  - A high-level summary of Project Requirements and solutions; timeline, Team size etc. It should be crisp, clear and succinct – like an elevator pitch. That is how will you quickly explain about your project if you suddenly meet your CEO in an elevator.
- Project Schedule
  - High-level info on Project timeline which mentions important milestones of a Project
- Business Goals and Objectives/ Need Statement
  - Crisp Bullet points or one or two paragraphs about project vision/Goal
  - Mention highlights of Need Analysis
- Stakeholder Details
  - A table or Organization Chart depicting Stakeholders with their contact details. The chart can also indicate Project Governance model
- Requirement scope
  - A high-level bullet points on highlighting the areas of work in Scope & Out of scope
- Functional requirements
  - A table of all the requirements along with names of stakeholders who gave that particular requirement.
- Non-functional requirements
  - A table of all the Non-functional requirements along with names of stakeholders who gave that particular requirement
- Data Migration/Management Requirements
  - A table of all the data requirement along with names of stakeholders who gave that particular requirement.
- Integration Requirements
  - A table of all the data requirement along with names of stakeholders who gave that particular requirement.
- Business glossary/Definitions
  - A table of all abbreviations, typical words with page numbers.
- Dependencies of existing systems

- A table of all the dependencies and their impact on requirements. You can map each dependency with the Requirement numbers which are impacted in a table.

- Risks & Assumptions
  - A Table of Risks with a Mitigation approach & the person responsible
  - Table of Assumptions

#2 – Project Charter/Project Vision Document

This document can also be called a Project Vision Document—commonly merged with a Functional Specification document (FSD). However, in many projects, this document is separately written by the Customer or the Project Manager and sometimes BA in collaboration with the Customer. The Customer or Project Manager owns and creates this document, but BAs must also contribute.

This document provides a bird's eye view of the purpose and intent of the project and states the business objective that will be achieved through the project. The Project charter also contains high-level information about the project scope, objectives, and participants/ stakeholders.

Project Charter/Project Vision Document Template: The document contains below Sections:

- Project Name & Confidentiality Clause
- Version History
  - A table of complete version history of the document with date and more.

Version No.	*Date*	*Version Changes*	*Name (Who did/ why)*
Document Name_V0.0	*23-11-2022*	*NA*	*NA*
Document Name_V0.1	*25-11-2022*	*Changed the Lead flow*	*Customer feedback*

- Introduction
  - Overview of the project describing problem and intended vision of the project
- Purpose
  - A paragraph about Purpose of this document
- Problem statement
  - Write about the problem that will be solved by implementing this project
- Scope
  - Describe Scope of the Project in Bullet points – Write clearly about what is in scope, what is out of scope

- Definitions & References
  - Put a table of technical/business acronyms and abbreviations used. Put a table of any reference documents that are mentioned in this document
- Business Case & Business Need
  - Reason for initiating this project. Write about business necessity/need for this project
- Business Benefits
  - Write about (bullet points) what business benefits are expected from the project
- Stakeholders
  - Put a Table with information about Stakeholders and their roles, involvement and responsibilities in this project. Ex: Name of the stakeholder, Organization, Business Unit, Project Role, Module, Contact details etc

Name of the stakeholder	
Organization & Designation/Business Unit	
Responsibilities	
Specialties/Expertise/Domains	
Project Role, Module	
Contact Details/Email ID	

- User Details (User Types & Profiles)
  - Put a table describing User Names /demographics that will use the system

User Type/Name	
User Profile	
User interaction area/domain	
Responsibilities	
Project Role, Module	
Deliverables/Expectations	

- High Level Requirements/Features
  - List of (A table) high-level Requirements/features that will be part of this project

- Timeline & Modules
  - Details about Project Timeline/Phases and modules (area within the project)

- Assumptions, Dependencies & Constraints

- List of all the assumptions; Dependencies & constraint that may impact the full-fledged delivery of the project

→ Cost and Pricing
  - This is an optional section. You may mention about Project Budget. Normally such financial details are not included in this type of documents. They are included in SoW or contracts

→ Quality Control
  - Details about the Process of acceptance criteria

→ Project Documentation Expectations
  - Type of documents expected from Project team

→ Any Other Information
  - Any other info that is relevant

#3 – Functional Requirements Document/Specification (FRD/FSD/FRS)

A Functional requirement specification or Functional Specification Document describes the intended behaviour of a system, including data, operations, input, output, and the properties of the system. In a BRD, the requirements are high level, but in an FRS/FSD, they are written in many more details to capture each and every aspect of a requirement.
Thus, a functional specification document becomes a more detailed, technical, accurate, and descriptive requirement document. Owing to their technical nature, FRS/FSD are equally used by developers, testers, and the business stakeholders of a project.

Functional Requirements Document/Specification (FRD/FSD/FRS) Template: The document contains below sections:

→ Project Name & Confidentiality Clause
→ Version History
  - A table of complete version history of the document with date and more.

Version No.	*Date*	*Version Changes*	*Name (Who did/ why)*
Document Name_V0.0	*23-11-2022*	*NA*	*NA*
Document Name_V0.1	*25-11-2022*	*Changed the Lead flow*	*Customer feedback*

→ **Introduction**
  - Overview of the project describing problem and intended vision of the project

- **Purpose**
  - A paragraph about Purpose of this document
- **Sign- Off**

Document **Prepared By**	**Reviewed By**
Name	Name
Title/Position	Title/Position
Vendor Name	Vendor Name
Date:	Date:
Reviewed & Approved (Sign-off) By	**Final Approval (Sign-off) By**
Name	Name
Title/Position	Title/Position
Customer Company Name	Customer Company Name
Date:	Date:

- **Table of Contents**
  - Create a Table of content with Page numbers
- **In Scope/ Out of Scope**
  - Describe Scope of the Project in Bullet points – Write clearly about what is in scope, what is out of scope
- **Assumptions, Dependencies & Constraints**
  - List of all the assumptions; Dependencies & constraint that may impact the full-fledged delivery of the project
- **References**
  - Details about documents referred
- **Content Matrix**
  - A Table describing how the information has been arranged by various Bus (When requirements are captured for various Bus) in this document. This table will be a guide for users to read only appropriate sections relevant to them
- **Business Problem Statement**
  - Write about the problem that will be solved by implementing this project
- **High Level Business Process flows**
  - This section is dedicated to represent overall process flows, if any. Ex: How a BU within an organization does the Sales
- **Actors /Users**
  - Describe each user role/Actor in a Table like below:

Description	Write about Actor roles, Responsibilities etc.		
Organisation Role	User Role		
Characteristics			
Number	Location	Growth	Notes
How many such users	Add User Location (s)	Frequency of User addition/deletions	

- **Business Hierarchy/User Hierarchy**
    - User Hierarchy diagram
- **Requirements/Use Cases/Functional Requirements**
    - List down the requirements and categorize them based on categories of users.
    - List the functional requirements that covers each user requirement.
    - Include the details as much as Possible. Each Requirement Has to be written in a clear & concise way as described earlier
    - Cover all possible scenarios so that all user types and all required functionalities are covered.
    - Give each user requirement a unique number. This is important for future tracking.
- **Data Flow Diagrams**
    - Wherever applicable & required provide the data flow diagrams or process flow diagrams. This is will be helpful during design stage as these diagrams will be further decomposed during design stage.
- **Wireframes & Mock-ups:**
    - As discussed earlier, Wireframes/mock-ups helps the client understand the future system, and as BA, it helps you to eliminate any understanding gaps between you and your customer.
- **Use case diagram:**
    - Use cases illustrate user's interaction with the system
- **Logical Data Model/Data Dictionary**
    - Creating the initial Logical Data Model is BAs job. He/she can definitely take help from technical team. But BA owns the data dictionary. Data dictionary defines the format of data aka, the field names, data type, etc. A typical Data dictionary table looks like below:

Display Name	Description	Data Type	Character Length	Required Filed?	Accepts Null value?

- **Interface Requirements (integration Requirements)**
  - Name the applications with which the system/application must interface
  - For each interface prepare a Source to Target Mapping (STM) – You may include a separate document for the same (See below)
  - Describe how the data flow will happen using the data flow diagram/sequence diagrams for each of the interfaces
  - Include high-level info about Integration approach—this information will be further decomposed in the technical design document (TDD)
- **Data Migration Requirements**
  - Define what data needs to be scrubbed or restructured
  - Details about Current Structure & status of Data
  - Document and list relevant data fields and what entities or tables should be moved along with specific fields
  - Complete the Data Mapping (You may have a separate document for the same)
  - Document how the Data Migration will be performed – Data Migration Plan
  - Document the Migration approach, size and scope clearly

#4- Requirement Traceability Matrix (RTM):

An RTM document is an important document prepared and managed by a BA. The RTM is usually created using an Excel sheet (in a tabular format) that lists the Requirements/Use cases along with their unique IDs and maps them to the corresponding Sections/IDs present in the other artefacts like Design Document (Design Section) Test Case Document (Test Case ID) Number, and more. RTM is utilized to monitor any modifications made during the project's implementation as well. The following Columns can be included in the RTM (Excel Sheet Columns):

- Software Module
- Requirement Id/Use Case Id/Section Numbers in FSD
- Requirement Description/Use Case
- Architectural/Design Document Section Numbers
- TDD ID/Section Numbers/Technical Specification ID/Sections
- Test Case Number

- Tested In (SIT/UAT/Pre-Prod)
- Status (Clarification/Design/Dev/Test/Closed/Deployed)
- Comments (If any)
- Delivery Phase

#5 – STM— Source to Target Mapping (STM) documents the mapping of fields between two systems to be integrated. A Typical STM Excel Sheet will look like this.

Target System			Source System		
Display Name	**Attribute Schema**	**Data Type**	**Display Name**	**Data Type**	**Column**
Account Name	Name	Single Line of Text	Name/Company	Free Text	ALIAS_NAME

#6- RAID—RAID log is an essential project management document to keep track of risks, actions, issues, and decisions. A Typical RAID log Excel Sheet will have below columns. You may also dedicate separate tabs for Risks, Actions, Issues, and Decisions separately.

- Serial No.
- RAID Type (RISK/Action/Issue/Decision)
- Date Raised
- Area
- Priority
- Description
- Cause (For Issues only)
- Probability (For RISK only)
- Impact (For RISK/Decisions)
- Mitigation Plan (For Risks/Issues)
- Responsible/Owner
- Approving Authority
- Deadline
- Current Progress
- Status (Open/Closed)
- Additional Comments

#7 – RACI— A RACI matrix is widely used responsibility assignment matrix to clearly depict who will do what (roles and responsibilities) in a project. Typically, A project Manager in consultation with his/team (Or Customer in a Vendor-Customer Scenario) will decide and assign these responsibilities to team members.

Acronyms used in RACI MATRIX are:

R: Responsible | A: Accountable | C: Consulted | I: Informed

Responsibilities	Description
R: Responsible >	Assigned person/parties can be single or multiple, as for a particular task/responsibility, more than one person/party can be responsible.
A: Accountable >	The person/Party gets the task done and is the final reviewer of the task. Only one person/party should be made Accountable. If multiple people/parties are taking accountability, then there can be conflicts.
C: Consulted >	Who all need to be consulted for a task. Consulted person/Parties give their input to the tasks
I: Informed >	Who all need to be informed for a task. Informed person/Parties should be kept in loop for certain tasks so that they are aware of the progress or what is coming their way...

The RACI Matrix For a Vendor / Service Provider* & Customer:

Project Phase	Tasks	Responsibilities	
		CUSTOMER	**SERVICE PROVIDER***
Requirements Workshops	Making sure relevant stakeholders are available	A	R
Design Activities	Technical Architecture / Design Documents	C,I,	R, A
Development Activities	Integration with an External System	C,I	R,A

The RACI Matrix For a Project Team:

Tasks/Roles	Roles in A PROJECT TEAM								
Project Tasks (Sample Tasks)	**PM**	**BA**	**Tech. Architect**	**Lead Developer**	**Software Dev 1**	**Software Dev 2**	**Integration Dev**	**Test Lead**	**Tester 1**
Produce a Project Plan	R, A	C	C, I						
Plan Requirements Workshops	C	R, A	C, I		I	I		I	
Documentation & Sign-off	R	R, A			I	I	I		
Design Documents & Sign-off	R	C, I	R, A	R	I	I	I	I	
Development Tasks	C, I	C, I	C, I	A	R	R	R		
Demos	C, I	R	R	R	R	R	R	I	
Test Planning & Test Cases Preparation	C, I	C, I	C, I	C, I	C, I	C, I	C, I	R, A	R, C
Testing Activities								A	R

#8 – Change Request Document

A Change Request (CR) is a "change in the functionality" the customer requests for an already developed or agreed upon requirement. Sometimes, customers suddenly realise their changed business scenarios and hence may request changes in the already agreed upon or developed features. This might delay or change the Project's timeline or plan.

Hence, before accepting and implementing the change, the BA will thoroughly analyse the CR and its impact on the Project in terms of timeline and cost/effort. Then, it goes through the necessary approvals before including them in the Project. Typically, during the project kick-off stage, the customer and the service provider mutually agree on how CRs will be managed. Generally, the BA will manage the CRs and recommend to the Change control committee when the change can be included in the Project, its impacts, and what it may take to have it. The BA can capture a CR by requesting the stakeholders officially communicate the change, which can then be included in the consolidated list of CRs. This "Change Request document" can be an Excel sheet with the below columns.

- Serial No.
- Change Initiated By
- Date
- Module
- Priority
- Original Requirement ID
- Original Requirement Description
- Changed Requirement ID
- Change Request Details (Description)
- Justification for the change
- Justification Provided by
- Cost/Effort Impact (Chargeable to Customer)
- Schedule Impact/Any other Impact
- Customer Approval /Sign-off
- Comments

What did You Learn in this Chapter?

- What is a Project Charter?
- What is a Change Request Document
- What is RACI? What is a RAID Log?
- What is STM? What is RTM?

CHAPTER 11

SCOPE MANAGEMENT

- *What Is a Scope?*
- *How Does a BA Arrive at Scope?*
- *What Is a Scope Creep?*

During my early days, one of my mentors said, "Managing the scope of a project commences right from the project's initiation. Please note, a project that seems simple initially can become a nightmare later, if the Scope is not properly managed!"

Let me describe a situation that happened.

"Why always customers ask for change or alter the Scope? Why do they want to squeeze us? This customer is ridiculous." A BA colleague of mine was cribbing about a customer.

I did not instantly nod my head with her concerns. Though her concerns are valid, as this customer had a history of frequently changing requirements, I wanted to understand the situation more.

Earlier, a set of requirements were discussed, agreed and signed off too. However, the customer has come up with changes to the initially captured requirements, which is now affecting other related functionalities, and it is impossible to accommodate everything within this Sprint/release. However, the customer is adamant that it will help users if released ASAP.

"Why wasn't this 'change' recognised sooner?" I inquired of my colleague.
"This was the requirement that the customer had written in the JIRA, which was very clear. We even discussed this, and since we didn't find any issues in terms of delivery, we finalised it," she said.

"Did you discuss all possible scenarios for this requirement?" I asked. "If a requirement has an action for another action, did we ask, what if one of the actions does not happen or if the action (or process) is different for different products., etc?"

"No."

"We did not ask right questions before we concluded the requirement, then," I said.

A BA should be able to see the requirements from a thousand feet above and at a granular level. We often focus on a granular level and forget to see the big picture. A BA should use the analysis tools/visualisation tools to analyse things clearly from all angles. Stakeholders sometimes cannot see through the situations; they also may not know what is better for them, and hence, one fine day, they will realise and come back to you with changes.

Now, whose fault, is it?

Can we even call such requests by Customers as "Change Requests"? Or "Scope Creep"? What is the way forward? What's important? Sprint Goal or the product goal? Schedule or the customer value?

Before we get into that question, let's get into the basics first. So, what is Scope?

Simply put, scoping arrives at the boundaries of a timebound project/ program/iteration. The Scope of a Project is an understanding that all the required stakeholders have about what will be delivered as part of the Project that defines the success of the Project. It is a set of product features, functionalities or tasks that must be finished to complete a Project.

The Scope is always finite and is measured against time. Hence, naturally, the schedule will be impacted when there is a change in the Scope via scope creep. The schedule impact will have a cost impact, too.

Change Request and Scope Creep are the same?

A Change Request is a "change in the functionality" the customer requests for an already developed or agreed requirement. In this scenario, the customer follows the agreed process to raise a Change Request; hence, additional timeline and cost will be allocated to implement the Change Request. Whereas "Scope Creep" is when a customer expects to include a different or additional functionality or item as part of a previously agreed schedule or cost. Also, in this scenario, the customer is bypassing the agreed process to include changes to the requirements.

Imagine this. Your Project has been progressing remarkably well, and as a BA, you feel content and satisfied. However, an unexpected challenge arises when someone from your management urges you to include a few additional features to impress the customer. Despite some resistance from your team, you agree to the changes without much deliberation.

Initially, it seems like a small set of alterations, but as time passes, you realise these seemingly minor adjustments have led to a cascade of changes. The situation becomes problematic, and you find yourself in a tough spot.

But fear not; the person who can pull you out of this predicament is yourself. Note that maintaining control over a project is crucial, as it can quickly spiral out of hand. This phenomenon is called "scope creep," which can be incredibly difficult to fix.

Scope creep occurs when a project's Scope expands unexpectedly or continuously without any corresponding plan for its delivery. While not always detrimental if managed appropriately, it can lead to inefficiencies, budget overruns, incomplete projects, and dissatisfied clients.

Have you heard about the project management "triangle"?—They are "scope", "time", and "cost". Something else will change if a change is posed to any of these elements. As a BA, you will collaborate with the Project Manager to keep the triangle in balance.

Scope Creep: What? Why? How to Prevent?

As the BA, your primary responsibility is clearly defining a requirement's "who, what, when, and how" by setting clear boundaries. It's essential to establish what is included and what is not. This will prevent others from encroaching on your scope territory and disrupting your peace of mind. So, scope creep often happens when stakeholders introduce additional requirements without proper authorisation as the Project progresses. Some common reasons include:

- **Unclear Scope:** When a project lacks a precise definition, stakeholders may assume details, resulting in mismanagement of Scope.
- **Conflicts Among Stakeholders:** When multiple decision-makers with different perspectives and priorities collaborate, scope creep can occur due to a lack of project direction.
- **Long-Running Projects:** Projects with loosely planned or extended timelines allow clients to introduce changes, leading to scope creep.
- **Weak Leadership:** A lack of strong, well-informed guidance or project management can make a project vulnerable to scope creep. The ability to be 'firm' in terms of Scope is essential.

- **Insufficient Client Involvement:** Failure to communicate clearly with clients early on can lead to misunderstandings and scope creep.

To prevent scope creep, consider implementing the following strategies:

- **Clearly Define Scope Boundaries:** Have a foolproof plan to deliver the defined and agreed Scope, including risk assessment and mitigation plans. Be firm with your plan. Hence, as a BA, locking the Scope by properly putting boundaries in terms of stating proper assumptions and drafting clear requirements that will be delivered.
- **Keep Communication ON:** Ensure that everyone involved in the Project understands the Scope and remains on the same page. Regularly communicate with your team to monitor progress and address potential scope creep early.
- **Own the Scope:** The BA should give confidence to his/her leadership (Project Manager) by owning the Scope and requirements.

Is The BA A Common Reason for A Scope Creep to Occur?

Yes. First and foremost, the reason is the BA. Yes, the majority of the time, incomplete and inefficient analysis will lead to half-baked requirements resulting in improperly defined or ambiguously defined Scope.

When the Scope is unclear, scope creep is bound to happen. In such situations, there is no one to save the BA! So, what are the other reasons?

1. When the originally stated requirements were not thoroughly analysed and understood
2. Ambiguously defined Scope
3. The BA failed to capture some implicit requirements
4. Lack of clear documentation
5. When Changes to the project needs, timeline, and budget happen
6. Lack of stakeholder communication and commitment

Scope creep can be the deadliest enemy of a project's success because it can lead to increased cost, delays, decreased quality, and decreased customer satisfaction.

How the BA can Prevent Scope Creep Then?

Clearly Define Project Scope: It is beneficial to understand a project's broader business needs, goals, and objectives to understand the project scope and the requirements it includes. For example, if the original requirement was to view, download, and print the invoice from a portal, but later, if the customer requests for the invoices to be emailed, then clearly, this is a scope creep.

Clear Documentation: In previous chapters, we have discussed the importance of documentation and how it should be done. Though capturing an explicit requirement is relatively more straightforward, implicit requirements create challenges for BAs. Most future problems can be avoided if the BA uses various documentation techniques such as Use case modelling, Wireframe, etc.

Have a Change Request Process: As a BA, you must inform the customer about change procedures and agree on a predefined process for managing changes. This process is typically established during the project kick-off stage, where both parties agree on handling modifications. The BA needs to take the lead in educating the customer about change procedures and establishing a clear process for managing them to ensure the success of the Project.

Have the Traceability of Requirements: Effective requirements traceability, or the ability to trace the requirement to its source and trace the requirement through the development process, can help identify valuable features and functionalities that can be traced back to a business benefit. This helps in eliminating unnecessary features and identifying any dependencies. It is essential for ensuring a project's success and that resources are being used effectively.

So, when customers request a Change or introduce scope creep, what steps should be taken? What is the best course of action? What takes precedence: the Sprint Goal or the product goal? Is it the schedule or the customer value that's more crucial?

As a general rule, it is essential to be cautious when considering changes to the Scope of a project and to thoroughly assess the potential impact and cost-benefit before making any decisions. This will help you determine whether a change is worth pursuing based on its impact on time and budget and the potential benefits to the client.

While it is generally best to avoid changes that could impact time and budget, it is possible to accept a change that does not impact these factors if it brings significant value to the client.

Scope or Change Requests, when not managed well, will significantly impact the Project's schedule and hurt the team's morale. The team members become frustrated and lose motivation, resulting in decreased willingness to contribute to the Project's success.

Reality!

➲ As far as my experience is considered, whatever scope creep management you do, ultimately if customer wants it and vendor wants the business – vendor has to budge! The Scope creep wars are very common in projects and there is NO end or perfect solution for the problem.

How Does a BA Arrive at The Scope?

Various methods can assist a team in reaching a consensus on the scope of a solution. These techniques enable the BA to formulate specific questions for stakeholders, helping them consider the real business needs and the most suitable solution.

Each technique involves creating a simple visual representation of the solution scope that can be used throughout the project to prevent scope creep. In the beginning, investing more time to clearly establish the solution scope makes project planning much easier and more accurate and helps reduce scope creep and delays during project execution.

Though the PM owns the scope, from a requirements perspective, the BA plays a major in this area by working with key project team stakeholders in collaboration with the Project Manager. The initial scope of a project is usually outlined in a business case or project statement by the Project Manager and other stakeholders. Still, this initial definition may not be detailed enough.

That's where the BA's initial analysis helps clarify the scope and may identify scope issues that the Project Manager, Customer, or Project Sponsor must address. It is essential to have a defined process for managing changes to the project scope, as unapproved "scope creep" can have negative consequences for the project.

Hence, especially regarding "Scope", the BA and project Manager should work together to ensure that the scope is realistic and aligns with the underlying business goals and objectives and that all stakeholders know what is within the scope of the analysis and what is not. The BA has a responsibility to help keep the business representatives and project team focused on the project's scope. Always, the Project Manager focuses on broader aspects of scope, and the BA focuses on finer aspects of requirements scope.

Here are the essential methods that can help a BA to arrive at an initial Scope:

1. Context diagrams
2. Use Case models
3. The Project Charter
4. Product Backlogs

Before beginning a detailed business analysis, the BA needs to ensure that the above models/documents, which stakeholders have approved and accepted, are in place. If these models/documents do not exist or have not been approved, the BA should prioritize creating or obtaining approval for them. This will help to ensure that the analysis is based on a solid foundation and that stakeholders are fully engaged and invested in the process.

Context Diagrams: A context diagram is a simple, high-level representation of a system that illustrates its boundary, users (human and other systems), and the high-level data that the system provides and receives. Here is an example context diagram/functional diagram of an e-commerce portal showcasing the in-scope functionalities at a high level.

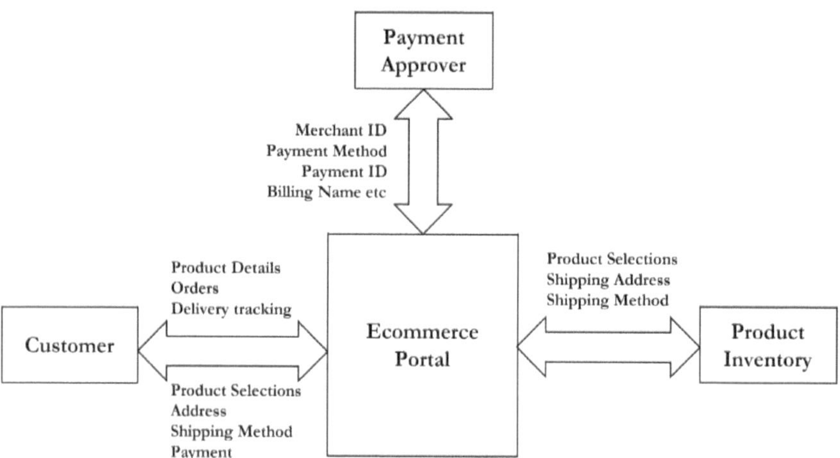

A context diagram effectively conveys part of the project scope to stakeholders when accompanied by detailed data definitions. While a context diagram only provides a broad overview, it is helpful for clearly demonstrating the system's relationships and components.

Use Case Models: We discussed the Use Case Model in the previous chapter. Use case diagrams illustrate the major units of functionality that the system will offer and the human and system users ("actors") who will benefit from or participate in these services. Here is an example of a Use case model of a Lead management system that will help a BA to arrive at a scope.

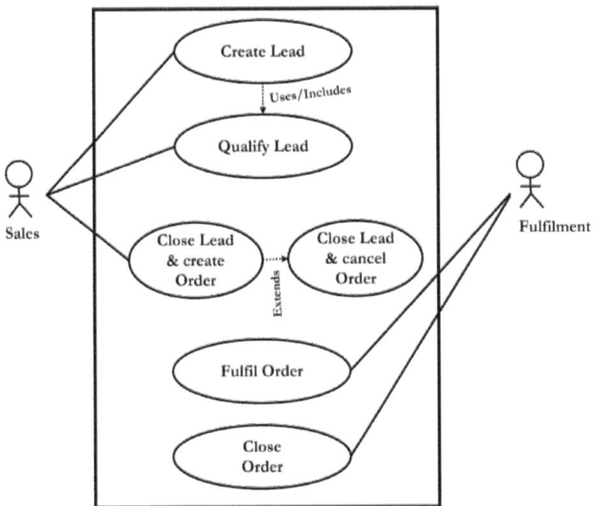

Using case models and diagrams provides a clear and structured approach to understanding the functional requirements of a system and how it will be used.

The Project Charter: We have learned about the Project Charter in the previous chapter. Normally, the customer-side BA or project sponsor creates this document.

However, in some cases, the BA also gets involved in creating this document. When a BA is involved, it's easier for him/her to start the scoping process then and there. If the BA is supplied with this document, he/she can refer to it as a base document, but the details in the document may not be enough for him/her to define the Scope. Hence, the BA must resort to some other technique or work with stakeholders to prepare a detailed scope document.

The Product Backlog: The product backlog is a collection of stakeholder requests used to scope the product and create a release plan. Each request is analysed briefly, and rough estimates are made at a high level. The team prioritises the requests based on value, impact, and dependencies and uses the product backlog to understand the Scope of the product and plan its development. Product backlog is one of the efficient ways a BA can define the Scope of a project/ iteration/sprint, etc.

Though the BAs can use the above tools to arrive at/conclude about the Scope, identifying stakeholders, making them aware of it, and obtaining their approval for project scope and requirements is a crucial step. However, sometimes, these techniques may be perceived as too high-level. A BA alone cannot define the Scope of a project. It's a shared responsibility of a project team's key members/ stakeholders. More importantly, when the Scope is defined and agreed upon, commitment from all the stakeholders is a must.

Change Requests and Scope Creeps: Good or Bad?

In essence, Change requests are Scope changes. When customers follow the process and raise Change requests, it is good. It can be an additional revenue for the vendor!

However, frequent Change requests are not good for the project's health, and eventually, the team members become frustrated and lose motivation, and this is just one side of the story.

Here is another way to look at it.

As part of project delivery, instead of just delivering a deliverable, if we consider it a value we are delivering, then yes, Change Requests or Scope Creep is a good thing because the customer wants it. Scope adjustments-removing some and adding some, keep happening in projects.

Do remember, always, that the Change Requests or Scope Creep are not negative words.

In Agile, requirements elicitation happens based on "how one can deliver value". Agile is all about delivering real value rather than Scope. In a nutshell, scope management and value management should go hand in hand.

A BA should collaborate with the customer or Product Owner to adjust deliverables for maximum value rather than assigning blame. The team must discuss the requirements again, re-prioritise, and, if possible, have some trade-offs to compensate for additional/lost hours so that the schedule remains intact as much as possible.

Mistakes will happen. Escalations happen. Despite that, a BA should have a goal and mindset to deliver a product or a service that should be usable and improve users' productivity—achieving the intended product vision and delivering value to customers.

One thing is for sure. Whatever you do, change is inevitable. Scope Creep and change Requests will come. They are part of a project. Hence, we need to account for it and plan for it! However, if they plan well and implement a process to manage the change, the impact on the project's health will be low.

Undoubtedly, the BA will be majorly accountable for Scope creep or Change Requests. Because of the way or approach BA adopts for requirements elicitation and management, leveraging various visual and modelling techniques will significantly impact the project and the deliverable's quality.

Note, a BA with strategic engagement and collaboration with required stakeholders will have comparatively fewer CRs and Scope Creep.

Learn to Say a firm "NO"!

Here is another side to the story—when customers/stakeholders enforce the scope creep.

"Why can't this functionality be delivered in this Sprint/ Release? It's just a minor change."

A BA faces this question very often from stakeholders. Sometimes, when a BA needs to act as a Product owner, the pressure on BA is huge. For a stakeholder, the changes he/she proposes would be minor. As a BA/Product owner, you also get carried away with his/her logic, and now, you start pushing your team to include the change within the current Sprint. A quick analysis of the dev team about the change revealed that it could impact previously developed features, and it is not advisable to include the new change/ functionality in the current Sprint.

This is one of the most common mistakes that BAs/Product Owners make. While Sprints are meant to be protected time boxes, the external pressure of changes can tempt you to disrupt ongoing work. However, as a BA/Product owner, it's also crucial for you to differentiate between essential changes and minor requests. You should be able to understand the impact a change introduced in-between the Sprint can bring, the usefulness & criticality of that change and so on. Yes, the new functionality or the idea may be great, but can it wait until the next Sprint? Most of the time, even though it is not that critical, stakeholders push you, and in turn, you push the team, which is not the right way.

To make your customer/stakeholder happy, you are now trying to jeopardise the Sprint, which is already ongoing. Do you think this is the right approach?

In such situations, as a BA/Product owner, you should learn to say a firm "NO," when you do so, you should have data to support your argument. Of course, accept the idea/change and document it in a backlog tool to prevent unnecessary interruptions during the Sprint.

Saying yes to every request spreads the team thin and hampers progress, as each yes is a no to something else. Prioritise decisively, explaining your choices for transparency. Balancing short-term urgencies and long-term goals is vital. Set clear product goals for focused direction and measurable progress. It's not always easy, but it's necessary to stick to your decisions and remember that you can't make everyone happy.

What Did You Learn in This Chapter?

- What is the difference between Scope & Change Request?
- Change Requests & Scope Creeps: Good or Bad? Explain.
- Explain common reasons for Scope creep
- What that key methods that can help a BA to arrive at an initial Scope?
- Is the BA a common reason for a Scope Creep to Occur? Explain.
- How to Prevent Scope Creep?

CHAPTER 12

ABCD OF STAKEHOLDER MANAGEMENT

- *Who Are Stakeholders?*
- *Understanding Stakeholders*
- *Managing Stakeholder Expectations*

There are various groups and individuals who hold a significant interest in the outcome of a particular project. These stakeholders include Customer Business teams, Customer IT team, Company executives, Sponsors, End users and Team Members.

Comprehending and actively involving the "right" stakeholders is vital to enhance the prospects of project success. These stakeholders might either strongly endorse or not support your projects. Therefore, it's imperative to pinpoint your genuine supporters among the stakeholders and swiftly garner their support.

Involving "right" stakeholders early in the project process is essential for its success. Ensuring that stakeholders are involved appropriately fosters a sense of ownership, accountability, and transparency. This is especially important because people naturally want to be understood and feel their input is valued. Hence, it is essential to set expectations, roles, and objectives in the beginning so everyone knows their responsibilities and role in the project. Creating a collaborative community that can build trust and ensure that everyone is working towards the common goal.

Hence, proper communication with the relevant stakeholders appropriately and managing these relationships is crucial in meeting the needs of all parties and achieving a successful outcome. That is where stakeholder analysis comes in handy. The BA plays a critical role in such analysis and stakeholder management.

Types of Stakeholders: Mainly, stakeholders can be internal or external. Internal stakeholders may include Project sponsors, End users, Members of Business Units Impacted, Project team members and more. External stakeholders can be External customers, Governments, Vendors, Subcontractors, Suppliers and more—as shown in the below illustration.

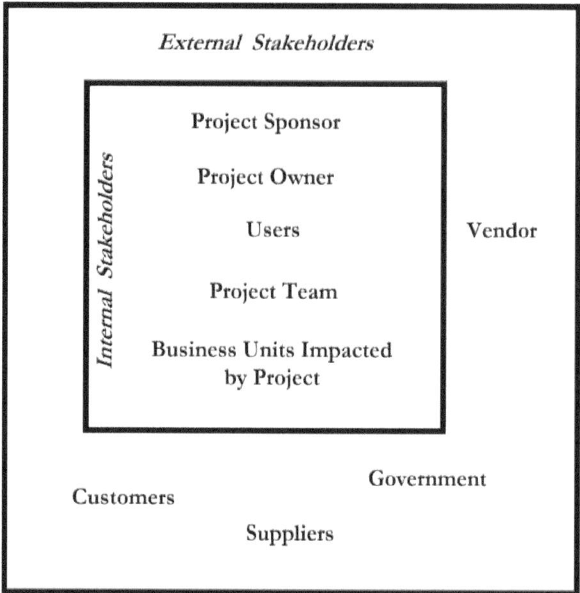

How to Identify and Categorise Stakeholders?

To identify and categorise stakeholders for a project, it's important to consider who will be affected by the project and who has the power to influence its outcome. Once you've identified your key stakeholders, you must continue analysing and understanding their characteristics to create a successful approach to working with them.

Engaging and collaborating with stakeholders throughout the project is critical for its success, as it allows you to get valuable input and feedback, build support for the project, and address any concerns or issues that may arise. By taking the time to understand the needs and priorities of your stakeholders, you can create a more effective strategy for working with them to achieve the maximum benefit for your project.

Hence, as a BA, you need to know how to deal with stakeholder attitudes, decision-makers, and stakeholders with power or influence. As you grow with experience, you should master and understand the art of collaborating and communicating with stakeholders based on their power, Influence/Interest and characteristics to keep them engaged throughout the project lifecycle.

That is why the stakeholder analysis is crucial and essential. This is not rocket science. When you follow a certain technique to identify the type of stakeholders, and once you identified the type of stakeholders based on their Influence/Interest, power and "characteristics", you can plan your tactic for effective collaboration, engagement and communication strategies.

Identification of Stakeholders: Now, let's see how to identify the stakeholders. The ability to accurately identify stakeholders is similar to identifying the cast for a fascinating movie. The BAs can begin the process by scrutinising the project landscape for all parties—individuals or groups—that either influence the project or are impacted by it. A stakeholder is an entity with a significant interest or influence over the project's initiatives or results.

The process of stakeholder identification typically can involve:

- Identification of Project Sponsor and then identify other stakeholders through him/her
- Analyse Org charts to identify various roles impacted by the project

The primary cornerstone for stakeholder identification is the project sponsor, who will clearly know the project's vision and purpose. This individual ideally possesses control of the Project budget, comprehensive project understanding, and the influence to efficiently organise the project team. Since the project sponsor knows the project vision and a high-level understanding, BAs can leverage the Project Sponsor and his team to identify the other stakeholders.

Although the initial information about the project provided by the sponsor might lack 100% clarity, this marks the exact starting point of the journey. The BA should leverage an organisational chart to transition from this conceptual stage to a comprehensive stakeholder list. By documenting the organisational chart and the hierarchy, the BA can map the real stakeholders who can contribute to the project in consultation with the project sponsor. This activity would typically be a kind of mini workshop with a project sponsor.

Engaging in discussions with the project sponsor and possibly other potential stakeholders within the customer organisation can be enlightening as the BA can gain clarity on the first level of stakeholders. These departments are then examined to identify potential interviewees who can explain their needs concerning the project. As a next step, list and categorise them appropriately based on their influence, power, Authority and interest towards the project.

Categorisation of Stakeholders: In this process, you can easily categorise the stakeholders based on their level of involvement by analysing their power and Influence/Interest towards the project.

As a first step, list down your stakeholders. As a BA, you are closely working with customers. Hence, you should gather info on who could be your stakeholders by understanding a set of people affected by your work, who have influence or power over it, or who are interested in successful/unsuccessful project completion.

As a second step, understand these stakeholders by talking to them directly or anyone from the customer side/your Account team to understand their power, Authority or interest in the project. See the figure below.

Lastly, categorise them in an appropriate bucket. Here is the approach gives an idea for you to allocate your stakeholders to a relevant bucket based on their Power/Authority and Interest/Influence:

- **Stakeholders with High Power, High Interest (Manage Closely):** Engage them Fully. You need to do whatever it takes to keep them satisfied. (Ex: Project Sponsor). Normally, they are the Approvers of major decisions and responsible for major sign-offs.

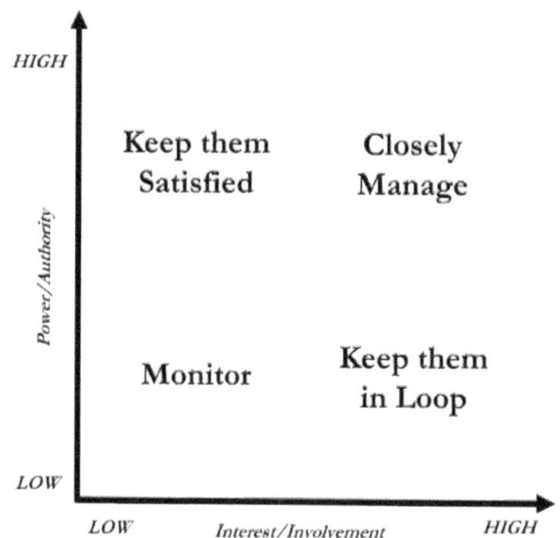

- **Stakeholder High power, Low Interest (Keep Satisfied):** They are key people. They come occasionally to your meetings. Keep them Satisfied. No need to give a lot of info to them. They want to know whether the project is going well or not. (Ex: Project Approver, that is, the Boss of your Project Sponsor)

- **Stakeholders with Low power, high Interest (Keep Informed):** Keep them informed in every aspect. These people are influential and may have a good rapport with top management. These people can be very helpful and maintain a great rapport with them. (Ex: Team member from an IT department)

- **Stakeholder with Low power, Low Interest (Monitor):** Keep them in cc. But they don't need to know each & every detail of your project. (Ex: Person /team who has a very low impact due to the project)

An easy way to summarize the level of support you may receive from your stakeholders is to have them segmented in a Word document or an Excel sheet. Colour code them if required. The below example diagram makes the concept even clearer:

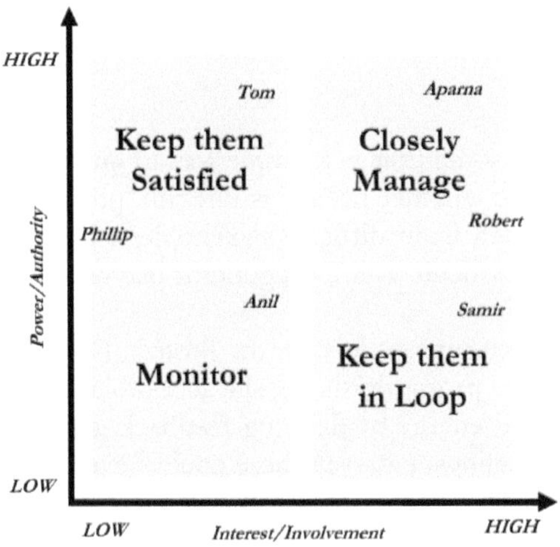

Another way to categorize stakeholders (and their responsibilities) is a RACI matrix. We have already discussed about the RACI Matrix in one of our earlier chapters.

Understanding Stakeholders

Understanding the "characteristics" of stakeholders becomes essential because it will help you know how stakeholders will likely respond to your communication/interactions and how you can get their support.

This seems easy but requires a bit of psychological analysis. A BA sometimes needs to be a good psychologist as well. As part of their work, they need to maintain a good relationship with stakeholders, and for this to happen, a BA needs to 'understand' a stakeholder.

I know, it's not a marriage or girlfriend-boyfriend relationship! Unfortunately, it's a love-hate relationship. However, if the rapport is great, it will be beneficial for the BA as well as for the health of the Project. It's plain & simple—if you share a great rapport with project stakeholders, collaborating and working with them will make mitigating risks easier, avoiding delays, and more.

Hence, how can you 'understand' a stakeholder?

Is it all about understanding their personality, behaviour, etc.? One of my colleagues said: "I cannot understand my girlfriend at all, despite being in a relationship for years. Now I need to understand my customer as well?"

I said: "Well, yes, you have to do it, to be in a better situation in the project at least!"

Observing them for some time is a simple way to understand a stakeholder. Look for hints about whether he/she is difficult/problematic. You are not going to benefit much from difficult stakeholders, but you need to see in what way he/she is difficult. Is it for a good or bad reason?

First off, observe their interest level in the Project. Does he/she respond to your communications promptly? Is he/she accessible? Also, if he/she is not showing the required energy by delaying feedback, ignoring emails, not attending required meetings, etc.—all these could be a warning sign, and you and your team/management should be made aware of this.

During meetings, do they (stakeholders) give constructive feedback? Or only negative feedback without appreciating the positive aspects? This could also hint that the stakeholder is a bit difficult, and such stakeholders should be managed carefully. It becomes problematic when stakeholders are rude and uncooperative for no reason—taking management help is one of the options in such situations.

Some stakeholders carry their style, where they become authoritative, sometimes dictators. You need to closely observe why they are like that. If it is because of their passion for the Project's success, you will significantly benefit from them. You may have to tolerate their tantrums (e.g., today, they will look happy and satisfied, but the next day, they will be unhappy for some reason), but they will go extreme to help you. However, if it is to squeeze more out of you, then you must be cautious—set the expectations clearly.

Ultimately, whether it is easy or difficult, stakeholders are part and parcel of our professional life. We can't dismiss them outright, but we should find a way to work with them. There could be some tiffs in between, but we professionals should avoid it and always try to defuse the situation.

Analysing Characteristics of Stakeholders

As described earlier, understanding the characteristics of stakeholders is of utmost importance. Once you understand the same, you can accordingly customise your communication strategy in terms of what information can be shared with them and what not, based on the characteristics of stakeholders to engage them effectively during the project lifecycle.

You can begin the analysis by talking to them directly or anyone from the customer side/your Account team to understand their characteristics, in addition to Power, Authority or interest.

Leveraging Positive Stakeholders: When evaluating stakeholders, assessing their attitudes towards the Project or initiative is essential. Supportive and positive stakeholders can be more easily engaged in discussions and collaboration.

As you work with these stakeholders, be sure to show appreciation for their contributions and respect their time by scheduling brief meetings and communicating with them in a way that is convenient for them. It is also important to remind stakeholders of their positive impact on the Project and organisation.

Dealing with the Negative Attitude of Stakeholders: To address a stakeholder with a negative attitude and to engage with them effectively (that, unfortunately, as a BA, you have to do), it's essential to have a plan in place. Start by openly and honestly communicating the importance of the initiative and the value it brings to the organisation. Ask the stakeholders if they have questions or concerns, and be willing to negotiate and find common ground.

If the stakeholder hesitates to engage due to other priorities or perceiving that you will be taking up too much of their time, try asking what works best for them and be flexible in finding a mutually convenient time to meet.

If these efforts fail to result in buy-in, you may need to involve your project manager or sponsor to help resolve the issue and find a way to work together effectively.

Arriving at a Communication Strategy: You can remember the questions/pointers during your analysis to arrive at a proper communication strategy for various stakeholders based on their characteristics.

- **Financial or Emotional interest** refers to a stakeholder's stake in the Project's outcome. This can be positive (benefiting from a successful outcome) or negative (negatively impacted by a successful outcome).
- **Motivation:** Understanding what motivates a stakeholder can help you tailor your communication and approach to them.
- **Information needed:** Different stakeholders may have different information needs. Understanding what information, a stakeholder wants from you can help you provide it clearly and concisely.
- **Current opinion:** Understanding a stakeholder's current view of your Project can help you address any concerns or misconceptions they may have.
- **Influencers:** Identifying who influences a stakeholder's opinions can help a BA to understand their perspective and tailor the communication strategy accordingly. These influencers may also be essential stakeholders in their own right.
- **Winning over opposition:** If a stakeholder is not likely to be positive, it is essential to understand what will win them over to support your Project. This may involve addressing their concerns or finding common ground.
- **Managing Opposition/Resistance:** If it is impossible to win over a stakeholder, it is vital to have a plan for managing their opposition. This may involve finding ways to minimise the impact of their opposition or finding alternative solutions.
- **Influenced Stakeholders:** It is important to consider any other stakeholders whom the opinions of a particular stakeholder may influence. These stakeholders may also be essential to consider in your communication and approach.

Hence, in a nutshell, to maximise stakeholder engagement, performing a stakeholder analysis is critical based on characteristics (Attitude like positive/negative, etc.) and the Power and influence/ Interest of a stakeholder (decision-making authority, and level of power or influence, etc.).

Each stakeholder is unique, so your approach to stakeholder collaboration and communication may change based on the unique characteristics of your stakeholder. The above-discussed techniques, such as stakeholder lists/maps RACI, can significantly help BAs.

> ➲ **Pro Tip**
>
> As a BA, cultivating the practice of expressing gratitude to stakeholders for the time they invest in the project should develop into a routine. Continuously acknowledging their significance in the project's crucial success can prove advantageous for both you and the project itself.

Etiquettes To Follow While Collaborating with Stakeholders

A BA must have a well-planned approach to collaborating with stakeholders. Start by checking schedules and calendars to ensure the stakeholder is available for a meeting at a mutually convenient time and location. If possible, try to meet face-to-face (if you are in the same office, never lose the opportunity to meet people one-on-one), but if you are in different locations, make sure to use the appropriate technology, such as Teams or Zoom Meetings and have a clear agenda so that the meeting time can be effectively utilised.

Before scheduling the meeting, consider contacting the stakeholder to determine what works best for them and demonstrate your willingness to accommodate their needs. This can help build trust and make the stakeholders more open to collaborating with you on your initiative. When working with stakeholders, asking questions to understand their needs and preferences is essential to collaborate effectively.

Here is an important aspect. I have seen many young professionals do this—which is seen as unprofessional. Unless you have such a rapport, avoid pinging, frequently chatting with stakeholders is not advisable. I would advise avoiding initiating a conversation without a purpose, plan, and agenda.

Well, that's one aspect of it. If we maintain professionalism at all times, how can we build rapport? Let's envision a scenario: you encounter one of your crucial stakeholders in an elevator or the office cafeteria, and you have an ideal opportunity to have a meaningful conversation with them for a few

minutes. Should you ignore them? Should you exchange pleasantries and continue on your way?
I agree that approaching stakeholders outside of scheduled meetings might make some BAs uneasy. They fear it may disrupt the established process or the stakeholders won't be receptive. But I assure you, there's nothing wrong with seizing such opportunities. These spontaneous interactions are a goldmine for insights and can significantly boost productivity.

The crux here lies in being discreet and respectful of the situation. Ensure that both parties are willing participants. Politely inquire, "Would you mind if I ask a question about such and such topic?" If they are open to it, proceed with the discussion. You are still professionally handling the situation – only your environment/settings are different here.

Nevertheless, it is imperative to uphold transparency and professionalism. Post your conversation, make notes, send a follow-up via email, chat via Teams, or comment on a user story. This not only aids in accurately documenting the information but also acknowledges the stakeholder's input and extends an opportunity for them to confirm your comprehension.

This transparent approach cultivates trust and guarantees that stakeholders won't hesitate to engage in future informal interactions. Additionally, it saves time – no need to arrange more meetings or dispatch extensive emails seeking clarifications.

Naturally, it's crucial to discern when and where to initiate these impromptu conversations. Refrain from approaching someone rushing to a meeting or attempting to catch a bus. Assess their readiness and willingness to engage.

Mastering the art of managing spontaneous interactions is integral to a BA's growth journey. It involves developing a sharp sense of when to seize the moment and when to await a more suitable setting. So, the next time you converse with a stakeholder near the coffee machine or in the lift, remember that these inconsequential encounters can unearth valuable insights.

Keep in mind, welcome the spontaneity, and you'll be amazed at the treasure trove of insights that can spring from the most unexpected corners. However, exercise caution – don't let this become habitual, as it can open the door to excessive intrusion into each other's domains and potentially affect your work dynamics.

Dealing with Peculiar Stakeholders

In this world, everyone is unique and peculiar in a way. On a Project, you see some weird people or stakeholders. Just because they are the clients (Project owners), they have a feeling in their heads that they are the kings or kingmakers. Indeed, it becomes challenging to work with such people. The pain is that, as a BA, you need them for various reasons, but they are pretty tricky to work with.

To manage such stakeholders effectively, as a BA, it's essential for you to be customer-focused and flexible and to use your leadership and influencing skills to understand their motivations and find ways to address their needs and concerns. This may involve identifying and including their pain points in the project requirements to show how the initiative will benefit them and make their lives easier. On the other hand, you may have to learn to ignore their behaviours. Do not take it personally. You keep them where you want to keep them. Whenever you need any information, collaborate with them and seek it. Do that professionally. Note that their peculiar behaviour is none of your business. They are behaving that way for some reason. Understand that and empathise with them.

Sometimes, while working with such peculiar stakeholders, you may lose patience, and some situations may prompt you to conflict with uncooperative or "peculiar" stakeholders. In such times, be selfish. Do not get into conflict with such stakeholders and waste your energy. Instead, as a BA, you should see your benefit first (for your work on the project).

It's essential to prioritise the project's success and avoid getting caught up in ego issues or stakeholder conflicts. Any escalated conflicts must be reported to the project board/management and your Project Manager.

However, it's also vital to be proactive in managing the stakeholder relationship and avoid escalating issues to their bosses or giving in to their demands, as this can lead to a loss of trust and even more resistance to the project.

Instead, try to work with the stakeholders to find common ground and make them change agents and project champions. Over time, you will learn to recognise potential critics, address their concerns, and change their mentality before they become antagonistic and influence other stakeholders.

Dealing with Escalations

Your project manager, who rarely calls you at odd hours, called you early in the morning and asked you to check an email. He/she also requests that you schedule a call as soon as possible to discuss the matter. You would fully awaken now and begin checking the said email and going through the email chain—at the bottom, you'll see an email sent to your top management from a top guy on the customer side (perhaps the project sponsor or his/her boss).

Escalation!

Fear, panic, anxiety, and whatnot—you are now engulfed with various such feelings. You immediately call your project manager and start explaining your innocence. And the real drama begins. Typically, an escalation is a situation where the intended parties cannot resolve/complete a task/issue; hence, the customer wants to bring it to the parties' attention at the next level.

It means that the customer thinks the situation is more severe, so urgent attention is required.

Fine. But is it essential to worry about that? Why does an escalation make most of us anxious?

The issue could be minor or not be an issue from your perspective. It could be a mistake on your end. Whatever it is, first and foremost, the reaction within you is triggered primarily because tens will ask you tons of questions from people from your organisation. Sometimes, you will get organisational support, sometimes not.

As a BA, please note there is no point in getting tensed or worried whenever there is an escalation. If you are worried, things will only get worse. Take a break and talk to your team about the mitigation plan.

Be positive, and more importantly, remain calm and don't take it personally. It's not against you. It would be best if you did not react but responded to it with an action plan.

Communication is key when dealing with escalations. Talk to your customers on call. If it is your mistake, acknowledge it. Everyone makes mistakes. It is not the world's end if an escalation happens in your project.

If it's not your mistake, then that could result from miscommunication. Clarify your stand. Be courageous. You don't need to be submissive. This will build trust.

There Are A Few Things to Remember as A BA Regarding Escalation:

- No matter how skilled and experienced you are, it is inevitable that you will encounter an escalation from a stakeholder in your work at some point. This is inevitable. So, have a process in place. Many times, customers/stakeholders are unaware of a few things, such as new processes. And out of panic, they escalate. Hence, establishing a process and making your customers aware of it are essential.

- If you respond to a situation with an action plan, rarely do escalations become an issue. Sometimes, customers think that escalations are a way to control the project team and keep them in fear so that they can deliver. Sometimes, such tactics do work. But in such situations, you should always be calm and respond with an action plan. If you have such customers, you will keep getting escalations more often! So, keep worrying every time about escalations isn't an option at all.

- Effective communication is crucial when dealing with escalations and addressing customer concerns. Communicate the status in every step during the resolution stage and keep every required stakeholder informed. When you handle the situation correctly, it will create an opportunity for your customers to trust you.

Can All the Needs of a Stakeholder Be Met?

Can a Project fulfil all the needs of stakeholders? Can BAs work in such a way that fulfils all the needs of all the stakeholders? Can we make everyone happy? Can all the needs of a stakeholder be met? Can we even think of that?

An interesting Whitepaper published on the IIBA website has some fascinating insights. The whitepaper makes very valid points about understanding and delivering the needs of stakeholders or customers.

As a BA, it is essential to understand the real customer expectations and, most importantly, what they expect from this project. Is it an improved business process? Or is it an enhanced efficiency?

Once you figure this out, as a BA, you should filter out the real needs and deliver those real needs. Business Analysis is heavily dependent on understanding and identifying the needs of stakeholders. Identifying these needs can lead to the pursuit of specific goals or the attainment of certain benefits.

Therefore, as BA, it holds significance to convey to stakeholders that not every requirement might be fulfilled. Crucial necessities like stakeholder needs, and at times, even fundamental ones like the need for air, water, sustenance, shelter, affection, and similar essentials, might remain unmet. This assertion from the whitepaper carries substantial weight. This is because constraints such as budget, time, or technical limitations may prevent all needs from being met.

It's crucial to remember that a need is not a tangible thing but rather an experience unique to each individual. Hence, it's definitely BA's job to make his/her stakeholders/customers understand the same.

What Did You Learn in This Chapter?

- How do you handle Escalations?
- How to deal with Peculiar Stakeholders?
- Explain a few etiquettes to follow while collaborating with stakeholders.
- How to Analysing Characteristics of Stakeholders?
- How to Identify & Categorize Stakeholders?
- Describe some challenges you faced while managing your stakeholders.

CHAPTER 13

CHALLENGES OF A BA

- *Key Challenges of Business Analysts*
- *Perceptions And Expectations*
- *Documenting The Undocumented*

Being a BA is a very demanding role. We all know that by now. Being a BA is a leadership role where you need to lead things. You need to take ownership, and you need to own the results – good or bad. The BAs encounter difficulties and challenges when collecting requirements, and often, these challenges persist into the testing phase, especially when user interaction is at its highest. Furthermore, throughout the entire project lifecycle, they grapple with numerous challenges.

Indeed, BAs are natural problem-solvers, and for them, solving problems is instinctive.

Numerous project-specific problems or self-induced issues can impact BAs in delivering their responsibilities. These include unclear requirements, non-cooperative stakeholders, scope creep, lack of user involvement, conflicting requirements, high expectations despite technical limitations, resistance to change, incomplete or missing information from stakeholders, lack of clear or conflicting priorities, insufficient BA skills, a business knowledge gap, and many more.

The Usual Suspects – Stakeholders

Typically, stakeholders are the usual suspects with whom a BA faces most of the challenges.

In the previous chapter, we covered the topic of stakeholder management. Now, let's delve into additional scenarios that offer insights from the perspective of challenges faced by BAs. Unfortunately, dealing with non-cooperative and sometimes over-enthusiastic stakeholders is part and parcel of a BA role. As discussed in the previous chapter, managing stakeholders and their expectations is a BA's primary KPI.

Sometimes, BAs need to tackle some of your users/stakeholders who attend meetings/ workshops regularly, but their participation in the discussion is zero. They just come with their laptop; they do their regular work there and go off. Even if you ask questions, you do not get any answers from them, or you may get some incomplete answers that are not trustworthy.

There are some users who send a set of documents for every question. Even for a simple clarification, they ask you to go through the documents. They do all these tantrums sometimes intentionally and sometimes unintentionally. You feel frustrated. Right?

Relax. It is normal. In every Project, you will find such specimens! How do we tackle such users? One thing is evident here. For some reason, these stakeholders don't want to get involved in the Project, so they are unwilling to share any info. But why?

As a BA, unfortunately, you should try to find the reason for their non-cooperation. As a BA, you are responsible for finding the root cause of their non-cooperation.

There could be three possible issues.

1. The change is always painful. It is common for users to resist change, especially when unsure how the change will impact them. Some users may be concerned that the new changes will increase their workload or have to learn new skills. Others may be uncertain about how the changes will benefit them or the organisation as a whole.

2. Is there any organisational internal politics that is making them not share info? Sometimes, users also fear that they cannot continue their kind of "corrupt" activities they are doing leveraging the loopholes of the current process and system. Hence, within the organisation, a few user groups sometimes lobby against the Project, leading to internal politics, making users deliberately not share info.

3. Stakeholders/users don't know the answers.

To address the first two issues, you may work with the customer PMO to educate these users about the benefits of the Project and the vision behind the same. It is essential for the team implementing the change to communicate clearly about its reasons, how it will be implemented, and the expected outcomes. It can also be helpful to provide training and support to help people adjust to the new processes. Once they are clear and the BA can gain the users' confidence, those users may start opening up.

However, it's not easy. For a BA, this is a very tricky situation. The BA could sense a lot of internal politics and gossip/talks against and in support of the initiative (the project the BA part of). When dealing with stakeholders, a BA might see numerous types of stakeholders having a variety of symptoms as below, who usually put up the resistance:

- Will this impact my job if my work is automated with this Project?
- I don't have time for contribute to this project.
- Not related to my KPI. Why should I support it?
- No one communicated to me about the Project. Why should I bother?
- The last Project failed. Will this work? I will not support & waste time.
- I am not clear about the current process

What can a BA do when he/she encounters a stakeholder having any of the above symptoms and is unwilling to collaborate/provide info or put up the resistance?

The BA needs to probe the real reason for the resistance and discuss the same with the Project promoter/owner—of course, the escalation channel will always be open in such situations.

However, this is the time; perhaps BA should get creative. He/She should be ready to change his approach to gathering requirements. If a stakeholder is not attending or not giving the required info, just ask for any related templates/documents and keep all the necessary stakeholders in the loop. Sometimes, these documents will have most of the information that is required. The BA can use the same to draft the requirements, present them to the stakeholders, get the required validation from stakeholders, and, in the end, take sign-off from them (customer).

For the third issue, you may have to dig a little deeper. You can ask questions in various ways to understand their perspectives about the requirements. The problem here is they may be just employees who follow already set processes. They just don't bother about a project's "why" aspects. They are just not qualified enough to answer your questions. Hence, they may not be able to answer your questions. You need to raise this issue with PMO and get the relevant/proper/correct users to answer your requirements-related questions.

The challenges won't stop there. There are more. These instances described here have happened to me multiple times, and I have also provided information on how I tackled them. So, all of these are based on real-life experiences!

A Project brings change or modification with a vision of improving a business process. If a change or modification is necessary to make a process more efficient, someone must be responsible for approving the change. If there is a lack of willingness among users to take ownership of the decision, it can be challenging to move forward. Similarly, it can be difficult to make progress if the elicitation process reaches a dead end due to a lack of decision-making.

To address such ownership issues, it is necessary to establish clear roles and responsibilities for decision-making and a process for addressing and resolving any roadblocks that may arise during the elicitation process. An explicit agreement on the Approval/Sign-off process must happen during the project kick-off stage. Note, this is the responsibility of a BA.

Conflict between a BA and Users can often arise when the BA proposes a novel or modified approach to a current process. This situation can be challenging, as it may involve changes to established procedures and require users to adapt to a new way of working. To address this conflict, establishing transparent communication lines and clearly explaining the proposed changes' benefits is essential. As a BA, you must not make it an ego issue. Ultimately, users will use the system; hence, their agreement in every step is essential.

Hence, always involve users in decision-making and allow them to provide input and feedback on the proposed changes. By fostering a collaborative and inclusive approach, it is possible to resolve any conflicts and move forward with the proposed changes in an acceptable way to all parties involved.

Conflicts among users who perform similar tasks across different organisational functions are common issues that can arise during the elicitation process. Each user feels that their approach is the best, leading to disagreements and potential conflict among themselves, which sometimes offers a BA the spectacle of fireworks during the workshop, which he/she can enjoy, at least for some time!

Jokes apart, to address this issue (of course, a BA should take the lead here), it is important to be open and involve everyone in the process to encourage collaboration and compromise among users. The presence of a neutral party such as you – a BA, to facilitate the resolution of any conflicts always helps. A BA's facilitation and analytical skills come to the rescue in such situations. Like a Court Judge, a BA should be able to view all balanced perspectives and gather relevant information about the Project and Scope. The

BA should make customers feel at least they have been allowed to present their respective views. If this does not work, the escalation becomes the last resort.

Irregular attendance of users can be a challenge when conducting workshops or meetings. Sometimes, a set of users attend one session and then skip a few, only to reappear, request changes, or ask to go back to where they left off. I have experienced this, and the frustration you get at that time is uncontrollable. This inconsistency in attending workshops can make it challenging to maintain momentum and disrupt the workshop or meeting flow. For a BA, these are real testing times.

To address this issue, you should establish a clear attendance expectation at the beginning of the workshop and follow up with users who are consistently absent. If required and the situation is severe and impacting the timeline, the escalation route must be considered. However, you should regularly communicate (keep informed) about the issues you face to the customer via your Project Manager so that they are aware—at least, you have proof that you alerted them well in advance.

As a BA, you can also highlight the impact of irregular attendance on the requirements-gathering process and the need to re-validate requirements if there is no continuity of user presence in the workshop. It is beneficial if you plan to address changes/ requests from users who have been absent to keep the workshop on track and ensure that all users can contribute and stay informed.

As a BA, you may encounter situations where an **unexpected Change Request** is made. This situation can be challenging, as it may require you to adjust your plans and priorities on short notice. When faced with an unexpected Change Request, it is crucial to consider its impact and the resources available to accommodate it. It may be worth considering if the change is necessary and can be implemented within the available resources. If the change is unnecessary or would significantly impact the Project, it may be wise to convince the customer why the requested Change Request cannot be accommodated.

We have already discussed about Change Requests in the Scope Management chapter. Accommodation of a Change Request always depends on the specific circumstances and how the Change Request will add value to the Project. In such situations, a reprioritisation of requirements should happen. We have already discussed various tactics used for Requirements prioritisation in previous chapters.

Sometimes, stakeholders cannot distinguish between what they need and perceive as their needs. Always real needs are typically the most obvious and easy to identify, as they are directly related to the essential functions and operations of the business.

However, many times, from the perspective of the business user, a perceived need may feel like a real need (for him/her) because it is something that the user wants or desires. However, from the perspective of the business as a whole, a perceived need may not necessarily be essential to the operation of the business. It may not directly contribute to achieving the business's goals and objectives.

Hence, as a BA, you should question the need. Dig deeper to understand the real need. To uncover the real needs of a business, you must ask probing questions and perform a thorough needs assessment to understand the underlying issues and priorities.

Every time, a BA should ask:

- Is this needed?
- If yes, why?
- If not, why?
- Is this part of the Scope?

If the BA is clear about these aspects, differentiating between real and perceived needs is easy. Clarity about the distinction between real needs and perceived needs is critical because addressing perceived needs may not always be the best use of resources, and it's essential to prioritise real needs that directly impact the operation of the business.

Lack of Interest from Stakeholders: In some projects, for some reason, stakeholders do not show interest towards the Project as they should be. Such situations are most challenging for a BA because he has to chase stakeholders most of their productive time—asking them to join workshops, UAT sessions escalating to PMO complaining about stakeholders not joining meetings, etc.

In such situations, other than escalating to their managers or Project owners, there is no other way. As a BA, you should work with your PM to escalate this issue. You can also start involving their managers in all communications till the required stakeholders fall in line.

No clarity of Scope coming from Stakeholders: When an organisation is big and has many business units (BU), the way each BU does the business also differs. So, users from each BU will have their requirements, and sometimes, each user will push for their individual needs. What can a BA do in such a situation?

This lack of clarity of requirements and Scope could be a severe risk for the Project. Clarity of Scope is one of the biggest challenges for a BA in most projects. Unfortunately, a BA has to face challenges while trying to establish a unified approach or achieve a unified business goal. Before the objectives and Scope of a project are agreed upon and defined, a BA can't ensure its success.

The Perceptions...Expectations

Many in the industry think that a BA is meant for document writing. However, the real fact is that writing and documentation are only a small portion of the actual work done by a BA.

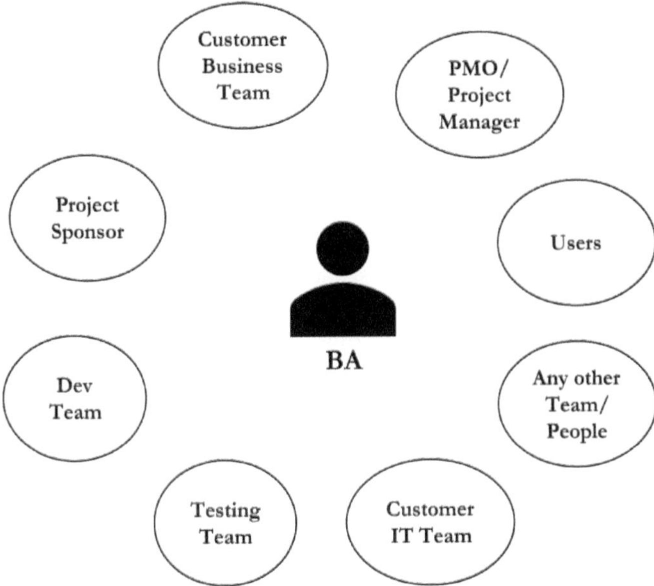

A significant amount of BA's time is spent understanding the customer's business, gathering and eliciting requirements, and building rapport with customer stakeholders. Mind it, a BA is not just a "Requirements Gatherer"!

Who is a BA, then? I repeat. A BA regularly interacts with people or teams performing diverse functions. A BA acts as a bridge between business and technical representatives from the customer side and the project team, including developers. The BA is omnipresent. He is "The Real Captain" of the project, helping the official captain, the Project Manager. The Project Manager is the official captain because he/she is responsible for making certain decisions.

Sometimes, customers do not understand the importance of Business Analysis and a BA. Many times, the customers think that BAs are not required for the entire duration of the project. Some customers have such perceptions or lack experience working on a project. They sometimes aren't aware of a BA's real responsibilities or deliverables. Due to such misunderstandings, a BA faces challenges in working with customers/ stakeholders.

When working on a project, business users may only have a high-level understanding of what they want, and it's the job of the BA to drill down into the details and fully understand the business needs and objectives. This process often involves uncovering hidden complexities and dealing with changing requirements and priorities. The BA is key in defining and refining a project's requirements and managing change requests throughout the project lifecycle.

The BA is also responsible for ensuring that the project stays aligned with the business objectives and meets the needs of the business users. This requires a deep understanding of the business needs of the project and the ability to communicate effectively with the business users and other stakeholders. The BA is a crucial member of the project team, involved throughout the project lifecycle, beyond just the requirements phase.

Hence, to avoid such misconceptions about the role of a BA, a clear responsibility matrix needs to be prepared and agreed upon with the customer. This will ensure what a BA will do in the project and clarify BA's responsibilities.

As a BA, you may find yourself in situations where the presales team who won the deal for the organisation had to accept a timeline that turned out to be very stringent or where stakeholders have unrealistic expectations of what is possible within the scope of a project. In such situations, it is essential to identify and address potential problems before they arise. This might involve evaluating the agreement's effects or the stakeholders' expectations and informing your management of any potential costs or risks due to an unrealistic timeline.

In such situations, as a BA, you should always be transparent and open with stakeholders about the limitations and constraints of the project. This might involve setting clear boundaries around what is and is not possible and being open to negotiating and compromising where appropriate. At the same time, for a BA, it's crucial to manage expectations so that it should not hamper the relationship with customers.

Documenting the Undocumented

Documenting the undocumented implementation processes as part of your project is always the trickiest job for a BA.

Though users follow the same business process across the departments, everyone will have their own version of processes because the rule/process is unwritten. Understanding and documenting the new common process acceptable to all would be the most stressful job for a BA.

Hence, to manage such situations, the BA should conduct a workshop in the beginning with users of multiple departments separately. The BA should understand the overall process followed by the users of each department. At first glance, it may appear that every user performs the work in the same way.

However, by asking the right questions at each stage of the process, you can uncover the unique process stages of each user. Now, you have a new challenge – managing the users who argue with each other in the workshop!

In each of these workshops, the BA should study the process, its variations and the wish list provided by the users. Once all the workshops are over, draft a common process that should be usable by all and compliant with the product/system you are building technically. Involve your project team.

Now, set up a common workshop for all the users from all the departments where you need to present your solution/process. Explain the new solution and its benefits to them and answer all users' questions confidently. Include feedback as required.

Yet. I bet you may not be able to get concurrence from the users, and each user will have their versions, and they will press for the same because change is irritating for everyone!

So, how do we resolve this situation?

Identify the key decision-makers from each department. Involve key system users – not all. Involve relevant project sponsors as well. Bring all these stakeholders to a common workshop, where you must present your proposed solution or process again. Highlight the differences you heard during earlier workshops and why you propose a common approach and its business benefits.

Somewhere, stakeholders must decide; they also need to own things. They also cannot keep things hanging. Also, now that all the required stakeholders are involved in setting up/designing an undocumented process, you may get the sign-off, perhaps as an outcome of this workshop or maybe later!

A BA plays an instrumental role in designing an effective solution or process and communicating the business benefits of the same to the stakeholders—thus enabling them to own things and contribute to the success of a project.

Always remember that a BA must focus on business needs and benefits rather than user preferences.

The Challenge of Skillsets and Knowledge

The learning journey for a BA is ongoing and never concludes. This principle holds for BAs and anyone aspiring to remain relevant in IT. Sustained learning remains exceptionally important.

BAs often find themselves straddling the worlds of business and technology, with the expectation that they are knowledgeable in multiple areas within both fields. This can be challenging, as focusing too heavily on one aspect may come at the expense of the other.

Continuous Learning: To navigate these challenges and attain sufficient competency in both domains, BAs with a technical background may benefit from seeking business-related training or educational opportunities, such as courses or certifications. Similarly, BAs with a business background may find learning about technical concepts and tools helpful through training or self-study.

In addition, staying up-to-date on industry developments and trends can help BAs adapt to changes in their work environment, such as moving from a structured systems analysis and design process to an object-oriented one or transitioning from a Waterfall to an Agile/Iterative methodology.

Seeking Mentorships: Importantly, seeking guidance from more experienced professionals, such as mentors, can provide valuable support as BAs navigate the learning curve and work to maintain competency in both the business and technical domains.

Cultivating a "Helping" Mindset: A lack of Mindset can pose a considerable challenge for a BA while executing his/her job. As a BA, one should know that a Project is all about building something new with a vision in mind. While building something new, the project may run into various challenges. It's always uncertain.

In such a situation, a BA must be prepared mentally so that he/she will face several challenges during the project. In addition, if you as a BA cultivate a mindset to "genuinely help people when in need", it will help you, too.

When you have that "helping" Mindset or that compassion, you will automatically get into that "caring" Mindset. This makes you ask the right questions to affected people/end users. This motivates you further to understand "why" and "how" end users do their work and why there are pain points/problems. This ultimately will make you come up with the right solutions to resolve those problems.

For a BA, there is nothing more important than solving the pain points of an end user. Technology is there to serve the people. A BA's job is to ensure that technology serves the end users effectively and improves their quality of work life! Only then will end users start using the technology; that's when a project can be called a success!

Becoming a Domain Expert: As a BA, domain knowledge is crucial as he/she is the one who will work closely with business users to fully understand their requirements. However, a BA cannot master the domains of each project he/she is part of. However, learning is essential to a BA's career, and trying to learn as much as possible about the new domain is necessary.

When you learn, your goal should be to learn just enough to add value to the project and understand the basic concepts and relevant processes related to that domain/industry. This may involve researching the industry, learning about the key players, and familiarising yourself with the terminology and processes specific to the domain. With time and experience, BAs can continue to build on this foundation and deepen their knowledge of the domain.

Technical Awareness: Does a BA need to be technically Strong? Even customers get confused with the role sometimes. If you have a technical background and know some basics of SQL, etc., it "may" help. However, technical or developer skills are not necessary to become a BA because, above all, a BA should think about business needs and problems that need to be addressed and develop an efficient solution for the problem.

However, awareness of the technicalities of how things are technically is essential. It is beneficial for a BA to understand how technology works, its limitations, and more. Because, as a BA, sometimes you may need to speak technology in a business language! A BA should know about the design of the functional architecture of a system, how a system works and how the logic behind a program or workflow works.

Hence, developing a good awareness of the technology is important. Ex: If any plugin is to be developed to introduce a functionality, a BA should know the logic inside and the data's operation.

Challenges That Come from Nowhere!

Here is a scenario. Based on the information available during presales activity, the sales/Presales team would have closed the deal with a certain timeline for a proposed project. However, when the actual project starts, the team realises that the time allocated for Business analysis is less. This is a challenge for a BA with no fault of his or her.

When you are faced with such a situation, alert it to the management and seek additional required time; otherwise, blame will come on to you if there is any problem that may arise later. Note that lack of adequate time to complete Business Analysis tasks can hinder the delivery of high-quality deliverables and result in implementing requirements that do not solve the business problem.

However, when no options are available, the BA should plan well and start early when working on a project with limited time. Everything should be black & white and crystal clear. This includes creating a comprehensive plan outlining key activity, prioritising tasks, and building in contingency time. The BA should also communicate any potential time constraints to the project team and stakeholders and work with them to find ways to mitigate any possible delays. In addition, the BA should identify any potential risks to the project schedule and develop contingency plans to address them.

In IT services set-up, typically, you, as part of the Vendor (implementation partner of a Project for your project) organisation, will become an extended team of IT team of the customer. Usually, the business team within the customer organisation gives requirements, and the IT team (including you) delivers the same. But sometimes, the IT department simply cannot deliver what the business wants due to the unavailability of resources or some other reasons like technological limitations.

However, the main reason for such high expectations from Business teams is the lack of understanding of the limitations of the technical infrastructure. Also, there was a failure from the IT team to communicate the same to the business team.

At these times, a BA who usually works with a business team to get requirements will face challenge as the BA may not be able to assess the technical limitations and accepts the requirements. However, the real picture emerges when the IT team gets involved and examines the technical feasibility. The catfight begins between business and IT.

That is why, as we read just now, as a BA, you must understand the high-level technical limitations of the current infrastructure. The BA should do a detailed study of the current status in collaboration with the technical team.

Note that you should never accept any requirements individually. The IT and project teams must assess requirements for technical feasibility before they can be accepted. As a BA, you own the solution design but lead the technical design in collaboration with the technical team. Also, all business stakeholders should be educated about any IT limitations.

Once the business stakeholders understand what is possible and what is not, people will be willing to accept any alternative ways to achieve the requirements. Suppose there is already no BA on the customer side or any collaborative environment between business and IT departments within the customer organisation as a BA. In that case, you must become a bridge between business and IT.

Becoming a Scapegoat!

When things go wrong, or if a project starts to experience issues, one of the first things that will happen is the launch of an investigation into the correctness of the requirements captured by the BA. If anything goes wrong there, you will be held responsible. That's the reason BAs are constantly under pressure because they must get things right.

If a system is implemented and does not meet the expectations of the business, you will be held accountable for the outcome. Hence, BAS needs to handle this pressure to deliver successful results.

In some cases, even if it is not your fault, you will become the scapegoat because you are the one who faced the customer first. So, whoever blames you will blame you only. At such times, if you have data points, artefacts, or proofs with you, they will save you.

Hence, as a BA, you must maintain written documentation for every decision made during the project lifecycle. Ex: Sign-offs, critical decisions on technical and business processes, and anything you think may create an issue later. Save the proofs to save you.

The Over Analysis: Analysis Paralysis

A couple of years ago, I had a colleague who had just moved from a technical role to a BA role. Though an experienced talent, he was doing the BA job independently for the first time. Suddenly, one fine day, his project manager called me and asked for help.

The project manager said: "Jay, our BA is not able to complete his documentation and deadline is already over. Could you guide him to complete his job?"

Since I had earlier worked with him, I guessed the reason for this delay.
He told me: "Hey Jay, the processes here is very complex. I have good information to draft good set of requirements. But I am not confident. I may need more workshops. Before that I need to go through this huge set of documents shared by customers."

I asked him a few questions:

- Can the project's goals be accomplished with the available info?
- With the available info, can you define/draft all the processes?
- Do you think stakeholders and developers can understand them?
- Once you draft them, can each of those requirements be tested?
- Do you have Acceptance Criteria defined?

He said 'YES' to all of them.

"Then what's the problem to complete the documentation?"

He said: "I feel I am missing some info. I think I need to incorporate some info from those documents, too."

Though his intention was right, he was worrying too much about a problem, making him not confident about the current status of his documentation.

My guess was correct. He was stuck in a loop. He was going through "Analysis paralysis"!

Due to the information load, he could not decide whether he could stop the analysis. He was excessively focusing on achieving perfection by risking the project timelines.

Simply, he was not sure where to stop. This is not only for BAs but also for entrepreneurs. When they overthink a situation, they cannot make a decision, causing delays in execution.

In business analysis, the information becomes unnecessary or redundant after a point. Hence, as a BA, he/she should understand when to stop the analysis and finalise the requirements.

Here are some learnings to prevent this mental state of "Analysis paralysis":

1. Involve stakeholders in every stage of the requirements gathering phase and have frequent feedback– which will give confidence to BA that he is on track.
2. Have a timeline for analysis and follow that strictly.
3. Agree with all stakeholders about the level of detail (or template of requirements document) you will provide.
4. Understand the vision/objectives of the project clearly. When you get into such a loop (Analysis Paralysis), pause, remind yourself of the objectives and introspect if those can be met with the information you have currently.
5. Whenever you are not able to make a decision, take a break. Discuss with a team/ manager for guidance – get a fresh perspective.

Top Risks of a BA

We studied all of these aspects already. Still, let's recap them in this small section. Indeed, a BA is like a bride's responsible brother helping his father to ensure the marriage event runs smoothly!

As a BA, if you think only project managers need to worry about "Risks" in a project, then you are mistaken. While it's a collective responsibility of the entire project team to tackle Risks, for certain Risks, BAs need to take ownership. Though gathering requirements, arriving at a scope, and managing them are the key tasks for a BA, he/she is also responsible for spearheading the solution design and implementation as per requirements by working with the project technical team. Hence, key risks automatically fall into a BA's bucket.

Requirements Risk: The main culprit of all. If requirements are not captured correctly, the entire project will fail due to incorrect design and implementation and not meeting the end-user requirements. Hence, it's entirely BA's responsibility to capture and manage the requirements correctly – the only mitigation for this risk. Involving customers at every stage of requirements and following best practices can help a BA to carry out this responsibility smoothly.

.

Solution Design Risk: There is always a possibility that despite the BA capturing the requirements correctly, the technical team understood it differently. This could be a disaster. A BA will closely work with the solution design team and the customer to ensure that design components satisfy the captured requirements. A BA must maintain a "Requirement Traceability Matrix" to map the journey of a requirement till its implementation.

Business Continuity and Impact: In many situations, the system users (impacted or being implemented during the project) may not have clear visibility into the future. Hence, it's BA's responsibility to work with customers to keep all end users in the loop about the possible impact and "Before vs. after" scenarios to make them understand the implications of new change. As a change agent, a BA should ensure that users are transitioned to a new system with minimum possible disruptions. A BA needs to work with Customers and the Project team to plan the implementation so that there are zero or minimal disruptions to ongoing business activities while ensuring all stakeholders understand the impact on the organisation.

The Risk of Change: This happens when the new implementation adversely affects the customer's business – perhaps due to users not being clear on how to use the system and being uncomfortable with the new process. Though the BA may not be directly responsible for any change management activities, he/she needs to proactively initiate such activities by working with customers and the project manager to develop a comprehensive change strategy to enable successful outcomes. The BA should lead this activity by bringing together all change management stakeholders.

Top 2 Things BAs Must Remember!

Every day is a new day!: For BAs, every day is a new day. Every challenge is a new challenge. Whether you are an experienced BA or not, your experience can help you tackle a situation to an extent, but not entirely. Every situation appears similar, but deep down, they are unique.

You just finished a project, and touchwood, all went well in that project, and you might be feeling super confident. You must! No harm. But do not get overconfident! Realise that every IT project is unique, and there's no guarantee that the approach or strategy that worked in your previous project will also work well with your upcoming project. Hence, leverage your learnings intelligently to tackle situations.

You are responsible for Requirements: many BAs complained that customers did not give the correct requirements. Never expect to get all the requirements from your stakeholders. They just can't define everything for you. Of course, if you are lucky, you will get all of them from stakeholders in some cases. However, in general, in most of the cases, it is not valid.

Remember that requirements evolve. Hence, you should not take and write precisely like what the stakeholder said in a workshop and finalise the same. It needs to be further analysed with the team and other stakeholders.

Hence, before finalising a requirement, various "checks" you need to pass through. These checks may not happen sequentially, so you should develop that "iterative" Mindset to make a requirement mature over a period of time. Ultimately, the success of your project lies in the business value you deliver. Business benefits your customers received.

What Did You Learn in This Chapter?

- Why usually stakeholders do not cooperate with BAs?
- How to handle Conflict between a BA and Users?
- How will you handle conflicts among users/stakeholders?
- How to you decide that it's now time to stop analysis?
- What are the top 4 common Risks of a BA?

CHAPTER 14

WORKING WITH TECHNICAL TEAMS

- *BA & The Development Team*
- *BA & The Testing Team*
- *Estimations & Collaborations*

"We discussed and agreed on this. What happened now? This is not acceptable."

The BA had earlier estimated the effort required to complete a set of user stories that are part of the current Sprint. However, despite having the full strength working, the team has realised that all the agreed user stories may not be delivered in the current Sprint and will require a couple of more sprints.

The BA conveyed this to the customer and the project manager as a person responsible. However, the customer is not very pleased with the BA's discussion.

There are various factors due to which estimations can go wrong. I agree that the most significant cause can be the lack of clarity in scope. However, the second biggest reason is the BA!

Really? How?

The BA did not include or collaborate with the project team/technical team for estimation. As a BA, even if you are technically strong, you must not estimate the effort on his/her own. Always consult the technical/ development team. Involve them and collaborate with them.

If a BA is technically sound, estimating alone may work, but make it a practice to consult the technical team because, ultimately, they are the people who will develop the user story or the requirements. Without taking them into confidence, as a BA, you should not agree on a timeline with the customer.

Another factor is that, as a BA, he/she should be aware that in projects, despite knowing the customer ecosystem dependencies with other systems (In integration projects), such slippages do happen. However, this should not occur frequently because of "your" reason (Because of the BA). If it is due to "customer's reason", as a BA, you will be under little less pressure.

This is just one of the scenarios depicting the importance of a BA working with a technical Team. Let's dwell a little more on this aspect.

The BA and The Development Team

We know the BA is a liaison between the business and technical teams. The BA's role is to understand the needs and goals of the business and translate them into requirements specifications. The BA is responsible for assessing the business and identifying the requirements that are essential for the smooth functioning of that business. Then, the BA will collaborate with the technical team to prepare technical specifications during the design stage.

However, whether you are part of an Agile or a Waterfall Team, making the technical Team or development team inclusive during the requirements stage or while writing Requirements is essential. Though the BA is the person who drafts and finalises the requirements, he/she should consult all possible types of stakeholders (Requirement owners within Customers, Testing Team, Developers, Architects, etc.). Whenever possible, include the key members of these functions during the requirements workshops wherein deep technical aspects are being discussed. This will help identify any technical bottleneck or complexity that you, as a BA, may not be able to gauge.

In contrast, there may be instances where the technical teams are unfamiliar with business terminology and how to address business challenges. The BA is critical in communicating business issues to the technical teams in such cases. The BA must present information in a way that is easy for the technical teams to understand.

Additionally, The BA is responsible for identifying solutions to business problems and communicating with the teams on how to implement them. The BA must convey to the technical teams the ins and outs of the business in a manner that can be understood easily and must be able to provide inputs to the technical solutions provided by technical teams for resolving business problems and guide them to implement them. The BA must ensure that technical solutions adhere to the captured requirements.

As part of their role, the BA must also be able to perform a system impact analysis in collaboration with the technical teams. This means they must be able to assess the potential consequences of implementing a given solution before it is implemented to anticipate and avoid any unintended outcomes. The BA should be able to conduct a pre-assessment of the impact of different systems that are to be implemented. This helps identify any issues that might come up and prevent them same. The BA must be proficient in performing system impact analysis working with technical teams to evaluate the outcome of any solution proposed to the business. He/She should be able to anticipate and mitigate potential negative consequences.

Hence, a deep collaboration with the dev team is a must. Once your Requirements Workshop is over (or during the stage) and once you are ready with your version of the Requirements document, you need to present the document to the internal teams, including key developers who will be part of the development of the same to perform any such pre-assessment on the impact of implementation, technically.

This will also be a perfect opportunity to identify any further gaps, including technical gaps you might have missed during your interaction with the customer at a workshop. Have those inputs gathered and then connect with the customer stakeholder again to clarify those points you have newly gathered from the technical team/developers.

This need not happen sequentially; instead, this can manifest as an ongoing dialogue involving your customer, development team, and potentially the Customer IT team. Such collaborative discussions frequently foster transparency and enhance customer trust in the team. The only potential drawback of this approach is that, over time, customers might begin reaching out directly to developers, bypassing you for inquiries or updates.

As a BA, you shouldn't allow such parallel communications as such direct discussions between Customers and the developer can be a distraction for the developer, and unknowingly, the developer would have developed a requirement as the needs of that customer, which was not at all documented by you. At a later stage, the testing team will catch this difference, and you will not know how this has happened, leading to an issue.

Hence, make it a point that any communication should go through you regarding Requirements and scope, and you are the 100% owner of the same. Involve your Project Manager in this matter and agree on a proper process of communication that should happen.

Typically, in Projects where the Waterfall methodology is used, the BA will experience the pressure of "Dev team is sitting idle" during the requirements stage, which is indeed awkward for a BA. A BA might have been still figuring it out (Requirements, etc.), and when in a status call, the Dev team says, "We are waiting for BA to deliver Requirements," the BA will feel that awkwardness or guilt-induced pressure - sometimes management may ask BAs, "Is there any way the dev team can start the work?" This may increase the pressure a bit more for the BA.

To avoid such a situation, usually, while the requirements are still being written, the development team is asked to start their work. This approach introduces risk, but continuous monitoring of the development activities by the BA can easily mitigate that risk. Trust me, most of the time, it worked for me.

The BA should own this "Requirements Risk", wherein the developers may develop something that will later conflict with the finalised Requirements Document. Hence, the BA should ensure that such risks do not happen, and he can do that by finalising the Requirements Document without delay. The final, approved version should be available to the developers before the developers have moved too far.

The risk can also be minimised by involving the development team while writing the requirements specifications described earlier. In this way, developers know what is required to develop what is missing. If the development team participates in writing the Requirements document, they will know how a requirement is being evolved and what may come. This way, developers will know very early on what the Requirements document will say so that they already know what to implement even though the Requirements document is not yet finalised.

However, the risk remains because Requirements can change anytime before it is finalised. And even after, many times!

Relationships and Collaborations

We touched upon this topic in earlier chapters as well. A BA needs to be able to identify and solve problems effectively. This may involve using analytical and critical thinking skills to understand the root cause of pain points or issues and then develop creative solutions that address them. Adapting to changing business needs and environments is also crucial, as BAs may be called upon to work on various projects and initiatives. To do this effectively, they need to be able to quickly learn about new domains and industries and adapt their approach as needed.

Hence, a BA should be good at building rapport with key people and stakeholders. However, it does not mean someone not skilled enough to build rapport or relationship cannot perform BA responsibilities. He/She still can. However, a relationship is very influential when it comes to business analysis.

The skill of making friends helps a BA the most. Building a good relationship with everyone associated with the Project, stakeholders or team members, is always essential for a BA. Such relationships help a BA collaborate well, especially with team members.

When it comes to collaboration, a BA must collaborate with technical resources to carry out the technical Analysis. If a BA is highly technical, then there may not be a need for another technical person to help the BA. Normally, very technical skills are not expected from a BA because his roles and tasks differ from technical roles.

Regarding collaboration, the BAs often need to collaborate with technical resources to complete technical Analysis as part of their work. While it can benefit a BA to have some technical knowledge, they are not necessarily expected to be highly technical experts. The BAs and technical team members often have different roles and responsibilities, with the BA focusing more on understanding the business needs and requirements and the technical team members responsible for implementing solutions to meet those needs.

However, a BA also must have moderate technical skills to assess the current situation and to conduct a system analysis. During the discovery phase of a Project, such assessment or Analysis usually takes place. This could be in collaboration with a technical Architect or a Technical Lead.

As a BA, it's important to analyse system and enterprise architecture to understand a system's underlying structure and functionality. System architecture encompasses a system's design, structure, components, relationships, and function. It is a high-level model representing a system's overall behaviour, structure, and features. He/She must be able to interpret the information on the model and know how to develop an improved version of the model whenever a requirement arises. It, however, is not necessary for a BA to be able to design the models himself/herself. All he/she should need is an overall understanding of system architecture.

Integrations are often a key part of any project and can enable different systems within an enterprise to exchange data and work together seamlessly. As a BA, it's vital to assess the current situation or set up and conduct a system analysis to understand the needs and requirements for integration. This might involve working closely with a technical architect or technical lead to identify the most appropriate approaches and technologies for integrating different systems.

A BA can help identify the most effective ways of connecting different systems to exchange data and provide a unified user experience by conducting a thorough system analysis. This might involve identifying common data formats and protocols and developing interfaces and other integration points to enable the systems to work smoothly. By carefully assessing the needs and requirements of the business and working closely with technical experts, a BA can help to ensure that integrations are implemented in a way that meets the needs of the business and delivers a seamless user experience.

Remember, BAs should never detach themselves from such technical activities. Though you are not a technical person as a BA, being aware of technical aspects always helps.

Though Dealing with business data is primarily the responsibility of customers (as they know their business well, and hence their data well), data analysis is an integral part of the BA's job, too, which involves examining, cleaning, transforming, and visualising data to uncover insights and inform decision-making.

A BA often needs to work closely with a technical architect or data analyst to conduct data analysis effectively, as these individuals may have specialised skills and expertise in working with data. As a BA, it's essential to be able to look at data obtained through various data collection methods and distinguish facts from beliefs. This involves critically evaluating the data and considering its sources and limitations to draw accurate and reliable conclusions. By conducting data analysis in a systematic and organised way, a BA can help to inform business decisions and identify opportunities for improvement.

Working with Testing Teams

The BAs play a crucial role in the testing process by supporting the team in several ways. The following are a few examples of how BAs can assist with testing efforts:

- **Defining the scope of testing:** BAs help identify what functionality should be tested and what should be excluded from testing based on the business requirements. They work closely with the test team to establish testing goals and objectives that align with the business needs.
- **Reviewing test scenarios:** BAs review the test scenarios prepared by the test team to ensure that they are complete and consistent with the requirements specification because, many times, understanding between the teams differs. A BA's main job is to ensure all the teams have a common and shared understanding of requirements. They also check that the test cases cover all the necessary functionality and that the test scenarios are appropriate for the intended use of the system. In smaller projects where a dedicated testing team is absent, the BAs themselves write the test cases and test the system.
- **Helping conduct User Acceptance Testing (UAT):** UAT is the final testing stage before the system is deployed to production. The system's end-users perform it, a critical step in the testing process. BAs typically help/support end-users in conducting UAT (sometimes in collaboration with the testing team) by guiding the stakeholders/end-users through the testing process, answering any questions that arise, capturing the feedback, analysing the bugs, root cause analysis and also capturing feedback on the system's performance and more.
- **Contributing to the Identification of The Testing Approach:** BAs help the test team decide which approach to take, whether manual or automated, based on the system and the specific requirements.

In addition to the above aspects, the BAs play a key role in testing by ensuring that the test team clearly understands the business requirements and that all testing efforts align with those requirements. This ensures the final solution meets business needs and functions properly.

Agile Teams and a BA

Technically, all the aspects we discussed so far also apply to an Agile team.

A BA in an Agile environment is a professional with expert knowledge in functional and technical aspects of product development and project delivery. The BA plays a dynamic role within the Scrum team, which allows them to adapt to the specific needs of the organisation and Project. In Agile scenarios, some of the primary responsibilities of a BA include:

- **Acting as a Product Owner (Or collaborating with Product Owner):** BAs may act as Product Owner depending on the Project's size and nature and the organisation's scale. In this role, they prioritise the backlog and work with the team to deliver a valuable, usable product. In cases where the roles of Business Analyst and Product Owner are distinct, the Business Analyst will cooperate with the Product Owner in Managing and prioritising the product backlog and related tasks such as backlog refinement, requirement clarification and more.

- **Identifying and resolving obstacles:** BAs are often the key point of contact between the development team and other stakeholders. They work closely with developers to identify and resolve any challenges during development, helping keep the Project on track.
- **Improving team performance:** BAs can enhance Agile team performance by providing technical expertise. They can help identify areas for improvement and assist the team in implementing best practices and industry standards.
- **Continuity and Consistency:** Having the same BA for multiple teams can be beneficial as they can maintain continuity and consistency across different projects. BA can interoperate various features and updates and analyse the product's credibility. This can help to ensure that the product is aligned with the business needs and that the final product meets the intended requirements.
- **Support Testing:** They assist in the scope of testing, review test scenarios, and conduct UAT to ensure the solution meets the needs of the business and functions as intended.

BAs are an integral part of any Agile-based team (SCRUM Kanban and more) and play a crucial role in the success of any project by bringing their technical expertise to the team and working closely with stakeholders to ensure that the product meets the business needs.

When You, as A BA, Join a Project in The Middle…

Here is a unique but common situation for a BA. Imagine you have joined a project (project team) that has already commenced. So, how do you plan to get up to speed?

✪ **Remember—**you are being monitored!

"It's been two weeks and your BA is not picking up. This is impacting the Project's progress. What is your Risk mitigation plan?"

The customer told the project manager, who conveyed the same to the BA. Both are under pressure now!

When an existing BA leaves the Project, and a new one joins the Project midway, every BA or project manager is bound to face such pressure unless the customer is very much accommodative.

As a BA, you are already under pressure because you joined a project midway. Your mind is still processing the information—you took knowledge transfer from the previous BA, read the requirements, scope, etc., and did almost all possible stuff that can be done quickly. Still, in a Requirements workshop, you cannot understand what the customer stakeholder is talking about and are struggling to connect the dots.

And the above feedback comes right after that.

What will you do?

If you are a seasoned BA or not, a situation like this will come to every BA.

First off, be calm!

Be honest with yourself. Are you trying your best to get up to speed? This phase could be overwhelming till you stabilise, unfortunately, & you might even have to spend some extra hours, perhaps.

You do not need to worry if you are satisfied with your efforts to get up to speed and confident about it. There will be some turbulence; however, you will land smoothly. This is often the "pressure tactic" the customer uses to keep the team on their toes!

Here are some tips to get yourself up to speed in such situations:

- In a workshop, ask the stakeholder if you are unclear about the process/requirements. Perhaps you can also say, "Because I am new and still processing the info, it would be helpful if you explain me once again."
- Use all the opportunities to gather information, even during a meeting with the IT team. Design or technical discussions will give you a different perspective, and you will start immersing yourself in the Project.
- Your team is your saviour. This does not mean you grab their time for your sake. Whenever you get a chance, try to get an understanding from team members. Be humble and ask them about things you want to know—requirements, scope, design, etc. No ego should come in between here.

- Build a rapport with customer stakeholders. During the day, just walk into the desk of a Stakeholder and casually talk to him, if the time permits (Or casually chat with them online). Here, too, be humble and ask what you don't know.

Please note rather than doing your study of documentation, asking people about them will provide more clarity. It also gives you confidence. Don't worry about what others will think about you or your credibility; no one can be an expert in everything. You need to seek knowledge first to become knowledgeable.

Suppose you don't know something. Accept. Ask. Clarify. It will improve your image and credibility.

Effort Estimation: Is the BA Responsible?

First off, effort estimation in software development is never accurate. That's why they are always called as Guestimates.

Effort estimation in software development is an intricate task, often perplexing technical and non-technical individuals. It's a challenging endeavour because, as many in the industry would attest, accuracy in these estimations is elusive.

Hence, to enhance the accuracy of estimations, it is advisable to employ a structured approach, breaking down the effort into key activities and seeking validation from experienced peers. By doing so, the software development process can become more transparent, manageable, and conducive to meeting project goals.

BAs usually collaborate with developers/technical teams to carry out estimations. Some BAs are technical or product experts (E.g., in the case of Product implementations like Salesforce or Dynamics 365) and functional consultants with the knowledge and ability to carry out Estimations. Despite this, even if you are technically strong as a BA, you must not estimate the effort on your own. Always consult the technical/ development team. Involve them and collaborate with them.

Always Remember a Basic Rule: Estimation is always subjective. It differs from person to person based on the expertise they have. If multiple people are involved in Estimation, it's better. Never do estimations alone. You may think, what's wrong with it? If you are technically sound, estimating alone may work, but make it a practice to consult the technical team because, ultimately, they are the people who will develop the user story or the requirements. Without taking them into confidence, as a BA, you should not agree on a timeline with the customer. Make it as a rule.

One big challenge arises when non-technical folks (like Project Managers or BAs without tech knowledge) try to estimate how long a software task will take. Usually, when non-tech people make these guesses or estimates, they're way off the mark. If developers can't finish on time according to these estimates, it's not their fault because they don't get all the technical details. This difference between what's expected and what happens can lead to frustration and disappointment.

Conversely, making accurate estimates in software work means you need to know the technical aspects well. Developers must consider how complicated the code is, what problems might pop up, and what might go wrong while building the software. However, this can make it tough for even experienced developers to guess precisely how long a task will take. Because of this uncertainty, developers often add extra time to their estimates as buffers. This is like a safety cushion. It helps them account for problems they can't predict and ensure they finish on time.

However, there are instances when this cautious approach by developers can lead to projects taking longer than necessary. Customers may not always agree with the estimate, and this scenario is quite common in IT projects.

That's why a proper review and analysis of estimates are essential to mitigate these challenges and arrive at more reliable estimates, there are two practical approaches to consider. The first involves using the developer's estimate as a starting point. It is essential to break down the effort into critical activities, providing a clearer understanding of the components that make up the estimate. For those activities that appear misaligned or unclear, further refinement can be achieved by breaking them down into smaller, quantifiable work units.

The second approach involves seeking validation from a more experienced developer or Architect within the project or company. A second pair of experienced eyes can identify discrepancies and offer valuable insights into refining the estimates.

This collaborative effort leverages the development team's collective knowledge and can lead to more accurate and realistic estimations.

Top 4 Most Used Estimation Techniques

Several methods are commonly used for requirements estimation in an IT project which should be typically led by a BA. The top four most used methods are:

- **Expert Judgement**
- **3-Point Estimation**
- **Bench Mark and Complexity Based Estimation**
- **T-Shirt Size Estimations**

Expert Judgement: This method can be used if you are a real expert in a particular area within a project, including functional and technical. Expert judgment estimation is a subjective approach used in various fields, relying on the expertise of knowledgeable individuals to make informed predictions or assessments when quantitative data is limited or unavailable. Experts, often with relevant experience, analyse the situation, consider past experiences, and provide their best-informed opinions. This method is valuable for decision-making, risk assessment, and project planning, but its accuracy depends on the competence and objectivity of the experts involved. It's commonly used in areas like project management, risk analysis, and complex problem-solving to fill gaps in data or information.

3-Point Estimation: When estimating effort in software development, it's common to encounter variations in the estimates developers provide. Depending on the specific circumstances, these variations can swing between overestimation and underestimation. A three-point estimation technique can be employed to manage this subjectivity in Estimation, particularly the best-case scenario calculation method.

To implement this technique, you should request the developer to furnish three estimates: the most optimistic, the most pessimistic, and the most realistic estimate. Once you have these values, you can apply the following formula to arrive at a more reliable estimate:

Best-Case Estimate = (s + 4b + c) / 6; Where:

- 'a' represents the most optimistic estimate
- 'b' stands for the most realistic estimate.
- 'c' denotes the most pessimistic estimate.

By plugging these values into the formula, you can calculate a best-case estimate that considers both optimistic and pessimistic scenarios and the most realistic projection. This method provides a more balanced and considered estimate for your software development effort.

However, it is advisable to seek input from multiple developers for larger projects. Each developer can provide estimates, and then you can apply the formula to these collective inputs. This collaborative approach ensures a broader perspective and a more accurate estimate for comprehensive projects.

Benchmark and Complexity-Based Estimation: This method is more suitable for product implementation projects (like Salesforce or Dynamics 365 implementation). This is one of the simple yet proven methods where requirements are classified as Simple, Medium and Complex based on the level of complexity level of each requirement. The BA and technical teams go deeper into each requirement or user story to understand and analyse the complexity. The team can further break down the requirements into smaller units if required.

Once this is done, based on the previous experience, the team would have already benchmarked the efforts (time or estimation numbers in hours or days) for simple, medium and complex requirements. Here is an example scenario—If a requirement is classified as simple, it may take 2 hours; if it is medium, it may take 4 hours; if it is medium, it may take 8 hours and so on.

T-shirt Size Estimations: In Agile project management, T-shirt size estimation is a simplified technique used to estimate the relative size or effort required for user stories or tasks during sprint planning or backlog grooming. Team members assign sizes like Small, Medium, Large, or Extra Large (S, M, L, XL) to represent the complexity or effort involved, analogous to T-shirt sizes. This method encourages quick, high-level Estimation without delving into precise timeframes. It fosters collaboration and helps teams prioritise work effectively. Over time, historical data from completed tasks with T-shirt sizes can improve accuracy in future estimations, aiding in better sprint planning and resource allocation.

In addition to the above, there are several other methods such as Parametric, Analogous estimation techniques that are in use. In Agile setups, people use other methods such as Poker cards, Story points, and more.

What Did You Learn in This Chapter?

- What activities a BA does during Testing & UAT stage?
- What are the top four estimation methods?

CHAPTER 15

THE AGILE WORLD'S NEW AGE BA

- *What Is an Agile Mindset?*
- *Cultivating The Agile Mindset*
- *What An Agile Ba Brings to The Table?*

Times are not the same as they were ten years ago. The world is much faster nowadays. The era of running projects for years to develop features is now a thing of the past. Every technology company now focuses on low-code and no-code concepts and harnesses the power of AI. As you know, such technologies enable people to create or build things swiftly.

Hence, whenever a requirement is conceptualised, the approach for building such requirements will be much faster nowadays by leveraging such technologies. Because building such things is easy and less effort-intensive, adopting any changes from customers also becomes much easier.

The point is that "Change" is no longer an "annoying" word. The "Change" is a value you deliver to your customer. To deliver "Value," you must quickly adapt and incorporate as per changing business scenarios. That's why you need to be Agile. As a BA, developing an Agile mindset is critical. As an Agile BA, delivering value is paramount at any cost.

What is an Agile Mindset?

An Agile mindset enables us to adapt to changes as they arise. Without this approach, we risk stagnating in the face of challenges, hindering progress and missing valuable opportunities.

For instance, consider a developer in a team who specialises in .NET. If a high-priority task requires proficiency in Python, and the team is not skilled in this language, they could learn (anyone within the team) Python quickly while continuing their regular work. This exemplifies the Agile mindset, as the team is not limiting themselves to their current knowledge but is open to acquiring new skills to deliver value to the customer. In this scenario, the value is realised when the high-priority task is completed and delivered.

The above example was just a hypothetical to illustrate the concept of an Agile mindset—an open, flexible, value-driven and always ready-to-solve problem mindset. Agile is not a set process or method but a flexible and adaptive mindset. In the above situation, there may be different approaches to responding to change, and Agile encourages learning and continuous improvement to reach business milestones. The key to understanding the Agile mindset is its emphasis on adaptability and growth.

To understand the Agile mindset, let's compare the characteristics of an "Agile Mindset" with our usual mindset; let's call it a "Traditional Fixed Mindset".

In contrast, a "Traditional Fixed Mindset" limits individuals' potential and confines them to their perceived limitations. This mindset leads to a belief that one is either good at something or not, and there is no room for exploration or improvement. Failure results from unchanging abilities, leading to resistance to challenges and a preference for staying in a comfort zone. The potential is viewed as predetermined and limited. With a traditional fixed mindset, individuals may cling to what they already know and give up easily when frustrated.

Compared to the "Traditional Fixed Mindset", the "agile mindset" provides far better results as this mindset provides growth—quick ideas, higher realised values, collaboration and many more.

Conversely, the Agile mindset fosters a growth mindset by encouraging individuals to try new things, explore and be inspired by others' successes. It provides direction and motivation to work towards growth while letting go of negativity towards changes. This mindset recognises that abilities are not fixed but can be expanded through effort and attitude. A failure is not a setback here—views failure as an opportunity for growth and feedback. The potential is not limited but is instead the ability to continuously learn and grow.

The Agile mindset is critical in an Agile environment as it helps individuals embrace change and continuously improve. The Agile approach values learning and growth encourages experimentation, and embraces failures as opportunities for growth. This mindset is central to the Agile philosophy, emphasising flexibility, collaboration, and continuous improvement.

So, how do things work in a typical Agile environment?

In Agile, work is completed in iterations, improving the solution. These iterations typically last two to four weeks, and Agile operates in a fast-paced delivery environment. The focus is on delivering value, and Agile emphasises collaboration and embracing changes as they come. That is why the "Value" mindset powered by empathy is extremely important to become a real Agile person—in terms of mindset!

The Agile approach values teamwork and empowers the team members to be self-organised. The respectful environment fosters a safe, fearless atmosphere where team members feel comfortable providing input and suggestions. The agile process also collaborates with stakeholders and cross-functional teams, who provide feedback and help shape the solution.

Agile is a continuous learning process, with techniques such as reviews and retrospectives used to elicit feedback and improve the solution. This feedback provides an opportunity for growth and improvement and helps to ensure that the solution meets the needs of the stakeholders. The Agile approach builds a strong foundation for collaboration, where all parties involved in the solution can work together towards a common goal.

In agile, customer satisfaction is of utmost importance. Agile prioritises delivering outcomes rather than just outputs. This means that the focus is not just on creating artefacts or meeting certain deliverables but on providing value to the customer through each iteration. The focus is always on delivering high-quality solutions that meet the customer's needs, not just creating documentation or charts. The customer's feedback is continuously considered through techniques such as reviews and retrospectives and is used to drive improvements and deliver better outcomes.

"Learn from yesterday, live for today, hope for tomorrow. The important thing is not to stop questioning." – Albert Einstein.

In my opinion, this quote from Einstein perfectly aligns with the agile way of thinking!

Business, Project or Life, NEVER EVER stop questioning. Who knows! Your one single simple question may drastically improve the product you are building. Certainly, continuous, consistent progress and improvement should be our primary objective as agile organisations, teams, and team members, of course BAs included.

It's a mindset. Agile is also a mindset first, methodology next.

Cultivating Agile Mindset

"One rotten Apple is enough to spoil the entire barrel".

Many say, as an organisation that wants to run an agile engagement or a team member who is part of a so-called "agile team", you should be careful while choosing the team members or when becoming one. While the agile way of delivery can provide you with the best value for the buck, if agile principles are not followed by the team, or even one member does not have that required "mindset" to be a part of an agile team, things may fail miserably.

I agree. The Customers and project team members should possess that "Agile Mindset" to make that project successful and thus gain the best business value from the engagement.

Because agile is all about being accountable, taking ownership, being responsible and being motivated all the time, this applies to every team member.

But my question is, can we "choose" the right kind of "Agile people"? Can large organisations that fight for human talent in the market even imagine "Choosing the right person" just for their projects?

Well, I do not have an answer for this.

In such scenarios, I have seen that priority was given to people with relevant "skillsets" rather than "mindsets". Then, these people are trained or "coached" to become agile. While I agree that coaching is one of the ways to make people learn to be "Agile", if they lack that required "mindset", will the "Coaching" be effective?

Can we enforce "Mindset" via coaching? I simply don't know.

I have encountered many such issues, not because of lack of "Skillsets", but the lack of "Mindset".

Can we bring a set of processes/practices into that "Agile" engagement in such situations?

The logic is simple. "Agile" follows 12 principles with four values. So, can we enforce (or implement) some processes/practices that more or less adhere to "Agile Principles"?

Probably yes. That's where SCRUM, Kanban, and such practices came into existence. This helps to make people follow the rules. These processes and rules are enforced to "manage" the mindset issues. One must understand that "Agile" is a thought process with some principles.

So, SCRUM, Kanban, XP, etc., are all "Agile" inspired frameworks or practices with their own set of processes, Frameworks and rules. It is a way to implement the Agile principles through project management methodologies that help teams achieve their objectives. Hence, the SCRUM can be Agile, but Agile is not SCRUM!

People can argue that your project can't be "agile" now.

It's Okay. If the above setup can deliver the best value for the buck for my business/Project, I don't care.

Many argue that "True Agile" is just on paper. Delivering a project using just "Agile Principles and Values" in its purest form is impossible. However, it is practically possible when the right people with the right "mindset" are in the team.

I sometimes feel any beautiful thing or experience—it just happens. Some projects, people coming together, etc., just happen like a miracle. You'll get that lifetime experience.

So, what is it that "Being Agile" truly means?

It is simple. Agile is all about value. Not just a delivery. It's the delivery of value. And to deliver value, one should possess that "Value Mindset" rather than just "delivery Mindset".

You should always consider how your work and your team's work will be a "Value" for your customer. So, at every step, you should think about how this action of mine or my team will add value to my customer. That's it. If you practice this, you will gain that mindset.

But if you are unwilling to practice or cultivate that mindset, you may not become an Agile team member.

That is why all the Agile-inspired methodologies/frameworks, such as SCRUM, XP or Kanban, have laid out their principles to instil that Agile thinking into the team.

All agile methodologies share some common characteristics, such as delivering value, fostering a culture of respect and creativity, prioritising rapid delivery, incorporating feedback and learning, promoting high levels of collaboration and communication among team members and stakeholders, and breaking work down into smaller, incremental, and iterative chunks.

Definitely, such principles or processes help make the team deliver value irrespective of whether they have the right (agile) mindset. However, they may not make the team agile because, for someone who doesn't have an agile mindset, it requires a willingness to cultivate the mindset.

Who is an Agile BA?

This is what I think. Being an Agile BA means being flexible and adapting your methods to suit the project's specific needs. This includes guiding the team to achieve desired outcomes rather than just completing tasks, using established business analysis techniques to establish a shared understanding of the Problem and driving the decision-making process.

It continuously gathers and incorporates user feedback into product development.

All the above traits are inspired or derived from the **12 principles of Agile**—famously known as the Agile Manifesto. Agile Principles are Value-driven. You will automatically get into that "Value" mindset mode if you get attuned to these principles.

Remember, current times need a "Value" mindset. Not just a "Delivery" mindset. That is, you should be able to demonstrate the value you delivered.

These are called 12 Agile Principles as part of the Agile Manifesto. *[Credit: Agile Manifesto]*

- **CUSTOMER SATISFACTION**: Deliver Customer Value. The feedback loop is frequent. Flexibility leads to more value and, hence, happy customers.
- **CHANGES ARE WELCOME**: Agile is iterative. Hence, incorporating change is quick. Any changes /feedback can be included in upcoming sprints (iteration).
- **FREQUENT DELIVERY OF VALUE**: Deliver something of great value quickly. Rather than spending a lot of time in preparation (documentation), deliver actual output bit-by-bit.

- **BREAK SILOS**: Because each delivery timeline is short, all the stakeholders involved should work together to achieve the common goal
- **BUILD PROJECTS AROUND MOTIVATED INDIVIDUALS**: It's like empowering your entire team. No Micromanagement. Making everyone feel that sense of ownership, and because everyone feels the same, there won't be any trust issues.
- **FACE-TO-FACE (1–1) COMMUNICATION**: Efficient & quick communication (1–1 OR Face-to-face) helps in eliminating any communication gap and hence any delay due to lack of communication among team members
- **WORKING SOFTWARE AS A MEASURE OF PROGRESS:** The Result of your hard work is in front of you. Your effort already started giving results. Your only job is to add incremental value to every Sprint.
- **SUSTAINABLE DEVELOPMENT**: One of the primary goals of Agile is to avoid overburn and optimise delivery plans accordingly. Hence, there won't be pressure to deliver a finished product as you are incrementally delivering it. This helps to respond quickly to new market needs & changes.
- **CONTINUOUS EXCELLENCE**: Continuous attention to design and development enables fewer troubles (Bugs, etc.) & allows the team to develop a high-quality product
- **SIMPLICITY**: Avoid complexity. Do what is required. Focus on the Problem & hence solution. Just don't do something for the sake of doing it.
- **SELF-ORGANISING TEAMS:** Agile Teams are always self-motivated. It's a group of self-motivated teams. Suppose you need to push your team for deliverables constantly. Then, your team is not ready for Agile.
- **SELF-REFLECTION**: The team frequently evaluates their performance and adjusts their behaviour to improve effectiveness.

When we read the above Manifesto, it is obvious that the values of the Agile mindset very well align with common human values. I would say all the above values are powered by "empathy".

It's that empathy towards others that makes us "help" someone. It is that helping mindset that is required for a BA to listen to customer problems and, hence, come up with the right solutions.

The Agile mindset applies to software development and other fields like project management, product development, marketing, and beyond. The core principles of the Agile mindset, such as flexibility, collaboration, continuous improvement, value delivery and customer focus, can be applied in any industry or organisation that wants to achieve better results, improved customer satisfaction, and faster time-to-market. The Agile mindset is a way of thinking and working that helps organisations and individuals adapt to change and respond to customers' needs in a quick and ever-changing business environment.

As a BA, you can cultivate an agile mindset by adopting simple principles in your day-to-day work. In a nutshell, you should be able to see the big picture and think like a customer to deliver something valuable. The big-picture principle of business analysis emphasises the importance of comprehensively understanding project needs and context.

Delivering Maximum Value Within the Constraints: As you know, Business analysis often operates within certain constraints, such as technological limitations, team skills, or a set timeframe for delivery. The principle of delivering value within constraints requires the BA to understand how to create the most valuable solution possible while working within these limitations. Through a thorough analysis, the BA assesses what is feasible within the given conditions and prioritises delivering a solution that meets these constraints. The goal is to deliver the highest possible value while working within the constraints.

Most importantly, it's also about continuously improving the deliverables. As a BA, you should always consider how to constantly improve your proposed solution and the processes to meet the customer needs to deliver real value.

Spend time only if there is a Value: As a BA, by carefully planning and focusing only on the required activities, agile principles help reduce waste and non-value-adding activities as they follow a lean and iterative approach. The focus is on delivering the minimum viable product (MVP) that provides the maximum value to the customer. This allows for continuous improvement and elimination of activities that do not contribute to the project's success, helping the BA to stay focused on delivering maximum value within the set constraints.

Thinking from a Customer Perspective: This is a simple principle. You need to just think like a customer. Just the way you would have wanted the solution to your Problem to be if you were the customer.

The Agile approach allows continuous improvement and adaptation to changing customer requirements through regular feedback cycles. The BA must have a customer-focused mindset and prioritise delivering value to meet their needs, continuously refining the solution through iterative development.

By keeping the customer's requirements at the forefront, the BA can ensure that the final solution meets their expectations and delivers maximum value.

What An Agile BA Can Bring to The Table?

The common understanding of an Agile team is that Agile is a self-sufficient team that can do all the required activities as and when required. Every team member is fully capable of and has the mindset to do what is required by wearing required "hats" as and when needed. Yes, that's correct. That's why the role of a BA in an Agile team is often questioned mainly for the "perceived" value a BA can deliver.

For example, a simple question customers ask is, "Why a dedicated BA is required when a Product Owner or a Senior Architect can do the required Business Analysis tasks?"

The question is indeed valid.

In a typical agile setting, developers (or any relevant team member) are encouraged to communicate directly with business users to comprehend their needs rather than heavily relying on BAs for documenting requirements. But, in an Agile team, various roles and skill sets are also required to successfully deliver customer value. One of the crucial roles is having individuals with strong analysis skills to carry out tasks such as discovering requirements, refining them, prioritising, elaborating, and delivering the solution. The title of the person performing these tasks (Whether he/she is a BA or not) is not as important as their ability to effectively analyse and contribute to the project.

So, can the team skip such an important " Analysis " process because it is an Agile team?

This could be a costly mistake.

On the contrary, the important point here to note is that if a BA assumes the conventional role and serves as a mediator between the development team and the users, focusing mainly on requirement documentation and note-taking (while documentation is an important aspect), then this role may not align with the Agile principles. It is also true that in practical scenarios, developers (or any relevant team member) may find it challenging to engage with business users for requirement elicitation, making the BA a valuable resource, particularly for complex requirements that require analysis rather than just documentation.

Hence, a BA is also relevant in an agile setup, but his/her role may not be limited to just being a BA. A BA working in an agile team should possess/cultivate a good agile proficiency to contribute to the project.

Certainly, a BA's roles and responsibilities in an Agile environment could be a little different than those of a traditional environment because the Agile team is a set of people with the mindset of a "Self-sufficient and Self-organising team". In an agile setup, a BA should also gel well with team dynamics, possess the right mindset and deliver value accordingly.

Regarding Agile, it is best to shift from focusing on job titles, like "Business Analyst", and instead consider the responsibilities and tasks required for success. As a BA, you should be aware of this fact. To the external world, you could be a BA. Still, your roles and responsibilities within the project focus on delivering value to the customer and collaboration among all team members, regardless of job title or function. The specific roles and responsibilities may vary from project to project. As a BA, you need to identify and improve your skills and experience, from time to time, for each role in each project—skills/ mindset such as facilitating decision-making, promoting collaboration and communication, and conducting in-depth analysis required to be a part of an agile team.

So, how can a BA bring value to an Agile team?

BAs are often regarded as problem solvers and advocates for delivering customer-centric solutions. They are often responsible for guiding the team in aligning data, systems, business processes, and people to achieve the desired outcome and connecting the organisation's systems and processes to the overall big picture.

This is exactly why the expertise of BAs is valuable to agile teams, who need to be individuals with skills in analysing user needs, defining and measuring solution impact, leading the team in customer-centric thinking, creating product visions and roadmaps, creating backlogs during the beginning of a project, refining backlogs by breaking down the requirements or user stories, prioritisation, elaborating on backlog items, facilitating conversations about project goals and user needs, Conducting and leading the customer demos, planning retrospectives, and leveraging customer/user feedback for continuous improvement. In a nutshell, the presence of a BA can greatly enhance any aspect of the Agile (or Agile-based process) process related to defining and designing work items/requirements or functional scope.

The BAs naturally have that entrepreneurial mindset that helps them resolve issues or problems. They are the real team players; their job is to break the barriers and build the bridge between teams. Their blend of skills spanning across technical, leadership, business, analytical, facilitation, and communication gives them a unique ability anyone else in the team to work effectively across different functions and various customer hierarchies and apply their knowledge and skills in various areas make them valuable assets to any agile team.

A BA's key job is understanding customers, their business, process, data, systems and requirements. Most of the time, in any given agile team, a BA is more skilled in this job than anyone—because that is his/her core skill. He/she is meant for that. Hence, a BA's unique perspective and understanding are valuable for the team. Without this perspective, teams may struggle to deliver solutions that meet the desired speed, relevance, and quality metrics. Hence, a BA can bring the team much-required clarity and focus.

A BA Vs. Product Owner

A common industry practice is that a person who acts as a Project Manager also acts as a Scrum Master, and the BA takes up the role of a Product Owner or vice versa. Ideally, it is a wrong approach. The people who handle such dual roles often struggle with "clash of mindset" issues on the job and lose focus and, thus, productivity. Hence, it is crucial to introduce a BA in the team to collaborate with POs to ensure that the customer's needs are met as the team prioritises and executes work. The role of BAs is to ensure that value is being delivered to the customer.

Though a Product Owner is responsible for the product backlog, he/she is more focused on product planning, release and working with the business for new features or requirements. The BA goes deep into the requirements, performs analysis for any impacts and can answer questions from development teams. This deep knowledge of product features or requirements gives a BA an upper hand. A BA's unique ability to prepare backlog items and work with customers for show & tell sessions or gather feedback makes it even better, as BAs are meant for that. This is essential for the success of a fast-paced, innovative, agile team.

In medium to large projects, a Product Owner alone cannot handle both Product Owner & BA responsibilities and, hence, requires a supporting hand. In my experience, when there is an effective collaboration between a Product Owner and a BA, the project succeeds, and the quality of the deliverables is very high. By collaborating with the Product Owner, the BA can help refine the backlog by focusing on the desired future state.

We discussed "Empathy", or helping mindset earlier. Assuming that every BA possesses such a trait—genuine concern, care, and empathy for customers and their problems—a BA can approach issues and challenges differently from a Product Owner, Project Manager, or Scrum Master. This makes customer engagement more positive. It's the nature of BAs to rise to the challenge and act as the user's voice within the team.

A BA is a business expert. He/she quickly understands the customer's business and proposes solutions for their problems. Usually, they understand the domain—if not fully, at least as much as it is required. The right domain knowledge helps BAs ask the right questions and initiate conversations. The team won't suffer from quality issues when you know and understand every feature/user story. In addition, a BA is typically very skilful in leveraging user-focused concept visuals such as models, Wireframes and charts that can spark discussions, conversations, and creativity among the team and stakeholders. Who else can do this better other than a BA?

As we discussed earlier, A BA is always a big-picture person. He is the one who keeps reminding the team about the vision and mission of a project. This keeps everyone on the same page about the direction of the project/project team. Isn't it the BA a Real Captain?

When working on large projects with globally distributed teams or stakeholders, it is crucial to have a dedicated person leading the effort. It could be a follow-up, a requirement clarification, a resolution of issues between stakeholders, or anything else. A customer-centric BA is the only person who can handle such thankless tasks and situations.

The speed of decision-making is crucial in Agile teams, particularly in a complex technology setting and fast-changing market conditions or requirements. Sometimes, a Product Owner cannot answer the questions from the development team at the level of detail requested by the development team. This will make the decision-making slower, and there may be a possibility of quality issues later on due to any gap that was not addressed.

This is where BAs or Agile BAs can pitch in for a collaboration with the Product Owner—as BAs are the people who provide a bridge between the development/Project team and various stakeholders. Their job is to keep the team informed of changes and ensure they have the right information to make quick decisions.

Hence, it is indeed crucial for any Agile project to have a BA (role names can be different) who can effectively drive the work in an Agile team other than the Product Owner, Scrum Master or Project Manager.

Transition to Agile Way of Working

Until recently, the Waterfall methodology was the widely used Project Management methodology (It is still being used). Since this was the traditional approach, we were used to executing things sequentially, transitioning to Agile, where we deliver things incrementally.

Considering this challenge, various hybrid ways of delivering things are also emerging, combining the best practices of Waterfall and Agile methodologies. However, in this chapter, we will discuss what it takes to be an Agile BA who is sometimes expected to jump from Agile to Waterfall and vice versa, based on project needs in an organisation.

As you already know, Business analysis has evolved over the years, and today, BAs face the challenge of adapting to the changes brought about by agile and traditional methodologies. It's common for BAs to get caught in the crossfire, struggling to balance both methodologies. They may feel like getting smacked back and forth between two different worlds. However, there is a way to reduce frustration and take charge of methodologies.

BAs must focus on what stays the same and different to survive in this changing landscape. Let's take a closer look at what happens when an agile Vs. Waterfall mindsets collide or conflict!

Team structures and operations/procedures are the primary differences between traditional and agile teams. Traditional teams tend to have a defined hierarchy, while agile teams have a flat structure with self-organised teams with loosely defined roles. Also, the agile teams may have different ways of collaborating, reporting progress, and sequencing tasks.

To cope with these differences, BAs need to learn to roll with them. Luckily, these differences do not affect the fundamental work of business analysis. The critical components of good requirements remain the same regardless of methodology. If BAs focus on the three areas mentioned below, they can reduce the frustration of switching between agile and traditional approaches.

Focus on the customer: Customer focus, understanding what is needed by the customer's business and delivering the same is paramount. Agile and traditional approaches demand that requirements should always be viewed from a customer's point of view. Starting requirements conversations with this approach is almost always successful. BAs are responsible for expanding the customer definition to include both internal and external solution users in agile and traditional approaches. They must also creatively address the changing needs of each customer.

Cultivate conversations: Successful BAs in agile and traditional environments use powerful conversations as the focus of their requirements process. Even in traditional/ waterfall approaches, conversations are critical to getting to well-defined requirements. Fostering open communication channels is essential to facilitate productive discussions between stakeholders, BAs, and development teams.

Be adaptable: In agile, the willingness to adapt and learn is key to success. A BA has to deal with new problems daily, and no two businesses or customers will have the same Problem, nor will they want the same solution. A key to achieving a successful outcome for a BA is to have the ability to adapt and change. It's important to remain open-minded and willing to explore new methodologies to find what works best.

Responding to Change: Agile is more about iteratively delivering value, and hence, the window for responding to a change is less, and hence, as an Agile BA, he/she must be able to respond to changes. This could be a little challenging for a BA, who still has the traditional mindset initially. Success for an Agile BA relies on recognising that requirements may change and delivering in short increments to achieve quick wins, mitigate risks, and remain responsive to changing circumstances. This mindset differs from traditional approaches but enables the BA to collaborate more effectively and handle changes more fluidly.

When you are flexible and customer-focused, no methodology can impede you because, as we discussed before, the fundamentals will not change. You just need to gel with the process as required. In addition, as long as you have the right skills, mindset and capability to understand and identify what remains constant and what varies and adjust accordingly, you as a BA will survive and excel.

The Conversations

The traditional mindset of a BA is focused on documentation, managing change through a process (often delayed), and delivering solutions that meet customer needs. While this approach has succeeded in a traditional waterfall environment, it can hold back BAs from being exceptional in an Agile environment.

The Agile BA mindset is centred around conversations rather than documentation. Agile BAs understand that written documentation can lead to misunderstandings and misinterpretations. Instead, they rely on conversations and user stories to convey information and ensure a shared understanding.

User stories are reminders to have conversations as the details are discovered in the conversation, not in the story. Well, that does not mean that Agile does not require documentation. Unlike Waterfall, where everything is documented in advance/before the development starts, in Agile, documentation is just in time and iterative. In Agile, they work in small increments, iterating based on feedback and adapting solutions to meet customer needs. Instead of doing a detailed design upfront, Agile BAs do just enough just in time. They seek feedback and adapt as they go, avoiding wasted effort on detailed analysis and planning that may change as they progress.

Now, let's consider a couple of scenarios. As an agile BA, when a stakeholder wants to add an item to the current Sprint, I would chat face-to-face with them and involve the product owner and iteration leader/scrum master to determine if it's possible to fit it in without impacting other items.

If the developer needs more detail, I would confirm our commitment to iterations and work on ensuring clear acceptance criteria, communicate user needs' intent and value through whiteboard huddles and drawings, and ask if a quick mock-up would help. The key is to prioritise face-to-face conversations over detailed emails or documents.

Have conversations. See what is valuable for the customer and what is feasible for delivery and just deliver it. Essentially, an agile mindset drives changes in behaviour that bring value to the team and improve the quality of solutions. If you think deeply, such conversations are the way to deliver customer value in Agile and Waterfall methodologies.

A few SCRUM Terms /Terminologies

Here are the key Agile/SCRUM Terms /Terminologies. Keep it handy for a quick reference in the future, before your interviews, etc.

- **Theme:** A high-level goal or vision of a product.
- **Epic:** A set /collection of work that can be further broken down into small pieces – User Stories.
- **User Story:** The smallest unit of work. It's the end goal
- **Impediment:** Anything (dependency, etc.) that prevents a team member from getting the task done
- **Bottleneck:** Tasks/Work piled up – Tasks waiting to be worked on by you – becomes a bottleneck for progress
- **Backlog:** A prioritised list of deliverables/Tasks/User Stories /Requirements. Backlog grooming is the process of adding/deleting/reprioritising user stories
- **Burndown Chart:** A Graphical tool giving you a measure of progress
- **Sprint Review** is the meeting that will be held at the end of Sprint to review what has been accomplished
- **Lean:** Best practices to make the process/project efficient and effective by leveraging only what is required
- **Definition of Done:** Criteria for a deliverable to be complete and ready for testing/use (Task Level)
- **Acceptance Criteria:** Conditions that need to be met to declare a requirement has been fulfilled (At a Requirement level)
- **Acceptance Test:** A Testing process by a team of Users (Testing team) to determine whether the delivered items meet Acceptance Criteria or not
- **MVP:** Minimum Viable Product – A usable product delivered with a minimum set of features
- **Product Owner:** Person responsible for defining User Stories and prioritising the backlog
- **Sprint:** A time-boxed period for a scrum team to complete a predefined amount of work. Sprint Planning is the get-together of the team to finalise and prioritise the User stories/tasks for the next Sprint
- **Retrospective:** Meeting at the end of every dev iteration to review what went well, what did not, and how to improve
- **Story Points:** A unit of measure to estimate the overall for a user story (Any piece of work)
- **Stakeholder:** Anyone outside of the project team who has a vested interest in the outcome of the project

- **Task List:** A board depicting a set of tasks with status (To-Do/In-Progress/Done
- **SCRUM Master:** A person who leads, trains, and coaches the organisation in Scrum adoption.
- **A SCRUM team** consists of roles such as Scrum Master, PO, & Dev team
- **Product Vision:** It is the long-term goal of the project or product described in a crisp & clear way.
- **Product backlog:** Collection of functionalities, enhancements, bugs, or requirements to build a product
- **Product increment:** Set of current & previous deliverables that were delivered during sprints
- **Product owner:** Team member who owns/controls the product vision & features to be delivered (in consultation with the Scrum Team)
- **Sprint Vision/Sprint Goal:** A *high-level goal or objective that describes the key outcome for each Sprint*
- **Sprint backlog:** Collection of tasks that require to be developed during a Sprint
- **Sprint Planning:** Collaborate with the Scrum team to plan sprint deliverables.
- **Backlog Refinement:** Organising backlogs to ensure whether it's ready for the next Sprint or iteration.
- **Sprint review:** Demo of a working software to the customer—items developed during the Sprint
- **Sprint retrospective:** Analysis of the sprint performance—what went well and what can be improved in future
- **Burndown chart:** Burndown charts are graphical views of tasks completed throughout a sprint (not an official scrum artefact)
- **Burnup Chart:** Graphical view of tasks the Scrum team has completed in the Sprint.
- Velocity: The rate of progress--indicates the amount of work completed by the team during a Sprint.
- **Scrum master:** Guides/leads the team—leads the scrum meetings, manages impediments, and works with Product Owners (or BA) on backlogs.
- **Daily Scrum:** A daily meeting organised by the Scrum master—max 15 minutes to discuss the previous day and the day ahead
- **Scrum board: A virtual/physical display of tasks that need to be done in a sprint**
- **Scrum team:** Project team (~5 to 10 ppl) with multiple skillsets
- **Definition of Done (DOD):** Set of conditions to call a user story complete

- **Kanban:** Another Framework to help teams. Here, the team works on tasks based on priority. The team caps limit the number of tasks it can deliver in an iteration. The is to get constant work without any bottlenecks/impediments.
- **Kanban board:** A virtual/physical display of tasks within the project with statuses.
- **Continuous Integration (CI):** A practice where the team constantly deploy their code to the production
- **Impediment:** Obstacle that can impact the productivity of a Project team.
- **Refactoring** is cleaning up the code by restructuring the existing code without modifying any new external behaviour.

What Did You Learn in This Chapter?

- How you will manage the mindset conflicts while transitioning to Agile way of working?
- Can a BA be Product Owner as well?
- Can a BA be Scrum Master as well?
- What An Agile BA Can Bring to The Table?
- 12 Agile Principles of Agile Manifesto—Explain a few.
- Who is an Agile BA?
- How to cultivate the Agile Mindset?
- What is an Agile Mindset?
- Why conversations are important rather than documentation?

CHAPTER 16

EXPECTATIONS FROM A NEW AGE BA

- *BA in Product Companies Vs. BA in Service Companies*
- *BA Vs. Consultant & Functional Consultant*
- *BA Vs. Presales Consultant*

By now, you would have clearly understood who a BA is and his/her roles and responsibilities. However, in some markets, the BA job roles could be vague & convoluted. In this new digital era, a BA is expected to do many things in many organisations across the globe.

Therefore, you must establish a clear definition of your identity and purpose. This involves identifying who you are and what you stand for and acknowledging who you are not and what you do not represent. Additionally, it is essential to recognise the potential roles you can undertake beyond your current responsibilities as a BA.

BAs in Product Companies Vs. BAs in Service Companies

Let's understand about two key areas where BA works. Predominantly, a BA works in two broad areas or types of organisations/ companies as below:

1. In IT Service companies (e.g., Accenture, Wipro etc.)
2. Product companies (e.g., Microsoft, Adobe, Salesforce, etc.)

Please note that most of the product companies also have their IT services division (and vice versa), where they provide implementation or other support services to their customers. IT Services are services offered by a company like Wipro to their customers by implementing a Software product per the customer's business needs.

In comparison, Product-based companies develop their products. For example, Microsoft has its Dynamics 365 Product suite. Let's compare the roles of BAs working in IT services Vs. Product companies:

BAs Working in IT Services Companies	BAs Working IT Product Companies
Primarily focus on understanding and analysing client requirements to deliver customized solutions. They work on their Customer Projects. They work on a project-by-project basis and collaborate closely with clients to gather requirements, document specifications, and ensure successful project delivery.	Typically work on developing and improving software products. They are involved in the entire product lifecycle, from conceptualization and market research to defining product features, creating user stories, and prioritizing development efforts.
They are client-oriented. They need to understand the specific needs and goals of each client and tailor their solutions accordingly. They often work on multiple projects simultaneously, serving different clients with unique requirements.	They are product-oriented. They focus on understanding the market, customer needs, and competitive landscape to shape the product roadmap. Their goal is to develop a comprehensive product that meets the needs of a broader customer base.
Frequently engage with clients to elicit and document requirements. They conduct workshops, interviews, and meetings to gather information and convert it into functional and technical specifications. Flexibility and adaptability are essential to accommodate varying client demands.	They also gather requirements, but they often have a more proactive role. They conduct market research, user interviews, and usability tests to understand customer needs and pain points. They work closely with product managers and development teams to translate those insights into clear product requirements.
They need to quickly grasp the specific domain and industry of each client they work with. They must understand the business processes, regulations, and industry-specific challenges to deliver effective solutions.	They need a broader understanding of the market and customer preferences. They focus on market trends, competitor analysis, and user behaviour to ensure the product's success in a competitive landscape.
Often encounter frequent changes in project requirements due to evolving client needs. They must be skilled in change management, adapting to shifting priorities, and ensuring effective communication between clients and development teams.	Work towards maintaining a consistent product vision while incorporating feedback from customers and stakeholders. They play a crucial role in prioritizing feature enhancements and managing the impact of changes on existing functionality.

As you have seen, the table provides a good overview of the contrasting roles of BAs in service-based and product-based IT companies. This will also help you decide on where you want to work. Of course, Money is more in Product-based companies, in general!

Naturally, BAs working in service and product-based IT companies have different roles and responsibilities due to the nature of their respective organisations.

Let's explore a few more scenarios. In Product companies (Let's say, a Food Delivery App Company), if you join as a BA, you may have to take up the role of a Data Analyst, where your primary Job is to play with data analysis and present the findings from the same. It is a kind of data analysis and research role. These roles require good technical skills in Python and SQL and an excellent technical capability to use and design Power BI and other such dashboards. In such cases, coding knowledge may also be required. However, do not fret. You may find a purely functional BA role as well in such companies. You should thoroughly study the Job description before you apply for such positions.

Nowadays, the role of a Data Scientist or Data Analyst is also called a BA, which is incorrect, in my opinion. A BA should also be able to understand and analyse data, but it's not his/her core competency. A BA can utilise the findings/reports a Data Analyst provides to make a business or technology decision in collaboration with his/her stakeholders. The fact is that, while a Business Analytics expert may fulfil the role of a Business Analyst, the vice versa is not always true, as the responsibilities and focus of the positions may vary.

Please note that this book may not be relevant for people in the roles of Data Analysis or doing a job related to dedicated data slicing and dicing. This book is for BAs, who work with stakeholders to elicit requirements and work with the technical team to deliver them, do stakeholder management and scope management, and act as a bridge between the business and technical teams.

So, there is no such BA role in Product companies?

Yes, there are. Usually, in such product companies, there is a specific role called **"Product Manager"**, who usually plays the role of a BA. In addition to BA skills, the product manager role will require additional skillsets that a BA can acquire quickly. There can also be cases where the BA and product Manager roles are performed by different people.

So, what's the exact difference between a BA and a Product Manager? Let's understand it very clearly, as this is also one of the questions that may be asked during interviews.

I have been working for IT services companies, implementing products or building something from scratch as a service as part of a project. Though I have done Business Analysis, Consulting and Project Management, I always felt that product Management" is equally interesting. I even had a chance to work with many product managers and learn from them.

In a nutshell, here is the difference I could figure out between these two roles:

1. BAs will have (most of the time) a service mindset. They offer their services to their customers by working on their projects to develop and implement capabilities by understanding the business needs. Hence, BAs usually act as a bridge between the business (or customers) and the technical teams of a project and ensure the requirements are captured correctly, understood correctly and appropriately implemented as per the business needs. The BA is responsible for functional solutions and will also be part of technical Solution design. The BA Controls/Manages the scope and thus acts as Gatekeeper (for requirements), so only requirements in scope are delivered as per the plan. Example: I have been part of many projects where we implemented Microsoft Dynamics 365 CRM apps as part of a project.

2. Product Managers are focused on developing Products by understanding the market's needs. The mindset of a product manager is slightly different. Though they go and pitch their product to potential customers, they may not be part of any implementations. For them, aspects like product performance in the market, how competition is faring currently, feedback from the market, what new features can be added, etc. matter. Developing and strategising the product roadmap is the core responsibility of a Product Manager (Imagine researching how the latest feature of a Food delivery app is being used by the end users, feedback and gathering data about the same with the help of Data analysts – A crucial responsibility of a Product Manager is highlighted here.). Usually, Product managers are also responsible for positioning a product in the market; hence, they closely work with their Sales and Marketing teams. They work with internal and external stakeholders to guarantee that the product delivers the value promised to its end users.

3. As discussed earlier, in a Product development setup, BAs work with Product Managers and Development Teams to develop a Product. These BAs do the same activities as mentioned in #1. Sometimes, the BA and Product Manager are the same person.

There are some similarities between a BA & a Product Manager, so skills are transferrable. Product managers, too, are sometimes responsible for Requirements management (mostly received from the market as feedback or as part of product roadmap and future strategy) like BA—this may happen when a Product Manager & BA are the same person. Interestingly, the skill sets are pretty similar regarding strategic thinking and communication. Ultimately, whether a BA or a Product Manager, they should first address the 'customer problem'. A Product or a Project must solve the 'customer problem'; otherwise, the entire endeavour will fail.

In Service companies (e.g., Infosys, Wipro, etc.), the role of BA is slightly different than BAs working in Product companies. Here, BAs are people-centric and working in a Service setup should be well-versed with people skills.

As we discussed so far in this book, a BA in service setup is the person who will gather requirements, work with the business and his/her technical teams to deliver those requirements and also act as a bridge between business and technical teams.

BA Vs. Consultant

Consulting and BA jobs also have overlapping responsibilities. Being a consultant is an additional skill. If you have expertise in certain Products (Say, Microsoft Dynamics or Salesforce or SAP, etc.) in addition to your BA skills, you can become a Consultant and a BA.

You can also become a Functional Consultant for that particular product (we will learn about that in the subsequent section).

If you can handle technicalities involving that product (customisation, extension of such products based on customer needs), you can also become a Technical Consultant + BA or Techno-Functional BA.

Now, let's learn the difference between the two Job Roles—Business Analyst Vs. Consultant. Long back, I was asked by an interviewer as well – can you differentiate between Consulting and Business Analysis?

Here is what I could figure out:

1. As we know already, a BA will analyze the problem → if required analyze the current state & Future state analysis →Work with customer to elicit requirements → Understand the Requirements → Work with internal technical teams → Suggest a best possible functional solution → Control/Manage the scope → Thus acts as Gatekeeper (for requirements) so that only scoped requirements are delivered (as much as possible!!).

2. However, Consultant is one level above. He/She may not work for a project. He may be an influencer for a project that may begin in future. When a customer has an issue in certain area and customers are not sure about what to do – that's where consultant (Management Consultant) comes into the picture. His audience mostly also involves C-level execs. In a nutshell, a consultant will listen to the problem → Analyses the problems using various tools and data to suggest a process improvement, if required→ Suggests process improvement→ May not suggest a product/technology for that improvement → But suggests an overall measure to overcome the problem and hence improve the overall business performance leading to an improvement in bottom line.

Although BA and Consultant may seem similar in function and responsibility, they are distinct professions. I believe, skill-wise, there is an overlap– typically, a BA is more of a technical/ product expert, while a consultant is more of an industry/ financial/ process expert. A single person can also perform these roles, provided the person has the required expertise, as mentioned above. Again, BA skills are transferrable/ interchangeable to excel in the field of Consulting as well, and vice versa is also true.

BA Vs. Functional/Techno-Functional Consultant

Which Job is better? A BA or Functional Consultant (FC) (or Techno-Functional)? I received this question from a couple of people in recent times. I have answered this query to many career aspirants in these areas (BA or FC). Though the skillsets required to perform these two job roles overlap, some differences exist.

Who is a BA? Let's ask this question again.

- A BA elicits, documents, validates, and manages business and stakeholder requirements.
- A BA comes up with relevant solutions to business problems.

- A BA Interacts regularly with business stakeholders as part of stakeholder management w.r.t managing requirements, scope, change requests etc.
- A BA is a technology agnostic – he/she can work on any project; for him/her, analysing business problems, capturing requirements, proposing solutions, and fulfilling requirements become the key focus.

Who is a FC?

- An FC works with BA to understand requirements. Sometimes, both BA & FC can be the same person!
- An FC and BA decide on a relevant solution to the business problems.
- An FC also interacts regularly with business stakeholders, BA w.r.t design, and other solution-related aspects.
- An FC is technology-specific—this is where the key difference comes in.
- The advent of software products in many areas (like CRM, ERP and much more) has given rise to many such product implementation projects. There are many products in the market in these areas, such as SAP, Oracle, Dynamics 365, etc., in the ERP area, and Microsoft Dynamics 365 CE, Pega CRM, Salesforce, etc., in the CRM area. An FC is a person who has great expertise in any of these products or multiple products. Ex: While a BA, I am also an expert Dynamics 365 CE Functional Consultant.
- As an FC, one needs to understand the requirements and analyse how those requirements can be implemented using the product he/she is an expert on. The key skill of an FC is to map requirements to the capabilities of the product being implemented.
- A BA is a Business Problem solver, and an FC is an SME of a software product. anA FC may be an expert in that technology in complex developmental projects.
- An FC may not be a technical person, but he/she knows how a product can be configured/customised/extended to fulfil requirements.

So, which role is better? As a BA, your marketability is higher as your skills can be usable in any project. As an FC for a specific product, your marketability becomes limited—but no harm if you want to be in a niche.

Suppose you have a BA skill, experience, and expertise in any of the hottest products in the market (e.g., Dynamics 365 CE or ERP, Salesforce CRM,

Pega, etc.); your marketability further increases, and it will help you do the Job better. In that case, you may become BA & FC for a project.

Here is My take: These (BA and FC) roles can be performed by a single person, provided the person has the required expertise mentioned above. Again, BA skills are transferrable/ interchangeable to excel in the field of Consulting as well and vice versa.

If you are an expert BA, gain expertise on any of the hottest products/skills in the market. If you are just an FC right now, gain some BA knowledge and experience—you don't have to struggle much, as your current skills are transferrable.

A BA Vs. Presales Consultant

When a BA is also an expert in some area or a product, a BA is expected to contribute to Presales-related activities as well. Though BAs and presales consultants are essential in any business organization, and both positions work closely with clients and stakeholders, their responsibilities, skill sets, and end goals differ.

We already know the roles and responsibilities of a BA. In contrast, a Presales Consultant is responsible for helping clients understand the value and benefits of a company's products or services. A Presales consultant helps the sales team to sell the products or services by understanding the potential customer's requirements, pain points, business challenges at a high level and, recommends a possible solution for the same and estimates the efforts required to deliver the same, in collaboration with the technical team.

The presales consultants also work with sales teams and clients to develop estimates and costs for the potential solutions that meet their needs and are feasible within their budget constraints. They provide technical support and expertise during the sales process, answering client questions and helping them understand how the product or service will help them achieve their goals.

While both roles require strong communication skills, the focus of their communication is different. BAs communicate with internal stakeholders, such as managers and executives, within a project to understand the organization's goals and priorities. They also communicate with external stakeholders, such as customers, within a project governance structure to understand their needs and identify areas of improvement.

The presales consultants communicate with clients to understand their needs and goals and provide technical expertise, helping them make informed decisions. They collaborate with sales teams to uncover prospects' needs and provide customized solutions.

In terms of skills, BAs require expertise in high-level data analysis, problem-solving, and project management. They must translate business needs into technical requirements and communicate effectively with stakeholders. Pre-sales Consultants require strong technical skills, product knowledge, and excellent communication and presentation skills.

A single person can sometimes perform both roles, provided the person has the required expertise and bandwidth. Again, BA skills are transferrable/interchangeable to excel in the field of Presales Consulting as well. However, the vice versa is not valid. A Presales consultant needs to upskill his expertise to become a BA.

BA Vs. Project Manager

As the IT world is leaning towards "Lean", organizations are experimenting with combining roles. For example, nowadays, a Lead Developer is also handling the tasks of a Senior Architect. BAs are doing Project Management activities as well. Fortunately, or unfortunately, the roles and responsibilities between such crucial roles are becoming very slim these days. Do you agree?

Let's list the responsibilities of each role at a high level: BA Vs. Project Manager. Let's understand/recall the basics first.

What does a Project Manager do?

- The role of a Project Manager entails overseeing the entirety of a project.
- A Project Manager creates a Schedule, Plan, Risks and constraints.
- A Project Manager takes ownership of the project issues to resolve them.
- Resource management is one of the primary responsibilities of a Project Manager.
- A Project Manager also manages scope, quality, budget, and time. They are the customer's primary contact for any issues/concerns.

As you can see above, the key strengths of a Project Manager are to deliver the project within the budget and timeline—Responsibilities include:

- Getting the work done by the team.
- Taking care of the team at the same time.
- Managing the customer—He/she owns the project.

The BA's strengths are his/her skill of understanding "what" is to be delivered per the business need & organization's vision. In a nutshell, the BA owns the Scope and the Solution. So, both roles have their sufficient share of work, though there are some overlaps. Can these two roles be combined? Can one become BAPM?

Well, in some cases, where the project is small, the risk is not significant, the budget is less, and there are no multiple teams to deal with—things are straightforward, and if it's just a plain vanilla implementation of business apps (Ex: Dynamics 365, Salesforce etc.) kind of scenario, combining the roles may be possible, provided the person who will be taking charge is well experienced and skilled to handle both the roles.

However, if we think deeper, it is risky. The Project Manager and BA are two different mindsets. Can a single mind handle two mindsets? The Project Manager's mind always says, "finish it off fast"; the BA mind says, "deliver it correctly". It's the conflict of mindsets within a mind!

Remember, the Project Manager and BA partnership always works, not the conflicts. This will require a whole different mindset. This is the one question you should ask yourself.

BA As a Trainer and Change Enabler

Typically, in a project set up within IT services organizations, a BA is also expected to play the role of a Trainer and serve as an enabler of change management. Though a BA is not entirely responsible for the Change Management aspects, because he/she is the person who knows the Project vision and owns requirements and plays an instrumental role in implementing and making it successful, he/she is considered a "Change Enabler" who collaborates with Change Management team.

As a Trainer, a BA's role involves preparing and implementing training strategies to facilitate the adoption of new systems and processes. This requires him/her to work closely with stakeholders to identify user needs and develop a comprehensive instructor-led classroom training material package.

Please remember that the BA trains the users to use the system. The Change Management team ensures the users use the system by conducting various change management activities. Hence, both BA and the change management team collaborate very profoundly.

To prepare for change, the BA works with the Change Management team to propose a change management strategy that involves forming committees and educating users about the new system's benefits. Managing change requires involving users and leadership/ evangelists who can influence users. A BA is also instrumental in feeding information about the benefits and purpose of the project to the Change Management team.

One of the biggest challenges in implementing a new system or process is resistance to change. To overcome this challenge, the Change Management teams, in collaboration with the BA, use various strategies, including conducting a visioning exercise with the team to help employees visualize how their work life will be positively impacted if they use the new system compared to the existing one. This exercise helps employees understand the new system's benefits and how it will make their work easier and more efficient.

Another important strategy for increasing user adoption is effectively communicating the new system's benefits to users, where the BA can play the lead role. This involves creating buy-in and maintaining users' enthusiasm throughout the implementation process.
A BA does this by conducting workshops, such as visioning exercises, that help employees understand the new system's benefits and how it will make their work more efficient and effective.

What BAs Are Not?

Though a BA has a kind of "Universal" skillset, there has also been a trend where organizations create positions labelled "BA" and use the role as a catch-all for tasks to keep costs down. Even if you have accepted that job, it may not work for you in the long term. Hence, you should know what a BA is NOT in the first place.

BAs are not testers: While part of their job is to create clear business requirements and functional specifications, test cases, and use scripts, they should not be completely managing the testing process. Dedicated testers are better suited for tasks like documenting testing methodology, scheduling equipment and resources, and configuring automation software. BAs can review test cases, but their focus should be addressing process issues found during testing.

BAs are not coders/developers: Although BAs may possess technical knowledge, such as knowledge about data architecture, network design, and programming methodologies, their focus should be on factors like Business needs, requirements, scope, solutions and more. On the other hand, developers are expected to code and develop the systems as per requirements. These two roles require distinct mindsets and must be kept separate.

BAs are not Support Executives: BAs often serve as the primary customer-facing team members, especially during the early stages of a project. While it's great to establish comfort and familiarity with customers during requirements elicitation, it's crucial to transition customers to the proper customer support personnel once the software is in production. Failure to do so will prevent the BA from moving on to the next project and inhibit customer service from taking ownership of ongoing support.

BAs are not Project Managers: A well-balanced project team should have separate individuals for each role—BA and Project Manager. Technical and business teams have different priorities that often conflict, and each team needs an advocate. The PM is responsible for keeping everyone on task, tracking the budget, updating the schedule, and managing risk. Whereas BAs manage the Business needs, requirements, scope, solutions and more. While BA and PM should work closely together, success is more likely when responsibilities are divided.

While companies may expect BAs to handle technical or PM aspects in smaller projects, fulfilling both roles is challenging. It's best to focus on being a specialized BA and work collaboratively with other team members.

Though BAs are not Project Managers, the current IT Job market expects people who can do both. Especially in small to medium Business app implementation Projects (Like implementation of Software Products rather than pure development projects), companies expect a BA to handle Technical or Project Management aspects too (Architect role or Project Manager role) so that the BA can be either Tech BA or BAPM. I have personally done that for some time, only to realize one should not do a BA and PM role together.

However, to be honest, this challenging stint gave me excellent and fast learnings and experience about the PM role. So, have you been the victim of organizations that use your role as a catch-all for tasks to keep costs down?

I have an honest tip for you. If possible, use such opportunities (as described above – using BA for a catch-all tasks) opportunity to learn new skills. It will help you somewhere in future. You always have the power to choose, no matter where you find yourself, and you must take responsibility for that choice. You can remain and give your best effort to the task at hand, and in due time, you can gradually increase your responsibilities and progress towards a BA. Otherwise, naturally, you can transition to a different role in a new department or company that offers more tremendous potential and opportunities.

Top 12 Project Management terms a BA Should Know
1. **Milestone:** A key event/achievement that signifies the completion of an important phase/goal 2. **Work Plan**: A detailed outline of the steps and tasks that need to be completed in order to achieve a specific goal or set of goals. 3. **Baseline:** A baseline refers to the initial plan that outlines the project's scope, cost, and timeline. 4. **Triple Constraint**: 3 constraints of a Project – cost, time, and scope. This helps project managers understand the impact that changes to one constraint can have on the other two. 5. **Project Life Cycle**: The project life cycle is the series of phases that a project goes through from its inception to its completion. Includes planning, Analysis, Design, Implementation. 6. **Risk Management**: The four strategies a organization can use to manage risk— Accept, Avoid, Optimize and Transfer 7. **Residual Risk:** It is the risk that remains after risk management activities have been completed. 8. **Critical Path Method (CPM):** Technique used to identify the tasks that are critical to the completion of a project and to determine the minimum amount of time needed to complete the project. **9. Planned Value (PV), Earned Value (EV), Actual Cost (AC):** → PV→ Refers to the budgeted cost for completing a task within a specific period. → EV→ Value of actual completed work → AC→ Actual Cost incurred to complete the work 10. **Contingency plan:** Commonly known as Plan B. It is a backup plan that is implemented when the primary plan does not go as expected. 11. **Fast tracking:** Technique used to analyse the project schedule to identify opportunities to adjust the project plan and accelerate the timeline. Perhaps, introduce some parallel activities, adding new resources etc. 12. **Feasibility Study:** A process used to determine the practicality of a proposed plan or methodology in achieving the goals of a project.

Is Solution Design the Responsibility of A BA?

Many think that the job of a BA is to gather requirements and pass them on to the development team. In many projects, once requirements gathering is over, the role of a BA gets removed as his or her job is over. The BA's real job starts after that, in my opinion.

Remember: A BA's job is to ensure that requirements meet stakeholders' business objectives and that real value is delivered. Hence, a BA has many responsibilities other than gathering requirements, and one such responsibility is "assessing" the solution that is being proposed! Yes, don't be surprised. It is your responsibility as a BA!

According to the BABOK, the responsibility of "assessing" and helping design the solution lies with the BA, not just the technical teams or developers. The task of "assessing" proposed solutions involves critically evaluating ideas and determining how well the solutions meet stakeholder requirements and deliver real value—the core responsibility of a BA.

Generally, the BA may not own the delivery of solutions (But will be part of it). However, the BA's role in designing the solution is critical to the project's success. They must take ownership of "assessing" proposed solutions and provide their input in designing the solution to meet stakeholder requirements. In addition, the BA must consider timelines, resources, and risks and ensure they align with the project's business objectives in collaboration with the PM.

It is critical for a BA to make sure how the solution is being designed and how it will affect his/ her stakeholders. That's where the BA will add value. The technical team and developers will focus more on how the system will work technically and efficiently. Still, the BA needs to be more focused on how his/her stakeholders (customers or users) will receive the solution because, ultimately, stakeholders are the people who will use the solution. Also, the participation of BA in solution design helps to avoid potential incorrect solution design due to incorrect understanding of requirements by technical teams.

Hence, whether the technical solution is simple or complex, the BA may need to schedule several brainstorming or whiteboard sessions or meetings to identify and assess several potential solutions, playing the role of a facilitator or custodian and bringing all the required team members together. Such sessions may involve elicitation, analysis, verification, and validation to ensure feasible requirements. Again, the key for a BA is to ensure that proposed solutions meet stakeholder requirements and make them happy, keeping developers/technical teams, PMs, and QA engineers focused on meeting stakeholder requirements.

What Did You Learn in This Chapter?

- Is Solution Design the Responsibility of A BA?
- Who are the BAs & Consultants?
- How do BAs differ from Functional/Techno-Functional Consultants?
- Explain the differences in responsibilities of BAs Vs. Presales Consultants?
- What are the differences in responsibilities of BAs Vs. Project Manager?
- What BAs Are Not?
- Why BAs need to collaborate with Change Management team?
- Why BA is called as Change Enabler?

CHAPTER 17

A DAY IN A LIFE OF A BA

- *Typical Routines of a BA*
- *Typical Day-to-Day Responsibilities Of A BA*

As you may already know, as a BA, each day is unique and brings new challenges. The role involves utilising technical, analytical, and interpersonal skills to connect business objectives with technology solutions.

In this chapter, let's explore what a typical day looks like in the life of a BA. Again, this is to give you a glimpse. The situations in your work/project may be completely different. However, overall, typical tasks will be similar.

A Day in The Life of A BA

Early Morning Routine: Most BAs begin their day with a routine checking/responding of emails, calendar, and prioritisation of tasks. They take this time to plan their day and focus on the high-priority items that require attention. This could involve meeting stakeholders, collaborating with team members, or reviewing data.

Workshops & Requirement Elicitation: Another essential aspect of the BA's role is gathering technology solutions requirements. This could involve conducting workshops, interviews, or stakeholder surveys to collect information. They may also use techniques such as user stories, use cases, or process flows to document requirements and ensure that they align with business objectives.

As we learned earlier, a BA will be planning for Requirements sessions, writing/re-writing requirements, prioritisations, Sprint plannings, meeting stakeholders for clarifications, planning and participating in demos and more.

Data Analysis: BAs analyse data and provide insights to support business decisions. This could involve reviewing data sets, creating reports, and presenting findings to stakeholders.

Please understand that not all the BAs do the data analysis. Data Analysis might be applicable for BAs in a typical data analytics role or who are already working on a Project involving Product development where data analysis is also a crucial part of a BA's responsibility. They may also use Excel, SQL, or any other data visualisation software tools to manipulate and present data.

Collaboration with Developers: BAs work closely with developers to ensure technology solutions meet business requirements. This could involve collaborating on technology solutions' design, development, testing, and implementation. Collaboration is crucial for delivering solutions on time, within budget, and meeting quality standards.

Product Demos and Testing: As a BA, the role in demo and testing depends on the organisation's process and methodology. Generally, BAs are the key people who are involved in planning & participating in demos and testing along with development and testing teams.

The BA may be responsible for demonstrating the features of a product to the stakeholders or end-users in collaboration with development teams. This can involve creating demo scripts and scenarios, coordinating with the development team, and presenting the product features to stakeholders.

The BA is typically responsible for identifying test scenarios and cases for the product. Though, most of the time, a BA will not be creating the test cases/or scenarios, his input and strict review will be necessary so that he/she can ensure that the testing is in alignment with the requirements. This involves collaborating with testing and development teams to ensure the product meets requirements.

The BA can also assist in user acceptance testing, ensuring the end-users are satisfied with the product. Overall, the role of the BA in demo and testing is to ensure that the product meets the requirements and specifications while also ensuring that stakeholders and end-users are satisfied with the product.

End-of-Day Wrap-Up: At the end of the day, BAs typically take some time to review their progress, update their task list and prepare for the following day. This could involve preparing reports, updating project plans, documenting requirements, sending meeting minutes, updating user stories and more. They also take this time to reflect on their performance, identify areas for improvement, and plan for professional development.

Onshore-offshore Setup: The BAs working in onshore-offshore setup (Typically in IT services companies) will have to adopt a slightly different strategy to manage their day to accommodate time zone differences.

Typically, the BAs need to work with developers in an offshore location or vice versa.

Hence, sometimes, BAs in onshore locations may have to begin their days early so that they can catch up with their counterparts in an offshore location – that is, if a BA in the US has to catch up with developers located in India, the BA might have to start his/her day as early as 6 am, which will be late evening in India. Or the BA might have to stay back late at night so that he/she can connect with his/her offshore colleagues in the mornings.

Hence, a typical day in the life of a BA involves a combination of stakeholder communication, data analysis, requirement workshops/ elicitations, and collaboration with developers, management, and stakeholders.

As mentioned in previous chapters, this role demands technical, analytical, and interpersonal skills and the ability to work independently or as part of a team. Each obstacle presents an opportunity to gain knowledge, develop, and make a positive impact.

Here is what a day in the life of a BA looks like, pictorially: In the subsequent tables shown in the chapter, I listed out typical tasks performed a by a BA in a day. Tasks & timings may vary from person to person.

First Half of The Day: From 9 AM To 12 PM

Time	Morning	Noon/Afternoon	Evening	Late Evenings
9 AM **(For an Onsite BA, the day may begin as early as 6 AM local time)**	▪ Status Call /Daily Scrum Meeting with PO/Customer Stakeholders for Status updates			
10 PM	▪ Send Minutes of Meetings ▪ Check Emails and respond ▪ Plan action items based on outcome of the meeting ▪ Look into any pending tasks /review and provide feedback			
11 AM	▪ Coffee Break ▪ Attend Requirements Sessions ▪ Backlog Refinement & Updates			

First Half of The Day: From 12 PM To 2 PM

Time	Morning	Noon/Afternoon	Evening	Late Evenings
12 PM		▪ Clarification Sessions with Customers ▪ Sessions with Development Team		
1 PM		**Lunch Break**		

Second Half of The Day: From 2 PM To 4 PM

Time	Morning	Noon/Afternoon	Evening	Late Evenings
2 PM		• Send Minutes of Meetings • Complete the User Story /Requirements Writing based on morning meetings • Updating the User stories/Requirements • User Story Estimations		
3 PM			▪ Meetings with Testing Team ▪ Meeting with Customer IT teams ▪ Meeting with Pos/Customer Stakeholders ▪ Check Emails and respond	

Second Half of The Day: From 4 PM To 6 PM

Time	Morning	Noon/Afternoon	Evening	Late Evenings
4 PM				▪ Coffee Break ▪ Sprint Planning (Not a daily activity) ▪ Retrospectives (Not a daily activity) ▪ Demos & Testing Sessions ▪ User Trainings (Not a Daily activity) ▪ Prepare Weekly Reports
5 PM				▪ Planning for the next day workshops ▪ Send Meeting Invites ▪ Finish off any documentation including BRD, SRS, UAT release notes, Go-Live release notes and more. ▪ Self-study, Self-skill enhancement activities, if any

Second Half of The Day: From 6 PM onwards

Time	Morning	Noon/Afternoon	Evening	Late Evenings
6 PM				▪ Weekly Status meetings with internal Team ▪ Weekly Status meetings with Customers ▪ Wrap-up
7 PM – 9PM				▪ Calls with Onsite/offshore Team as required ▪ Wrap-up [**Note:** These meetings sometimes go until late night. Accordingly you need plan your working schedule]

Typical Tasks of A BA In a Real-Life Setup

A BA with around **4+ years** of experience in a Product company will have below daily tasks and he/she may use below tools – a typical scenario.

While this list outlines common tasks, it's important to note that the specific responsibilities of a BA can vary depending on the organization, project, and industry.

However, these tasks provide a broad overview of what a BA with several years of experience in a product company might encounter in their daily work.

Daily Tasks	Tools
To-do Lists	Excel Sheets, Word Docs, Power Points
Daily SCRUM/Status Meetings	
Market Analysis / Research	
Daily Reports Preparation	
Attend Meetings & Documentation (Requirements, Retros etc)	Lucid Chart, Visio, Draw.io, Miro Mind Mapping tool etc
Send Minutes of Meetings	
Bugs Analysis/Resolution/	JIRA, Azure DevOps/QA Tools
User Trainings	Teams, Zoom, In-Person
IntegratonTesting (API testing etc)	Postman

A BA with around **6+ years** of Experience in a Service company working for a Banking Customer will have below daily tasks and he/she may use below tools – a typical scenario.

Daily Tasks	Tools
To-do Lists	Excel Sheets, Word Docs, Power Points
Daily SCRUM/Status Meetings	
Requirements Sessions, Workshops	
Requirements Backlogs, Prioritisations, Conduct Impact Analysis	
Attend Meetings & Documentation (Requirements, Retros etc)	Lucid Chart, Visio, Draw.io, Miro Mind Mapping tool etc
Finish off any documentation including BRD, SRS, UAT release notes, Go-Live release notes and more.	
Bugs Analysis/Resolution/L1 support and analysis	JIRA/QA Tools/Azure DevOps
User Trainings	Teams, Zoom, In-Person
Technical Testing (API testing etc)	Postman
Weekly Report Preparation	
Data Analysis (Optional)	SQL etc.
Skill Enhancement	

Do You Believe That a Reading Habit Is Required for A BA?

A reading habit is a skill and a practice that can significantly impact a BA's career. BAs are responsible for collecting and analysing data to provide insights that assist organisations in making better decisions. In today's fast-paced business environment, business analysts must keep themselves informed on the latest trends and advancements within their industry. Reading is one of the most effective methods of staying informed and current.

There are numerous advantages to reading for BAs. Reading helps broaden their knowledge base, allowing them to analyse and interpret data more effectively. By reading widely and diversely, BAs can develop a more extensive perspective on various topics, assisting them in coming up with innovative solutions. They can also learn from the experiences of other analysts and industry leaders, avoiding common mistakes and pitfalls.

Additionally, reading can improve a BA's critical thinking abilities. They must analyse complex information and identify patterns and trends that can assist organisations in making better decisions. Reading helps in the development of critical thinking, the evaluation of information, and the making of sound judgments. This can significantly impact a BA's career as they become more effective in their roles.

Reading can also assist business analysts in improving their communication skills, which are crucial in their work. BAs must communicate complex information to stakeholders and team members clearly and concisely. By reading, BAs can learn how to communicate effectively, using the appropriate language and tone and ensuring their message is well understood. Individuals can learn to tailor their communication style for various audiences, including executives, team members, and clients.

Finally, reading can help BAs stay motivated and engaged in their work. By reading about industry trends and innovations, they can remain enthusiastic and passionate about their work, resulting in better performance and increased job satisfaction. Hence, reading is crucial for BAs to develop critical thinking skills essential for sound judgments. Reading enables understanding of complex information, as well as to identify and solve problems. By reading widely and diversely, one can develop a broader perspective on various issues, which helps them to come up with innovative solutions.

For BAs, reading comprehension is a crucial skill that allows individuals to understand and interpret written material effectively. It involves identifying key ideas, drawing inferences, and making connections between different pieces of information. Developing this skill can help individuals to read more efficiently and retain more information.

Just like we used to do in our college days, a BA must possess a "reading skill," which can be called "Attentive Reading", which involves engaging with the material actively, asking/ answering questions, and taking notes. Active reading can help individuals retain more information and better understand the material.

However, if a person has issues with reading due to health reasons or any other reasons beyond his/her control, obviously, the latest technologies and digital mediums help, as suitable for their needs. Nowadays, people use technology to read – audiobooks, dictators to transcribe and more. While in the meetings, people use recorders to record the discussion and later transcribe it or write it. The evolution of AI has made writing easier for BAs nowadays. As a BA, you should never forget the habit of reading as it has its benefits. Don't ever think that reading is outdated. It is a must for a BA, in fact, for everyone in the knowledge industry.

Remember, to write 100 words, you must read 10000 words or more.

What Did You Learn in This Chapter?

- ✪ As a BA how you spend your typical working day?
- ✪ As a BA what are your tasks in your typical working day?
- ✪ Do You Believe That a Reading Habit Is Required for A BA?

CHAPTER 18

DEVOPS FOR A BA

- *What Is Devops?*
- *Responsibilities Of BA in a Devops Setup*
- *My Experience with Using a Devops Tool*

DevOps allows companies to deliver high-quality products that meet customers' needs on time while eliminating waste, most of the time. The concept of DevOps mainly came into existence by keeping the Agile way of working in mind.

DevOps brings customer feedback to the forefront, ensuring quality from the beginning. In a DevOps environment, the BA's role is as important in ensuring successful releases.

The cloud dominates everything, and cloud technology is currently in high demand. As more organizations start to adopt cloud-based applications, the frequency of "change" is increasing.

In this fast-changing world, technical systems and applications also need to adopt a continuous process of changing the applications as per business needs or customer requirements. This is happening more frequently than ever.

Hence, the delivery process needs to be streamlined to deliver such frequent changes and maintain the quality of delivery and the product. This is where DevOps comes into the picture, and this is the purpose of the DevOps methodology.

What is DevOps?

DevOps (Derived from "development" and "operations") describes a type of agile relationship between Development and IT Operations/Support activities. DevOps is a way of developing software where the people who make it and those who run it work together to make it faster and better. It's like a team that uses teamwork and technology to make software that is always improving.

The diagram shows a continuous loop that goes around six steps: Plan, Build, Integration, Deploy, Operations, and Continuous feedback.

However, to achieve success using DevOps, all the team members, including BAs, should be aligned, and of course, it requires a great level of adaptability from all of them.

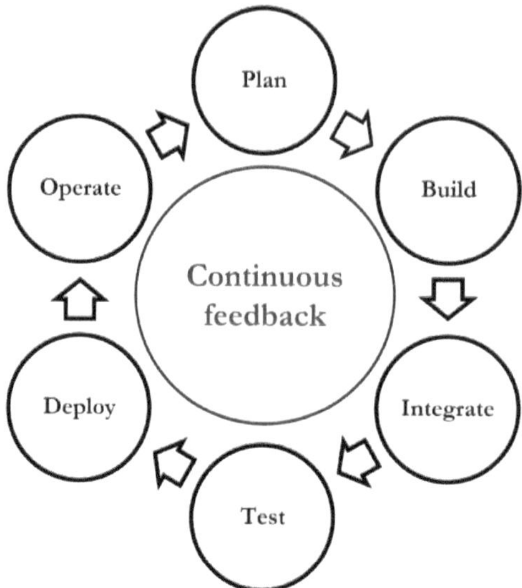

Responsibilities of a BA in DevOps

What is the role of a BA in this scenario or in DevOps based Project? Nothing different.

The role of a BA remains the same, regardless of whether in your project leverages the DevOps concepts and tools or not.

Here too, the typical role of a BA is to keep the communication and collaboration ON. Like in any projects, BAs here too expected to do all the required activities. In the discovery phase, the BA resumes their usual tasks such as defining scope, analysing requirements, and designing solutions while collaborating with various teams.

As we understood in the previous chapters, the BA also needs to have a wide variety of Agile project skills such as Kanban, Scrum, and technological knowledge. They need to have a basic understanding of DevOps (tech fundamentals) and the ability to write requirement artifacts using techniques such as user story map, epics, user stories, backlog management, and acceptance criteria. The BA needs to ensure that acceptance criteria are well-defined, and also need to track traceability and dependencies despite constant flux.

During the Development and Implementation stage, the BA needs to pay specific attention to maintaining and monitoring requirements. They need to ensure continuous feedback not only from the management but also from the implementation teams. Active participation in testing and UAT is also necessary.

In a DevOps project, typically, the BA's involvement starts from the initial or transformation phase where they contribute in various tasks such as providing inputs in building the DevOps transformation roadmap, providing inputs to planning stages, building process models for transformation phases.

A BA plays a critical role in setting up a DevOps process and lifecycle in collaboration with technical teams. Hence, a knowledge of configuring and DevOps based on the Project needs is advisable.

My Experience with Using DevOps Tool

As a Dynamics 365 consultant and BA, I have used various DevOps tools (sometimes called Work management tools), including AzureDevOps and others (e.g., Jira). I've been primarily utilizing Azure DevOps since its inception, and our focus in this section will revolve around the features and advantages it offers for work and requirements management.

Hence, I will share my experience and best practices of using Azure DevOps in this section. Certainly, these best practices will be useful and adaptable to any DevOps tools you use in your Project. We will delve mostly into requirements management only in this section.

It's important to note that there is no one-size-fits-all approach to managing requirements in DevOps. Each client and Project are unique, with different levels of understanding and cultural differences. You must adapt and choose the best practices that suit your Project and client's needs.

The Traditional Approach: One common method for managing requirements is using Excel spreadsheets, which I have used. I don't recommend using Excel nowadays to manage requirements unless you are compelled to use it due to budget reasons.

A few years back, I started working with a customer. We opened an Excel spreadsheet containing their requirements during a meeting with the product owner. However, due to its size and complex formatting, the spreadsheet took a long time to open and froze. When opened, for some reason, the data were missing. There are options to upload Excel sheets in SharePoint for collaboration; however, sometimes, people with higher privileges (Access) and open documents from the PC can delete the document unintentionally. Collaborating with multiple users using an Excel sheet is always cumbersome, even though it is efficient. Hence, if you have a dedicated tool for the purpose, as a BA, you should leverage it and always suggest customers use it if they are unaware.

Azure DevOps is a web application that allows you to subscribe to it from Azure and create projects. As per Microsoft, "Azure DevOps offers a comprehensive suite of services and tools designed to facilitate the seamless management of software projects, spanning from initial planning and development all the way to rigorous testing and successful deployment."

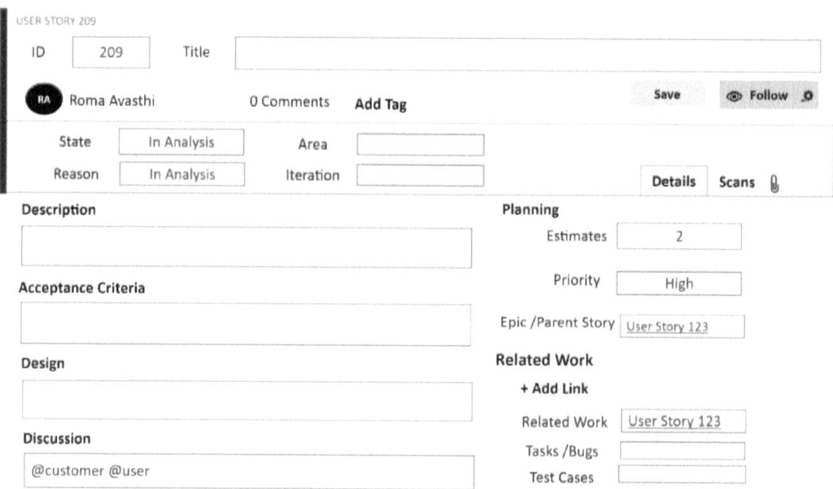

Within Azure DevOps, the Azure Boards are a central place to manage requirements. Azure Boards offer a versatile and tailored toolkit designed to empower software development teams in project management. Its extensive functionalities include seamless integration with Agile, Scrum, and Kanban methodologies, calendar-based perspectives, customizable dashboards, and integrated reporting capabilities.

The backlog, accessible through the board, is where you can structure and organize your requirements. It offers features for writing detailed requirements, collaborating, and tracking progress. We have seen a wireframe of a typical Azure DevOps board in one of the earlier chapters (as below)–the screen to capture a user story.

Structuring requirements: Depending on whether you start with no requirements or have an existing list, there are different approaches. If you start with no requirements, you can begin by identifying high-level business processes that must be addressed. For example, suppose the project involves requirements to develop a Loyalty management system for a retail company. In that case, the typical set of business processes may include Inquiry submission, Loyalty points management and Redemption processes. By decomposing these processes, you can refine and prioritize the requirements. You can then have these requirements in Azure DevOps, organizing them into epics, features, user stories, tasks and more. If you have existing requirements, you will need to map them to the Azure DevOps structure. The categorization used by the client can be used as epics, while groups of user stories can be treated as features. This way, you can work on related stories together for improved productivity.

Managing ever-evolving Requirements: Capturing requirements is an essential step in any project; however, in Agile development, where the requirements constantly evolve, the process requires a more dedicated approach. Any missed information in between can pose a delivery risk. Hence, it is essential to have a clear, "shared" understanding of requirements and the know-how to structure and capture requirements to ensure the project is successful.

Always, it is crucial to establish requirement ownership. In Agile projects, the requirements should be owned by the client and the Product Owner (Sometimes a BA will act as Product Owner & BA). While others may assist in writing the requirements, the Product Owner should make critical decisions, approve or reject requirements, and validate the acceptance criteria.

There are different sources or origins for requirements. In a new project, requirements may come from an existing list or need to be planned. For projects in progress, new requirements may emerge during workshops, client conversations, demos, or even after going live. User stories are often used to capture the details of the requirements. It is important to focus on the "what" and "why" rather than the "how" when writing user stories.

Capturing Requirements in Azure DevOps: Several fields are commonly used when capturing requirements in Azure DevOps. You can configure the structure & process lifecycle as per your needs. As a BA, you need to work with customers to establish this. The title briefly describes the requirement, while the state indicates the stage of the requirement's lifecycle.

The description field is used to write the user story in the format of "as a [role], I want [action], so that [benefit]." Documents can be stored in Azure DevOps, but storing them in a SharePoint folder and referencing them in the user story is often more flexible. Acceptance criteria help confirm a shared understanding of the requirements, and limiting them to around ten bullet points is advisable.

Once the requirements are captured, it is important to manage them effectively. Requirements go through different stages in their lifecycle. They start in the "new" stage when they are just an idea or a suggestion. As conversations and discussions happen, the requirements evolve, and more details are added. The stages may include analysis, design, development, SIT, and UAT. The state of the requirement changes as it progresses through these stages. Documents, discussions, related work, and tasks may be added or updated throughout the lifecycle.

Tags, story points, and priorities can be used to manage and categorize requirements throughout the lifecycle. For example, tags like "to be reviewed" or "ready for demo" can be used to further categorize requirements. You can search by tag to get those sets of Requirements. The discussion field allows communication and tracking conversations related to the user story.

Tips & Best Practices:

- ✈ **Give a unique ID for epics:** Instead of using the full name of the epic, using a number or some other identifier can make it easier to communicate and track progress.
- ✈ **Add Custom fields if necessary:** Custom fields in Azure DevOps allow for the addition of extra information or the linking of external documents to epics, features, and user stories, enhancing the flexibility and functionality of your setup.
- ✈ **Definition of Ready:** To streamline the development process and prevent misunderstandings or rework, I recommended using a "definition of ready" in Azure DevOps. This involves clearly defining and validating acceptance criteria before proceeding from analysis to development, promoting a shared understanding and smoother transitions.
- ✈ **Keep User Stories Crisp & Concise:** Keep the user stories always crisp. Any additional details or documents can be placed in linked SharePoint or other accessible locations.

- **Mention customers:** Whenever a discussion or clarification is required, you can Mention (@customer) your customers and request them to clarify in writing in the tool.
- **Delivery plans:** Azure DevOps offers delivery plans for tracking features and setting dates, providing a valuable tool for managing project timelines and dependencies
- **Technical documentation:** It is essential to update the document as and when there is a change or update. Technical documents are living documents. Documenting technical solutions and system configurations related to user stories is recommended when they become more stable. This is what Agile principles suggest, too. Azure DevOps provides options such as wikis in Teams or Azure DevOps itself to structure and store documentation.

What Did You Learn in This Chapter?

- What is DevOps?
- What are the responsibilities of a BA in a DevOps setup?
- What are some of the best practices for managing requirements in DevOps tools?
- Can you describe some of the best practices you have used while managing requirements in DevOps tools?

CHAPTER 19

FUTURE OF BA CAREER

- *Ba As a Strategic Role*
- *Various Opportunities for A Ba*
- *Artificial Intelligence & Ba*

The evolution of the digital workplace has been marked by significant changes in how projects are planned and executed. We used to practice the Waterfall approach for Project delivery earlier (even now, this exists), where requirements gathering was a linear process that involved extensive documentation and formal sign-off from customers. However, with the rise of Agile methodologies, this approach has become less common, as requirements can "evolve" throughout a project in response to shifting business scenarios.

Today, the role of the BA has evolved to become more strategic and comprehensive. BAs now concentrate on user context, impact metrics, and collaborative team efforts. Successful business analysts are characterised by their curiosity, willingness to learn, and fearlessness in asking questions and taking risks with new ideas and technologies. As we have seen in earlier chapters, they should possess excellent communication skills, build strong relationships, and be dedicated to delivering value and satisfaction to the end customer. Remember, a BA job is more of a delivering a "Value" than just a deliverable.

To remain effective in the digital workplace, business analysts should be open to adapting their mindsets and behaviours to new methodologies and working environments. While traditional skills remain important, they must learn to incorporate them into Agile teams' collaborative and dynamic nature. This requires a willingness to learn and master new modern skills like user experience design, data analysis, and the latest technologies and trends.

In Waterfall, projects were scoped out initially, and stakeholders would schedule weeks or months of elicitation sessions to gather requirements. Agile has replaced this approach, which emphasises collaboration and user-centric discovery. BAs and stakeholders work together to discover user needs as they arise, peeling back layers of complexity to reveal the most important and relevant details. Weekly meetings are held to discuss feedback and refine project priorities.

What is interesting is that agile methodologies are now the prominent approach companies use. This methodology is more flexible and easier to use than the traditional waterfall method. The BA role is becoming less defined as companies move towards agile methodologies. The title of BA doesn't even exist in Agile. Instead, you have a product owner, a team, and a scrum master.

So, where does the BA role fit in? In agile, the BA role is a combination of everything. You need to be flexible and wear many hats. We discussed these aspects earlier. You might be asked to take on some of the responsibilities of a scrum master, product owner, or even the development team (what I meant is you will be called as part of the development team; you will not be asked to develop or code). The key is to be adaptable and willing to take on new challenges.

Remember, you can do all these jobs if you are a BA. Your skills are transferrable. Of course, there might be some responsibilities that are not similar. Still, as a BA, you can always adapt and leverage your skills to fulfil the responsibilities of these roles, like a scrum master product owner.

Hence, what can you do to prepare for the future of the BA role? Firstly, you need to understand agile methodologies and how they work. This will give you a better understanding of where the BA role fits and what you need to do to stay relevant. Additionally, you should be willing to learn new skills and take on new responsibilities. The future of the BA role is all about being flexible and adaptable.

To pursue a BA career, you must stay on top of these changes and be willing to learn and adapt new skills. Doing so can ensure that you remain relevant and valuable in the future.

Observing users and analysing data insights are critical to the success of modern digital projects. BAs must be able to experiment with unknowns and assumptions about users, data, and systems and use their insights to drive hypotheses and experiments. They must be willing to take risks and embrace new technologies and tools to stay ahead of the curve.

The future of Business Analysis as a profession is bright, but BAs must remain adaptable and open to change. In today's modern digital workplace, BAs are emerging as the "Real captains" of projects, taking on leadership roles that require them to deeply understand their craft. They must be willing to take on new challenges and master new skills while remaining focused on the end user's needs.

By focusing on user context and impact metrics, BAs can drive successful project outcomes that meet the needs of both the business and the end user. By embracing the dynamic nature of modern projects and teams, BAs can continue to add value to their organisations and remain relevant in an ever-changing landscape.

Opportunities for BAs

The role of a BA presents incredibly promising opportunities due to the specific set of skills and abilities it demands. As a BA, one must possess critical thinking skills, comprehension of diverse business models, a forward-thinking approach, and exceptional consulting and customer management skills.

Customers seek individuals who can understand their businesses and develop systems that align with their processes, a task that technical experts may not always be able to perform. Consequently, BAs play an essential role in designing systems according to the specific requirements, making their presence indispensable in any small, medium, or large project. It is highly unlikely that robots will replace this role anytime soon. The advent of AI tools like ChatGPT & other AI-powered tools will only help a BA further improve productivity.

Hence, as we already know, they can advance their career in any direction due to the nature of a BA's broad set of skills, resourcefulness, and a high level of technical expertise. Of course, knowledge of one industry is beneficial and makes it easier for them to work in that industry only, but with little effort, they can easily move to new sectors/industries or take on new roles.

Here, the core fundamentals of the BA will remain the same. However, the BA needs to learn about the new industry in which he/she is moving. As one gets more and more experience, the BA can become an Industry expert (SME). They can get a new executive-level role where they contribute to developing business strategies, IT strategy setup, process setup and program management-related roles – which all are very highly rewarding job positions that can translate into a higher level of job satisfaction and great growth in the career.

Business analysis has become an increasingly important function in modern organisations, leading to the role and job market growth for BAs. Historically, the role of a BA was poorly understood and undervalued. However, many organisations now recognise the significance of skilled BAs in achieving business objectives, and the demand for these professionals has risen steadily over the years.

Moreover, becoming a BA does not require professional qualifications, as certain skill sets coupled with common sense can equip one for the role. The acquired skill set is valuable and provides opportunities for career progression to other senior and strategic management roles, such as strategic program management, business architecture, and strategy.

Becoming a BA provides an opportunity for lifelong learning and addressing business problems by providing solutions. The career is versatile, as BAs can work in different sectors and industries. The role of a BA is not monotonous, as each day comes with varying tasks, domains, projects, and industries.

A key question that many individuals ask when considering a career as a BA is, "Do BAs make good money?" The answer to this question can be found online!

I would say, "yes, they make good money".

Business analysis provides a solid foundation for individuals seeking to advance their careers. The acquired skills can be transferrable to various strategic management roles and leadership positions in project teams and organisations over a period of time. This career progression is achievable through experience, professional development, and exposure to different projects, industries and domains.

Business Analysis Certifications

IIBA (International Institute of Business Analysis) and the CBAP accreditation (Certified Business Analysis Professional) are the most well-known global BA education and certification-providing bodies. Here are the best BA certifications for beginners or aspiring BAs. You may research more about these certifications online:

- IIBA Entry Level Certification in Business Analysis (ECBA)
- IIBA Certification of Competency in Business Analysis (CCBA)
- IIBA Certified Business Analysis Professional (CBAP)
- IIBA Agile Analysis Certification (AAC)
- IIBA Business Data Analytics Certification (CBDA)
- IIBA Cybersecurity Analysis Certification (CCA)
- IIBA Product Ownership Analysis Certification (CPOA)

Does Certification Really Help?

I know this could be a bit controversial, but I am stating my experience. Do you really have to do a certification to get a job or get a high salary?

I would say, "NO". Certification never helped me get a job or a high-paying job.
Recently, I ran a survey on my LinkedIn, and many of my fellow connections have echoed the same. Here are the facts about certifications.

People who sell certifications with a "promise of Job or as a prerequisite for a high paying Job" – I would say, they are just selling their certifications. It won't get you a Job or high-paying Job directly.

You should be an expert in a subject or area along with some experience to get a good Job. Just doing certification won't fetch you the experience or the job.

I agree that certifications help you get the subject knowledge. It may offer you that structured learning. If you have time and aim to get knowledge and learn, you can do that certification, provided the certification gives that value fully, and you need to ensure that.

Certifications may help you in getting shortlisted for an Interview. That, too, is not all certifications. Some select premium certifications may help. Getting a high-paying job completely depends on how you perform in an interview, how the interviewer perceives your experience and the availability of a suitable position.

Most of the time, certifications are pricey. Please do the certification if you want to do those and can afford them. Do check the "value for money" regarding knowledge from that certification.

If you are working in an organisation, the organisation may want you to do some certifications for various reasons. In this case, as the organisation is sponsoring the certification, please do the same. Many times, it's not worth spending your own money for certifications.

Freshers should try to acquire knowledge about the subject they want to master via some real courses that can provide them with practical knowledge – Just gaining theoretical knowledge is not enough; while they are also important – practical experience has more value. Follow the Blogs of various industry experts who offer content filled with practical scenarios and try to learn from those. If you have the required budget to do a certification, you can do one of the above-mentioned certifications. The key advantage is that certification provides you with focused learning.

Certifications are not mandatory. Premium certifications can add weight to your CV and make your CV look fancy, but in the end, what matters is your knowledge and practical experience as you grow in your career. As an experienced BA and someone accountable for recruiting and supervising BAs, I commend those who invest the time and effort to attain certification, demonstrating a willingness and dedication to keep progressing. However, it is not the sole indicator of one's potential to be an excellent BA.

Note: Views are strictly personal.

What Did You Learn in This Chapter?

- Do you have any BA Certifications? How much value did it add in your career so far?
- What are the major skills the BA should possess?

CHAPTER 20

DO YOU HAVE THE PERSONALITY TO BE A BA?

- *Key Traits of a BA*
- *Various Must Have Skills of a BA*

So far, so good. But do you have the personality to be a BA?

As you have acquired a significant amount of awareness and knowledge about the skillsets required to become a BA in the IT industry, it is time to evaluate yourself.

Take this self-assessment by answering the questions below and assess whether you have the required mindset and ability to be a BA. Considering roles like BA are very demanding, possessing suitable personality traits is essential. I am not a psychologist. However, we can self-assess if our personality really suits us to be a BA or not!

Here is the set of questions—they are not all, but only a few important ones. Just answer them honestly to yourself. Please write it down. Wherever you have negative answers (a NO!), consider that those are the areas you must improve upon to become a good BA.

✪ **Remember, BA is a demanding role.**

Note: This is based on my experience; people will have different perspectives.

Interpersonal Traits

- Do you like to talk to people? Can you build a decent rapport/good business relationship with people?
- Let's say you are an introvert, but at least for your job (BA), can you talk to people and build and maintain a good relationship with them?
- Can you subtly understand the customer organization's political (w.r.t project) environment through your relationships?

Communication Leadership

- Do you like continuous/back-to-back meetings? Do you even like meetings/ workshops etc.?
- Do you have confidence in yourself that you SPEAK and WRITE clearly?
- Can you lead a meeting & express ideas clearly? Can you clearly express ideas/concepts using a whiteboard from scratch if required?
- Let's say you are building a house. Do you get a clear vision of how your home should be? Can you express your idea clearly to others?

Focus & Listening

- When you are thinking deeply about something, do you get out of the crowded place and sit alone quietly somewhere to work/write for hours to give shape to your thoughts?
- When you talk to someone, do you give equal importance to what they say? Do you listen to them actively?

Critical Thinking & Problem Solving

- Are you a quick self-learner? Can you resolve a problem by figuring out what is required (by researching, asking people, etc.), & by quickly learning new things/techniques? In essence, can you own the problem to resolve it?
- You don't feel stressed to choose the best option when you have multiple options. Do you use any tactic to choose the best?

Curious & Creative Mind

- Do you feel thrilled to understand your customer's business, etc.?
- Do you get curious when you see any product, not necessarily a software product? Do you have thoughts about improvement areas as well?

Collaboration & Situation/Crisis

- Do you have the patience & perseverance to slowly build something while collaborating with others, including your team & customers?
- How good are you at managing a situation? When a customer shouts at you, do you maintain your calm?
- At the moment of crisis (escalation/major issue, etc.), you don't panic but feel like, "let's understand the issue first"?

Others/Analysis

- Do you have the habit of believing anything if it comes from the customer without any due diligence and further analysis? Do you jump to conclusions quickly?

How was the test? Would you like to be a BA?

Being Introvert—Not an Impediment!

Some personal traits are hard to change, such as "being introvert" or you are not a people person, so you may have to put a lot of effort into coming out of your comfort zone. Remember, introverts can also become a BA; however, if you have a nature where you don't like people, want to be alone, or be an individual contributor, a BA may not be suitable for you.

BA's job is teamwork. People will keep bugging you for various reasons throughout the day, and that's the nature of the job.

Yes, introverts can become BAs. The ability to work independently, focus on details, and analyze complex data are all qualities that can be found in introverts. Introverts may excel in certain aspects of the job, such as conducting research, working with data, and thinking deeply about complex problems. However, introverted BAs need to develop their communication skills to collaborate with others and present their findings to stakeholders effectively. With the proper training and experience, introverts can make excellent BAs.

Hence, you must hone those "people" skills and possess those other required skill sets.

Get ready; all the Best!

If you have decided to become a BA, it's time to prepare a compelling CV/resume. It is crucial to present yourself in the best possible light during the application and interview process, and the upcoming chapters will provide you with valuable tips and strategies to achieve that.

Preparing for a job interview can be intimidating, but you can approach the process confidently with proper guidance and preparation. Keep yourself motivated and focused on your goals, and with determination, you can secure your dream job as a Business Analyst in the IT industry.

Good luck!

CHAPTER 21

HOW TO START A BA CAREER?

- *How To Transition to A BA Career?*
- *Can A Non-It Person Get into Ba Role*
- *Framework For Career Transition Into BA*

Numerous individuals have found themselves in the role of a BA, thanks to their inherently refined skills, which are essential for success in this field. Some may have been fortunate enough to receive guidance from a senior or mentor. However, not everyone is bestowed with such opportunities. While few possess an innate aptitude for these skills, most individuals must actively cultivate them.

Therefore, if you believe you possess the necessary skills to excel as a BA, it's crucial to highlight and demonstrate them. You must also master the art of effectively promoting your abilities.

To be a successful BA, you need "common sense" and good stakeholder interaction skills. For IT BAs, some IT knowledge is also required. Successful BAs come from various backgrounds, not necessarily an MBA or IT/Engineering degree. As we have seen in the previous chapters, in a nutshell, to become a BA, one must be good in the aspects /personal traits:

- Business acumen—the ability to understand business; this comes with experience
- Willingness to look into the problem and eagerness to solve the same
- Should be a good communicator – verbal & written
- Storytelling—the ability to present complex topics in a simple way and document the same
- People skills—stakeholder management, facilitation, conflict resolution etc.
- Good at creating decent visuals—wireframes, flow diagrams, charts, etc.
- Some awareness about Technology

If you are a Fresher, learning to code and deliver the same is comparatively easy. Because someone will tell how an App should behave, what is required and more. You will code it/build it, and test it; your job is over. Even if you are an experienced technical person (developer or Architect), predominantly, your job is done when your code or App fulfils the requirements. Of course, as an experienced technical person, you should also possess analytical skills to analyse the code dependencies and conceive and deliver efficient technical architecture—but predominantly, you, as a technical person, are still thinking technically.

Now, as a technical person (Fresher developer/experienced developer/lead, etc.), your state of mind should be different if you want to get into Business Analysis. You should be able to shift to the "BA" state of mind or mindset, where you will be thinking more about solving business problems through your (or your team's) technical solutions.

That's where you need an additional skill upgrade. That's when you should start thinking like a BA. Act Like a BA and Sleep like a BA. Because you are now looking after the entire technical ecosystem that will make or break your customer's business!

The Career Transition—To Be A BA

If you are a Fresher, to be honest, opportunities are comparatively less. To be a BA, one should know how a typical IT project works, and he/she should get some exposure. Hence, I would suggest, for a couple of years, continuing wherever you are (If you are doing a developer job or are currently skilled in development) and observing, getting yourself groomed well in the skills required to execute BA responsibilities. There is no harm in seeking mentorship from any senior BAs within your organisation or outside, if you know anyone, and slowly prepare yourself to get into a BA role.

But please note there are companies (especially product companies) who recruit freshers for BA roles, too. If you get it, your life is set. You can also approach reputable small to mid-level IT services companies to see if you can join them as a trainee in the Business Analysis domain.

Remember that many such companies may not readily hire freshers for this role due to the complexity of training candidates for Business Analysis, which can be more challenging than training developers or testers or hiring candidates with at least one year of experience.

If you are an experienced person (Technical or any other area), you know how a typical IT project works and more. Your job is to ensure you have the personal traits required to be a BA. If you are lacking, get a mentorship from experts and get a proper knowledge of BA responsibilities through self—learning or any courses you want to enrol in.

For anyone who wants to switch industries or roles, his/her first duty is to understand and learn how a typical IT project lifecycle works in IT. Learn/read about how BAs work in an IT project. You may leverage online resources, courses, or certifications; it's up to you. But your primary goal is to become a person who understands the nuances of the industry to a certain degree.

- First and foremost, you should think like a BA. Act Like a BA and Sleep like a BA.

- Explore if you can perform some activities in your current job that you should do in your future BA job—at least some aspects. Ex: You can analyse your existing IT system and applications and prepare your analysis document on improving the current process. If you have a mentor or a friend who can help you with feedback about work, that is even better.

- If you already have a BA in your current organisation, offer to assist him/her on top of your everyday duties. Talk to your manager about your aspirations. Get some work, even if it adds to your existing responsibilities. Utilise that opportunity to the fullest to learn about the BA job.

- Don't forget to highlight such activities/experiences in your CV so that you can demonstrate your experience during the interviews.

- When you change the industry/role, it's obvious that you need to completely revamp your CV. You must write your CV so that your current job role is almost the same (or relevant) as your aspired role—BA. You need to highlight the appropriate activities you are doing in your current job. On top of it, if you get relevant knowledge (learned online, courses, etc.) to back it up, the interview may work in your favour.

- Typically, in IT organisations, people are under pressure to hire someone quickly because they have a new project requirement that needs to be fulfilled. Though they prefer experienced people from the same industry/similar IT companies, sometimes, if you are shortlisted and, in the interview, you can showcase your confidence, skills, and commitment, there is no reason they will reject you. However, in the job, you should be ready to put extra effort to get up to speed as you face real-life situations and problems.

- ✈ Keep networking. Connect with relevant people on platforms like LinkedIn. They may not help you immediately, but it is essential. Try the referral route via any contacts/friends. The referral is one of the most powerful ways to land a job in the IT industry.

Can A Non-IT Person Get into IT As A BA?

Many people have asked me this question. First off, YES, this is possible.

As we discussed earlier, it requires a good effort from your end to learn the tricks of the trade. You have an advantage if you have a non-IT background but good industry experience. You can become an excellent domain BA—like a healthcare person can become a Healthcare domain BA.

Again, for anyone who wants to switch industries, his/her first duty is to understand and learn how a typical IT project lifecycle works in IT. Learn/read about how BAs work in an IT project. Your primary goal should be to become a person who understands the nuances of the industry to a certain degree.

Framework for Career Transition into BA: Any transition, transformation, or upgrade/switch of the domain or job role will not happen overnight. Be it transitioning to a BA job, PM role, or any role or job you aspire to be in from your current situation or position!

In addition to your knowledge-gathering activities, be it self-learning, attending a course, getting a mentorship, etc., you need to make sure "you" are 100% determined and dedicated to becoming that person you aspire to be (your desired role).

✪ Remember: It Will Take Its Own Sweet Time.

However, of course, you can speed up the process. But it depends on how much time you set aside to dedicate to that, how well you grasp the concepts and understand the nuances of your aspired role, and how well you present yourself, your "knowledge", and your "confidence" to your future employer—"why you are better suited for the role."

When you are on a journey to become someone (your aspired role), the first thing you need to do is "become that role," that is, "start thinking you are already doing that role" and align your mind as per that role. Once you start doing that, other aspects will fall into place automatically.

Here is my recommended framework for career transition, which applies to BAs and everyone on their career transition journey.

First and foremost, the rule is to have PATIENCE throughout your journey. The Next Steps are as depicted in the diagram/below:

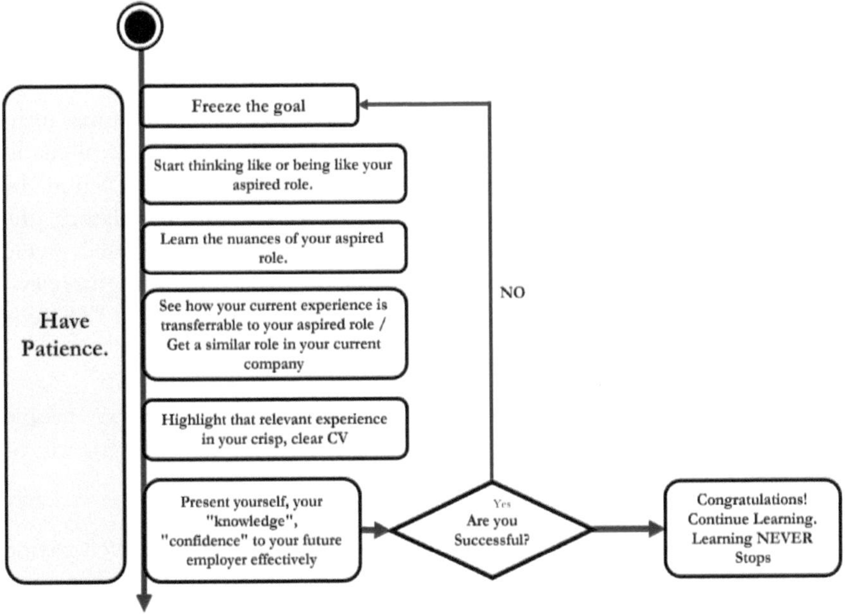

1. Freeze the goal.
2. Start thinking like or being like your aspired role.
3. Learn the nuances of your aspired role.
4. See how your current experience is transferrable to your aspired role / Or get a similar role in your current company, if feasible.
5. Highlight relevant experience in CV – a crisp CV is crucial.
6. Present yourself, your "experience", "knowledge", and "confidence" effectively to your future employer.
7. If you are successful, continue your learning. Learning NEVER stops.

If you are unsuccessful this time, incorporate your learning and repeat the steps. Again, and again.

If you are dedicated, do the right things and have patience, you will one day become what you aspire to be. 100% True. Believe my words. All the best.

Be Honest. One Day, You'll Get There!

You are mistaken if you think you can put some fake experience in your CV and get the job with your dream salary. Even if you managed to get it, that is the biggest fraud you are committing, and it can ruin your career and life sooner or later. This could be for any Job, BA or technical consultant jobs.

Faking work experience has become a common problem in the IT industry. This is not the story of recent times but has existed in the IT industry for a long period.

I have seen people making their brilliant friends attend the telephonic technical interview rounds. Once they crack the interview for them, real candidates attend the HR round for salary negotiations. To curb such actions by candidates, when organizations made the Video rounds mandatory, the candidates got even more intelligent, wherein their friends started giving "voice-overs" to the actual candidates on a Video call. When the Interviewer gets suspicious about missing lip-sync, the answer they get is: "There is some lag in my network"!

There is another set of candidates. When asked for verification, people mention fake organization names in their CVs and provide their friends/or some paid agents' contacts.

I've seen many such "fake experienced" candidates who obtain well-paying jobs in the IT company, join the company, and then get fired when their background checks fail. However, there could be some exceptions; some people succeed, don't get caught and make their careers great. I would say they just got lucky. That's why people get the confidence to put the fake experience in their CVs to move up fast or gain a high-paying job!

But beware! Organizations are more innovative now. People who interview are even more brilliant now. Despite this, sadly, the "Fake Stories" still happen.

A long time ago, one of my friends asked a ubiquitous question—"If I don't fake it, how can I get into IT?" "I don't have any experience, though I have some knowledge."

It is like the classic "chicken or egg" situation: the job mandates experience, and you can't get experience without a job!

However, there is always a way to overcome such "chicken or egg" situations in the knowledge industry, like IT. Committing fraud by faking the experience is not the solution at all. I strongly advise against fabricating your work experience.

For example, consider a scenario wherein a person from a non-IT industry wants to enter IT as a BA. Nothing wrong with that. In IT, we need people who have domain experience. They can be excellent domain BAs—like a healthcare person can become a Healthcare domain BA.

Hence, for anyone who wants to switch industries, as described in the above example, his/her first duty is to understand and learn how a typical IT project lifecycle works in the IT Industry. Learn and read about how BAs work in an IT project. You may leverage online resources, courses, or certifications; it's up to you. But your primary goal is to become a person who understands the nuances of the industry you are getting into (IT, in this case) to a certain degree. Once the person is equipped with the proper knowledge, it is in this stage where people are tempted to put some fake experience so that they can get shortlisted and at least get the interview. Well, still, I would say that is not the right way. It is unethical to put fake experiences.

So, how can you gain some real experience in such a scenario?

As we discussed previously, your first duty is to understand and learn how a typical IT project lifecycle works in IT. Learn/read about how BAs work in an IT project. Your primary goal should be to become a person who understands the nuances of the industry to a certain degree. There are no shortcuts, unfortunately!

To gain knowledge and experience, you may also consider taking up freelance projects or accepting positions at smaller companies with lower salaries to gain practical experience, provided you are fine with that. If you are a fresher, have only a little experience and need more experience, this is the best way. This will provide you with the right knowledge and some real experience. Be aware that any mature interviewer can figure out whether your experience is real or fake by sometimes looking at your CV or talking to you. Hence, keeping your "career" genuine and honest is always the best way to excel in your career and life because a career founded on honesty and genuine experiences endures forever.

CHAPTER 22

AI REVOUTION AND BUSINESS ANALYSIS

- *How AI Tools Can Be Assistants to Business Analysts?*
- *Writing A Great Prompt*
- *Top Six Areas Where BAs Can Benefit from AI*

As technology advances, AI-powered tools such as ChatGPT are becoming more widespread. These tools offer various benefits to professionals in different domains, including BAs.

So, how AI, Generative AI can be a boon for a BA? How can a BA leverage the latest AI tools to his advantage?

Note that this chapter is written in the Sept-Oct 2023 timeframe, and if you are reading this after this timeframe, there might have been drastic developments that could have occurred. AI is a very rapidly changing area nowadays.

As you already know, BAs collaborate with stakeholders to understand needs and develop solutions aligned with organisational goals. BAs possess business knowledge, communicate effectively with technical and non-technical audiences, and employ strategic thinking and creativity.

Artificial Intelligence to Assist BAs

While AI can assist in various Analysis activities, it cannot replace the strategic thinking and human judgment integral to many aspects of business analysis. BAs' critical thinking, problem-solving, and communication skills are challenging for AI to replicate. AI serves as a tool to enhance the work of BAs rather than replace them.

An AI tool like ChatGPT can be a valuable resource for BAs in several ways:

- **Draft Requirements:** Use cases are crucial in capturing functional requirements and understanding user interactions. When gathering and analysing requirements, the BA can tap into the power of ChatGPT during stakeholder interviews. By employing ChatGPT, the BA can automate the creation of essential documentation like functional specifications and use cases. For instance, if a stakeholder verbally describes how the application should notify service providers of new customer orders in their vicinity, ChatGPT can automatically generate a functional specification outlining this specific functionality. ChatGPT can help BAs generate initial drafts of use cases by providing a starting point with descriptions, actors, pre-conditions, and user system interactions.

- **Asking Questions:** BAs often need to develop relevant questions when preparing for stakeholder meetings or requirements-gathering sessions. ChatGPT can generate role or feature-specific questions to assist in the process. This helps ensure comprehensive coverage of the topic at hand.
- **Writing User Stories:** BAs can break down complex use cases into smaller, manageable user stories for development cycles. ChatGPT can aid in this task by providing user story templates that capture different aspects of the feature or functionality.
- **AI Scribes:** An interesting application is the AI scribe. It involves using a transcribing tool to convert meeting recordings into text, which ChatGPT can then process. By doing so, ChatGPT can generate Meeting Notes that include Action Items and future steps. And this is already happening as per my research online. Nowadays, Microsoft Teams has developed a live transcribing feature—where it transcribes the conversations (during Team online meetings) live. At the end of the meeting, it also suggests the Meeting notes. This is one of the key features as part of Microsoft's Viva feature for teams.

How a BA can leverage an AI tool for Drafting Requirements (Use Cases)?

BAs can leverage AI tools to their advantage and improve productivity, enabling them to focus on higher-level knowledge-intensive tasks and strategic decision-making. To obtain the desired results from AI tools like ChatGPT, Bard, or similar AI systems, one can achieve success by providing queries along with context and then precisely instructing or prompting the AI tool on what is needed.

Hence, before you start, you need to describe the scenario to the tool by feeding it with relevant info and then provide prompts or questions to get the output for your tasks. This way, the AI tool can optimise its answers to your needs.

While ChatGPT assists in generating initial content, human analysis and expertise remain crucial for refining and tailoring the use case. Let's delve into the process of drafting a Requirement titled "Convert a Lead to an Opportunity" using ChatGPT.

Example Prompt: "Please draft a Requirement titled Convert a Lead to an Opportunity."

Response from ChatGPT:

- The Convert a Lead to an Opportunity use case enables sales representatives to transform potential leads into actionable opportunities within the CRM system. This process ensures proper tracking and management of the sales pipeline.

Now analyse the generated Requirement (Use Case) and make appropriate changes yourself or ask again by prompting ChatGPT to further finetune and enhance the Requirement (Use Case). While the generated use case provides a solid foundation, it necessitates customisation to align with your needs. BAs should incorporate additional details such as lead qualification criteria, required information for opportunity creation, and validation rules.

In addition to generating Requirements, ChatGPT can facilitate the breakdown of Requirements into use cases (or user stories), enabling more granular development scenarios.

Example Prompt: "Please provide a user story for the Convert a Lead to an Opportunity use case."

Sample Generated User Story:

- As a sales representative, I want to convert a qualified lead into an opportunity to efficiently manage and track potential sales within the CRM system.

Again, as you can see, while the AI tool aids in generating initial content, it is essential for a BA to combine it with human expertise and analysis to refine and tailor use cases (or user stories) to meet the project's unique needs.

Note: Accurately prompting to get the required output is extremely important.

Generally, the use case generated by ChatGPT will encompass essential elements like below. By giving required prompts you can get the elements as per your needs.

- Description: The use case outlines the purpose of lead conversion and emphasises its significance in maintaining an organised sales pipeline.
- Actors: It identifies the key user role as the salesperson responsible for converting leads.
- Pre-conditions: The use case assumes the salesperson is logged into the CRM system and can access leads.
- User System Interactions: Steps include identifying a qualified lead, updating lead information, associating relevant data (such as contacts, opportunities, and accounts), and transitioning the lead status to an opportunity.

How Can AI Tools Be Utilised to Generate Targeted Questions for Stakeholders?

ChatGPT is valuable in generating pertinent questions to ensure comprehensive feature coverage during stakeholder discussions. The prompts I have provided here are very basic. You must keep prompting the tool until you get the required matured output. As you may already know, using the latest version of the AI tool is always good for a better output.

Example Prompt: "Please provide 10 questions I could ask the sales team about lead conversion."

Sample Generated Questions:

- What are the criteria for determining if a lead is qualified for conversion?
- How should we handle leads with incomplete information during the conversion process?
- Are any specific fields or data that must be captured when converting a lead?
- Can a lead be converted to multiple opportunities, or is it limited to one?

Happy with these questions and responses?

Well, I am NOT. So, keep prompting or editing the prompt/query until you get all the questions you want to ask. It gives you a starting point and many options, saving you time. Agree?

In addition to the above activities, during the development of an application, the BA can also utilise ChatGPT or other tools like Bard for process and data modelling. By providing a verbal description of how the application should retrieve and display data from other systems (in an integration scenario) providers, ChatGPT can generate process flow diagrams and data models (Table structure field names, etc.). This automates the modelling process and assists in visualising the desired functionality.

Please note that currently available (At the time of launching this book - Q4 2023) free tools cannot generate flow diagrams or wireframes; however, over time, such tasks will be done by an AI tool, thus saving a lot of BA's time. Regarding stakeholder communication and management, AI tools like ChatGPT can prove invaluable during project management. The BA can use ChatGPT to generate reports, presentations, and other communication materials.

Microsoft 365 Copilot is the latest addition in the market where all your Windows office products including Word, PowerPoint and Excel (all Microsoft 365 products) are now AI powered and you can develop content, Presentations or Excel sheet with medium to complex formulae in minutes. Microsoft's AI-powered Microsoft 365 Copilot (Azure Open AI-powered) can help you generate content on Word, Outlook (To draft emails), Teams (to capture meeting minutes, transcribe the conversation, etc.), PowerPoint (prepare slides) and Excel sheets (content) can make your life easy.

All these Copilot or Azure Open AI-based features will be part of work management Apps like Azure DevOps, Jira can now provide suggestions for writing, rewriting and rephrasing content and more.

Many Task and Project Management tools are now equipped with the power of AI to help BAs and Project Managers. There are several AI powered Project management tools which are leveraging the data and information gathered from stakeholders to automatically generate a weekly report for the management and development teams, highlighting the project's progress and outlining the subsequent steps.

Tools like Wrike, StepSize, Trello, Ayanza ClickUp, etc., are now AI-powered. These tools now offer capabilities to streamline processes, analyze, sort, prioritize tasks, offer insights, use case creation, User story creation, Proof reading, content creation help and such many features and boost productivity in business analysis and project management. BAs can also leverage such tools to their advantage.

Gartner predicts that by 2030, 80% of processes (Business analysis, Project Management and others areas) will be AI-driven, transforming traditional roles. Hence, AI is an ever-evolving area, and many tools will come to the market to help a BA increase his/her productivity. As a BA, one needs always to be aware of this fact and prepared to learn and upgrade.

Though many such above mentioned AI tools offer attractive features as described, the real help such tools can offer to a BA have limitations. Currently, they provide just an outline for a presentation or report or mere illustrations, which a BA can leverage to further improve and customise as per his/her needs. AI tools like ChatGPT can be valuable assets for BAs when used effectively, offering benefits such as increased productivity and improved bandwidth:

- **Increased Productivity:** ChatGPT streamlines the drafting process, saving time and allowing BAs to focus on critical thinking, analysis, and stakeholder relationships.
- **Improved Bandwidth:** By leveraging AI tools for routine tasks, BAs can concentrate on areas where human expertise has the most impact, such as relationship building and aligning business value.

However, it's important to be aware of the limitations and use AI tools judiciously:

- **Outdated Data:** AI tools may rely on outdated data and lack access to the latest information, potentially limiting their responses on recent topics or capabilities. Using paid or latest versions of the tool may solve this problem.
- **Ethics:** AI tools lack human ethics and values, requiring BAs to ensure organisational norms, diversity, inclusion, and social justice principles are incorporated in the requirements development process.
- **Stakeholder Alignment:** AI tools cannot determine specific stakeholders' needs and relevance, relying on BAs' expertise to align expectations and priorities.
- **Validation:** The AI tool's output serves as a draft or starting point, and hence, a BA should make sure to get the required output to a stage where it meets expected business rules, preferences, and stakeholder requirements.

[The AI arena is getting exciting every passing day with the release of the paid version of Chat GPT/ other Premium AI tools and the release of thousands of plugins enabling the automation of various repetitive and process-oriented tasks. Remember, AI is a very fast-changing field.]

Writing A Great Prompt for AI Models

Crafting an effective prompt may require experimentation and iteration to achieve desired results. It is crucial to critically review and evaluate the generated responses, considering the AI model's limitations and biases. You need to apply all your best practices of writing a clear requirement here, too.

- ✪ **Remember**—consider the AI tool as an Intern; hence, you need to guide the tool/instruct the tool to get the desired output. It requires practice, which over a period you can master. If the initial response is not as expected or you want the model to focus on a specific aspect, provide additional context or refine your prompt. Iterative conversations often benefit the model's understanding.

A great prompt should follow below aspects:

- **Be Clear:** Ensure your prompt is clear, specific, and provides relevant context to guide the model's response. Avoid ambiguous or vague language that could lead to misunderstandings.
- **Purpose:** Explain the conversation's goal or purpose in your prompt. Are you seeking information, opinions, suggestions, or creative ideas? Clearly stating your objective helps the model understand the direction it should take.
- **Context:** Provide relevant background information to set the stage for the conversation. This helps the model understand the specific scenario and generate accurate and relevant responses.
- **Instructions:** Include any necessary guidelines or instructions for the model to follow. For instance, if you want pros and cons, a comparison, or brainstorming, mention it explicitly.
- **Constraints:** If there are specific limitations or constraints, such as time, budget, or criteria to consider, mention them in your prompt. This helps the model generate responses that align with the given constraints.
- **Be Concise:** While the model can handle various prompt lengths, keeping it concise and focused is generally helpful. Lengthy prompts may confuse the model or result in less coherent responses.

- **Tone:** Chat GPT/AI Tool responds to the tone and language used in the prompt. Reflect on your prompt's desired tone (polite, formal, casual). Be mindful of the model's biases and potential for generating inappropriate content. Always review and moderate the responses.

Example: I want you to act as an experienced BA who understands and knows how to write a Requirement well. Write a Requirement crisply based on the text provided – [Provide the requirement text you have written] Keep the word count under 100 words. Keep the language simple in English with a simple, formal tone.

Top SIX Areas Where BAs Can Benefit from AI Revolution

Documentation Aspects

- Writing Requirements, Use Cases, User Stories, etc.
- Various Diagrams like Flow diagrams, Process Diagrams
- Creating Wireframes
- Review Documents (As part of Document Analysis)
- Analyse & Summarize documents
- Grammar checks and reviews
- Email Drafting & Communication Aspects
- Generate Document Templates based on the Prompts.
- Preparation of Presentations/PPTs: When BAs input data and insights collected from stakeholders, AI tools like ChatGPT can automatically generate reports, presentations, and other communication materials.
- Prepare Questions to be asked during Requirements workshops

Problem Analysis / Solution Suggestions: Prompt AI tool with Business Problems and AI may suggest a solution based on the experience/ knowledge fed to the tool. (This is not a reality now, but I believe this may happen very soon.)

Estimations & Planning: Normally, a BA or Presales person does Effort Estimations (Effort required to fulfil Requirements, User story or tasks, etc.) based on certain mathematical models, experience and a gut feeling. Generally, people use Excel sheets to carry out such tasks (in certain organisations, they also have some tools). Now, if all these mathematical models, parameters and boundaries essential to estimating a requirement are fed to the AI tool.

Certainly, it will be a useful tool for a BA. AI tools can help estimate the time and effort needed to fulfil requirements. They can be made to look at things like how complicated the requirements are, how many people are on the team, what skills are needed, and what other things might affect the project. They can also consider different ways of doing the work, any limits or rules for the project, and what is considered standard in the industry.

✪ **Remember**—AI tools are only there to help. They can give you a good starting point for estimates, but human experts still need to check and adjust them. Also, all these may not be available now, but soon they will be.

Project Management & Planning: Already, AI is helping BAs and Project managers in many ways. AI is helping streamline processes, analyse, sort, prioritise tasks, offer insights, and boost productivity in project management. Several tools provide AI features like AI-assisted task management, Gantt charts, time tracking, and performance reports, summarising discussions and brainstormed ideas leveraging Generative AI, AI-assisted Content, Grammar check, change the tone, translation and more.

Build POCs/Apps/Technical Analysis: With Azure Open AI services gaining momentum, the configuration of Azure Apps or Power Apps (MS Power Platform Low code no code Apps) creating an App can be easy just by giving prompts; the tools can be instructed to build screens, workflows and much more. This will help BAs come up with POCs on the fly and can help BAs immensely. Not only for BAs, this could be a boon for developers to build excellent Apps quickly.

AI tools can serve as valuable assistants to BAs, particularly in technical aspects. They can help BAs with tasks like generating SQL queries, creating HTML code, designing Excel formulas, and providing sample JSON. Interestingly, AI tools can even identify patterns within XML messages. Not only Microsoft but every product vendor (be it Salesforce, Pega SAP, etc.) is coming up with its own AI infrastructure to help its users

Test Strategy & Test Cases Preparation: As a BA, he/she works with the Testing team. Hence, a BA's contribution to testing is important. A BA or testing team can also leverage AI tools for their needs. However, human testers are still essential, and Human judgment and creativity are crucial for designing effective test strategies, evaluating test cases, and making critical decisions based on results.

- **Test Case Generation:** They can assist in generating relevant test cases or test Scenarios based on system requirements, improving test coverage efficiently; it all depends on how a human tester gives a prompt to the AI tool.
- **Test Data Generation:** AI tools generate diverse and representative synthetic test data, particularly useful for complex or large datasets. Again, this is envisioned; at this moment, this may not happen as desired.
- **Bug Triage and Classification:** AI tools like ChatGPT can help automate bug triage by analysing and categorising bug reports based on severity, priority, and relevance to specific components. Again, all these are not a complete reality today, but they will be soon.
- **Test Automation Script Writing:** Just by giving prompts to the AI tools, perhaps testers can write test scripts more intuitively

Very soon, such functionalities will be built by Vendors of such BA tools (By building Plugins, etc.). Or BAs themselves will be able to feed such parameters to an AI tool via their plugins, etc. I believe five years down the line, though the BA fundamentals don't change, many aspects of "how a BA functions" will change. The BAs should be vigilant about such advancements going forward.

Final thought: BAs should recognise AI tools as supportive collaborators. These tools can automate repetitive and time-intensive tasks and can effectively handle activities that involve analysing extensive data sets and organising information.

- **Remember**—even when using such tools, a BA's "common sense" matters, and it is essential. No tool will come with that 'common-sense' that a human possesses.

LAST CHAPTER (23)!

TOP 45 BA INTERVIEW QUESTIONS

- *30 Typical Questions—For Answers Refer This Book*
- *20 Scenario Based Questions with Guidance to Answer*
- *Tips To Write Your CV & LinkedIn Profile*
- *Is Certifications Really Worth It?*

"**W**hat is the "Business Value" you delivered as part of your Job?"

One of the typical questions asked during a BA Interview. Through this question, the Interviewer is looking for the skill maturity of a BA and expects the answers with qualitative and quantitative information.

Your answer to the above question should cover the following:

- What was the Problem?
- Why was the Project started in the first place?
- How did you gather the required information/requirements?
- How well did your customer receive your solution?
- What was the duration of the Project?
- What was the ultimate business value that was achieved?

A BA who understands the BA concepts well and knows his/her deliverables will crisply answer this question by connecting the answers to all the above pointers.

For example, the customer was struggling with entering Lead information in a complex legacy system, which was taking a lot of time, thus losing productivity. We understood this problem and drafted a clear requirement from the customers by understanding current pain points and processes through a working session and a workshop. We then developed a well-designed "Lead capture process" by integrating a relevant system for quick data sync, which reduced their Lead capture time from 15 minutes per Lead to five minutes per Lead—thus increasing the productivity of an end user. This was possible because we understood "Why the problem was occurring" & "What was missing".

The above answer succinctly covers aspects like—how a BA understood the problem and captured the right requirement and how a business value (Productivity increase) was delivered to the customer.

Hence, whenever you answer a question in an interview, structure your answers well. Make sure you understand the question well → State the problem → How did you arrive at a solution → How it helped your customer with some quantifiable numbers. This shows your maturity as a BA.

This approach is inspired by the well-known "STAR framework for answering questions", which involves four key steps: S (Situation) – provide context, T (Task) – specify the task or problem, A (Action) – explain the actions taken to address the task, and R (Result) – present the outcomes or results achieved. It's commonly used in job interviews to structure responses effectively.

In this chapter, I have listed the Top 50 Questions usually asked during a BA interview. Thirty are on the BA topics, and the remaining 20 are scenario-based questions. This is not an exhaustive list, but it will help you prepare well and give you an overall idea about the questions asked during interviews. Also, I have not provided detailed answers to these questions, but this book will have the answers for the questions—thus, "you must read and digest this book" to get the answers. However, I have provided basic guidance on how to answer the questions.

When you go for a BA job interview, they will assess three main things: your understanding of business concepts, BA Skills, People Skills, technology skills, and, of course, how well you'd fit in with the company. As a candidate to do well in the interview, follow these tips:

- About the Company & Job: Understand what the company does, its goals, and its challenges. Tailor your answers to show how you can help them.
- Job Requirements: Look at the job responsibilities and find examples from your past that match them. Prepare to talk about these examples during the interview.
- Improve your knowledge: Review topics like business analysis best practices, high-level understanding of Reporting and analytics, processes, methodologies, etc.
- Practice common questions: While you can't predict all the questions, practising common ones can help you feel more prepared.

Top 30 Common Skills-Based BA Interview Questions

1. Which BA tools do you consider the most important and have used so far?

   ANS: Refer Chapter 9: Techniques of Documentation

2. As a BA, describe two diagrams you frequently use and how they impact your work

   ANS: Refer Chapter 9: Techniques of Documentation

3. Explain requirement prioritization and discuss various techniques used?

   ANS: Chapter 6: Techniques of Business Analysis

4. When designing a use case, what are the necessary steps you follow in the process?

   ANS: Chapter 8: How to Get Requirements Right?

5. Define scope creep and explain your approach to avoiding it in projects.

   ANS: Chapter 11: Scope Management

6. How does a BA handle change to requirements?

   ANS: Chapter 16: Expectations from A New Age Ba

7. Differentiate between User Stories and Use Cases

   ANS: Refer Chapter 8: How to Get the Requirements Right?

8. Define UML modelling and its significance in the context of Business Analysis

   ANS: Chapter 6: Techniques of Business Analysis

9. Explain what is Non-functional Requirements are and provide examples.

   ANS: Refer Chapter 8: How to Get the Requirements Right?

10. What is the purpose of the Requirement Traceability Matrix (RTM)?

    ANS: Refer Chapter 8: Sample Document Templates for BAs

11. Discuss the various types of Requirements that a BA encounters

    ANS: Refer Chapter 8: How to Get the Requirements Right?

12. In your opinion, should a BA be involved in testing? If yes, why?

ANS: Refer Chapter14: Working with Technical Team

13. What are the essential qualities of an Agile BA?

    ANS: Refer Chapter15: Agile World's New Age BA

14. State the top FIVE reasons motivating you to pursue a career as a BA.

    ANS: Ch. 1: Who Is the Real Captain? & Ch.19: Future of BA Career

15. What preparatory activities would you undertake before requirements sessions?

    ANS: Chapter7: Techniques of Requirements Gathering

16. Do you think a BA's involvement is necessary during implementation? Explain.

    ANS: Chapter 5: Project Lifecycles & Role of a BA

17. Which one is your favourite requirements gathering techniques/methods and why?

    ANS: Chapter7: Techniques of Requirements Gathering

18. Define whiteboarding and discuss any previous experiences you have had with it.

    ANS: Chapter7: Techniques of Requirements Gathering

19. Explain the concept of active listening and its importance for a BA

    ANS: Chapter3: Skills of a BA

20. How can a BA effectively handle difficult stakeholders?

    ANS: Chapter12: ABCD of Stakeholder Mgmt.

21. Enumerate the various diagrams that a BA should be knowledgeable about.

    ANS: Chapter 6: Techniques of Business Analysis

22. How do you influence multiple project stakeholders?

    ANS: Chapter12: ABCD of Stakeholder Mgmt.

23. What is a Project Charter?

    ANS: Refer Chapter10: Sample Document Templates for BAs

24. How will you write a requirement without ambiguity?

    ANS: Refer Chapter 9: Techniques of Documentation

25. To visualize relationships with stakeholders (customers), what modelling technique would you employ?

    ANS: Chapter12: ABCD of Stakeholder Mgmt.

26. What documents are typically prepared by BA's? Please tell us about examples of documents you have prepared in your previous work.

    ANS: Refer Chapter 9: Techniques of Documentation

27. How do you, as a BA, determine that you have gathered all the requirements?

    ANS: Refer Chapter 8: How to Get the Requirements Right?

28. How would you plan the analysis for a project where the customer's expectation is to modernize their existing processes?

    ANS: Refer Chapter 8: How to Get the Requirements Right?

29. How will you ensure you have a required BA Mindset?

    ANS: Refer Chapter 2 – The BA Mindset

30. What are Top Risks of a BA?

    ANS: Refer Chapter 13 – Business Analysis Challenges

Top 20 Common Scenario Based BA Interview Questions

1. Imagine, the customer has escalated against you to your management saying that, 'the competency of your delivery team is not as expected and your BA has no experience and lacks the competency to handle or manage our requirements'. Though you have experience, the industry this project belongs to is new to you and you are doing your best to get things right. At the same time, your customer is also not supporting as expected to gather or elicit requirements due to their own political reasons. Now, you are being blamed for not so matured output from your side. As a BA, what would be your plan of action to diffuse the situation?

    - **ANS:** I will take the situation with a CALM mind. Examine myself what went wrong. Gather data about the situation and show them the real situation. At the same time, work hard to correct your approach and come up with better version of your work. Indeed, it will be a challenging situation and it's an opportunity to demonstrate our skills, leadership, ownership and learn from the situation.

2. Describe your communication style and indicate whether you prefer written or verbal communication in professional settings.

    - **ANS:** You are free to answer this question based on your preference. However, as a BA, you are expected to be good in both written and & verbal communications.

3. If stakeholders have differing opinions or conflicting perspectives on project priorities, how would you go about establishing consensus among them?

    - **ANS:**
        - Organize a requirements workshop with all stakeholders to discuss needs and find a balanced solution through open dialogue and prioritization exercises.
        - Facilitate compromise discussions to address the majority of stakeholders' requirements effectively.
        - Reach a consensus by ensuring all voices are heard, leading to a well-rounded solution

4. How do you typically handle challenging stakeholders when working on a project?

    - **ANS:** By bringing them to an open forum. A BA can answer this like this: For example, in a project to implement a new system, I faced resistance from team members accustomed to current manual processes. To overcome this, I conducted vision workshops which helps stakeholders to understand what a to-be status will look like. Also, I gained stakeholder buy-in through successful pilot projects and continuous support.

5. Elaborate on your approach for effectively conveying complex, technical information to stakeholders who may not have a technical background.

    - **ANS:** Approach can involve simplifying complex technical information into non-technical language, utilizing clear visuals and examples to aid understanding, and actively listening to stakeholders' concerns to address them effectively.

6. Provide an example of a situation where you dealt with sensitive information and explain your approach to handling it

    - **ANS:** To ensure confidentiality, I obtained explicit consent from participants, securely stored the data within customer specified locations, and shared it only with authorized stakeholders, adhering to data protection guidelines.

7. In your view, which holds greater importance: being an attentive listener or an effective communicator, and how do these attributes contribute to successful interactions and collaborations?

    - **ANS:** Refer Chapter 3: Skills of BA

8. Can you share an instance where you had to communicate negative information to a client or colleague? Please elaborate on how you approached the situation and the outcome.

- **ANS:** This will be a tricky situation for any BA. As a BA he/she would clearly explain the situation, the reasons behind the negative information, and offer potential solutions or alternatives to mitigate the impact. The outcome would depend on the specific circumstances, but with an open communication and a willingness to address concerns constructively can help a BA to build trust and foster a collaborative approach to resolving issues.

9. A Stakeholder shouts at you in a workshop for some reason. How would you react and manage the situation.

    - **ANS:** As a BA you can keep calm rather than shouting back. In a calm manner you can communicate your viewpoint and be firm on that but be open to listen to feedback. If the situation demands escalation to a higher management it needs to be done as a last resort.

10. You as a BA need to do an assessment or a feasibility study to automate current manual processes in a company, what steps would you take to gather the project requirements effectively?

    - **ANS:**
        - Stakeholder Engagement: Identify all relevant stakeholders involved in the manual process, including task performers and

managers. Conduct stakeholder interviews to gather information about pain points, challenges, and expectations for automation.
    - Document current State: Create process flow diagrams to visualize the current manual process and identify areas for improvement.
    - Document To-be State: Work with stakeholders to define clear objectives and goals for the automation project, considering efficiency and accuracy improvements. Analyze technical feasibility and constraints, as well as regulatory requirements. Define specific functional, UI, data, and integration requirements. Validate and iterate on the requirements through regular feedback sessions.

11. As you lead the implementation of a new CRM system for the Customer Service team, how will you approach effectively managing the associated change to ensure a smooth transition and successful adoption? Provide key strategies and steps.

    - **ANS:**
        - Conduct stakeholder analysis to identify affected individuals/groups, including sales reps, managers, and IT staff, to tailor the change management approach for the new CRM system.
        - Develop a comprehensive communication plan with regular updates, training schedules, and feedback opportunities to manage expectations and address resistance to change.
        - Implement user acceptance testing, train the customer service team with tailored programs, and appoint change champions to advocate for the CRM system while providing ongoing post-implementation support to maximize user adoption and success.

12. As a BA assigned to optimize inventory management for a spare parts company, how do you plan to approach the project and what steps will you take for requirements gathering? Provide an overview of your strategy and methodology

    - **ANS:**
        - Understand the current inventory management process by analyzing it, identifying pain points, and interviewing stakeholders.

- Define clear project objectives for inventory management optimization, considering reducing stockouts, improving turnover, and minimizing carrying costs.
- Engage stakeholders, elicit and prioritize requirements, and manage them throughout the project lifecycle using validation, verification, and documentation processes.

13. How would you conduct a feasibility study for the implementation of a new online Portal & CRM system for a Health Insurance company? Outline the key steps and factors you would consider to determine the project's viability.

    - **ANS:** The steps include defining scope and objectives with key stakeholders, identifying technical and operational requirements, evaluating economic and legal compliance, analysing schedule feasibility, and preparing a comprehensive feasibility study report for a final recommendation on implementation.

14. As a BA, what are the key activities involved in implementing suitable new software to digitize the organization's sales management and reporting, starting from the project initiation to its completion?

    - **ANS:** Conduct thorough analysis, collaborate with stakeholders, and develop clear objectives and requirements for system implementation while managing expectations. Ensure effective communication, user training, and post-implementation support throughout the process.

15. You have been assigned to a project where your team needs to implement a CRM system to digitize the Sales process. You have two weeks of time to before the project kicks off. What preparatory activities will you perform in these two weeks as a BA?

    - **ANS:**
        - Study Existing documents. Prepare a Set of questions for customer.
        - Prepare documentation templates and get it approved by Customer, if it is feasible.
        - Plan customer sessions and schedule workshops, if feasible
        - ...and more.

Have A Great CV That Highlights Your Experience Accurately

To create a compelling BA resume, craft a captivating profile showcasing your best qualities, and list relevant work experiences and educational background. Here are the basic rules to follow a compelling Resume/CV:

Mentioning essential skills and keywords in a CV is utmost important to make your CV Applicant tracking system (ATS) compliant. An ATS compliant CV adheres to the reverse-chronological resume format, ensuring ATS and recruiter-friendly readability. The fonts are clear and organized, using different styles to direct the recruiter's focus.

Always customize your CV for each employer needs and highlight your skills & experiences matching the job description.

This will make sure your CV is ATS compatible as your CV has high chances of getting shortlisted. Always upload your CV in Word format and keep it one page or maximum two pages.

Include additional sections for achievements, projects, and activities that set you apart from other candidates.

Every section is distinctly recognizable, with the resume profile at the start, followed by experience and education. The certifications section closes the resume, providing extra insight into the candidate's qualifications. The key distinction between an ATS-compliant resume and a generic one is that the former is always tailored for a specific job opening.

Do not forget to include essential skills as mentioned in the Job description and also highly sought after skills/keywords including Stakeholder Mgmt., Requirements Elicitations, Stakeholder collaboration, Agile development, testing support, UAT Support, Scope Management, Documentation, and implementing effective change management strategies, among others.

Here Is an Example Format:

Name & Contact Details

- - -

PROFILE OVERVIEW: A Powerful paragraph with 2 to 3 lines which should highlight your overall experience, roles held, skillsets and any major certification that you possess.

Example (You may Write better than this too): Seasoned Business Analyst with (X years) of extensive experience in diverse industries, including finance, healthcare, and technology. Held crucial roles in facilitating successful software development projects, conducting comprehensive stakeholder analyses, Requirements Analysis, Scope Management, Documentation, and implementing effective change management strategies. My skillset includes exceptional problem-solving abilities, strong communication skills to bridge the gap between technical and non-technical stakeholders, and expertise in process modelling and data analysis. ABC Certified.]

- - -

EXPERIENCE (Write your Recent 5+ companies Experience)
[Job title, Company] [Month, Year – Month, Year]

- **Write about Key Responsibilities**
- **Write about Results Achieved**

- - -

Education
[Degree or certificate earned, University/College Name] [Graduation Year]
[Relevant courses]

- - -

Skillsets
[Technical skills]

- - -

Certifications

- - -

Awards & Appreciations
[Award1] [Award2…]

Have a Great LinkedIn Presence

LinkedIn is a powerful platform where you can connect with relevant experts and potential Employers—Use LinkedIn for professional reasons. Connect with Recruiters, or Potential professionals whom you think can help you get a referral in an organization—by sending them an InMail or Direct message with proper context. While LinkedIn offers all such privileges, keep in mind, do not spam. Follow LinkedIn rules and policies when on LinkedIn.

To do all these, building a good trustworthy profile is key. As a first step, include relevant keywords in the headline, summary, and experience sections, focusing on skills, industry-specific terms, and job titles. Showcase achievements and results in the work experience section, using quantifiable metrics to demonstrate impact.

Profile Pic: Always upload a "professional" high-quality headshot. Avoid casual pictures taken at a party, in restaurants, or during trips or outings.

Headline: Mention your current role or area of expertise in a very clear manner. Include industry keywords to enhance your discoverability.

Summary: In the summary section, you need to make it very interesting. Use a narrative approach to narrate your professional journey, achievements, and aspirations. This text or content needs to be a bit engaging and must include relevant industry keywords for better search visibility. Encourage readers to connect, collaborate, or get in touch. If possible, include how potential people can connect with you, whether via email or direct message.

Experience: Include all the job roles or positions you have held so far in chronological order. Provide a concise and to-the-point description of your experience, job roles, and responsibilities in each of those positions. Write down the time spent in each job or position. Include good industry keywords; this will help your profiles come up on searches when potential employers search for candidates by skills and experience.

- **Highlight a few quick, quantifiable achievements** or results. If available and shareable, attach relevant work samples, videos, articles, or presentations—but it's not a must.
- **Seek "recommendations"** from colleagues, clients, and managers to build trust and credibility. Regularly update your profile to incorporate any changes or recent achievements.
- **Maintaining an up-to-date profile** guarantees an accurate reflection of your evolving professional journey.
- **Skills:** List the skills most pertinent to your profession and career aspirations.

Education and Certifications: Do not forget to include your educational details, certifications, and accomplishments. It is always good to highlight any patents, awards, or publications to showcase expertise.

Engage & Socialize:

- **Share:** If you want to turn Creator mode on, go for it. Sharing your thoughts on your expertise can be helpful for you as it showcases your expertise. Post industry news and insights.
- **Engage:** Interact with your network through comments, likes, and shares.
- Connections: Actively connect with professionals, alumni, and colleagues to expand your reach.
- **Groups:** Join industry groups, participate in discussions, and showcase your knowledge.

Settings: Customized LinkedIn URL: Always use the personalized LinkedIn URL. This will look professional, and you can easily share the link with others. In LinkedIn settings, you can easily customize the URL.

- **Visibility:** Make your profile visible to everyone.

In A Nutshell, Don't Forget These:

- **Use Proper Keywords** that is relevant to Business Analysis as discussed above
- **Powerful Opening Line:** Essential info for desktop and mobile viewers
- **Concise LinkedIn Summary:** 3 to 4 short paragraphs with key skills in bullet points.
- **List Relevant Skills** with bullet points, focusing on demand and applicability.
- **Emphasize Industry Expertise** and recent achievements for employer value.
- **Showcase Passions, Professional Interests**, hobbies, and social work involvement.
- **Leave No Rooms for Any Grammatical Errors**. Proof read. Keep it concise.
- **Include Contact Info** (email, social links) for easy recruiter communication.

One Last Advise!

Never Let a Failed 30-Minute Interview Round Bother You!

No one in this world can judge you with a so-called 30-minute conversation/interview. Don't get demotivated by such rejections. Instead, learn from them, if any. You will find a better place soon. Period. In 2009, Facebook turned down Brian Acton, a co-founder of WhatsApp. The rest is history.

This is not just a motivational rant, but a fact. If you are confident in your skills & abilities, and if the interviewers are not able to figure it out in 30 minutes, then it's their fault – they couldn't truly understand you in that short time. It's their loss.

Sometimes, despite doing best in the initial key rounds of interview, someone in the end will reject you. It happens not necessarily due to your fault. It is just that they may think that you may not fit the role or not a company culture fit. But remember that doesn't mean you are unfit for the role. It is a fact that sometimes interviewers have their own agenda, constraints or even bias. So, no matter how much you know, you may not be selected, even if you are currently performing a similar role. In this situation, you should not worry at all. Just learn from that experience and move on.

When you are in a journey of transition, that is, for example, if you want to get into BA career from your current role, and if you have a little or no experience as BA, you may have to face such several rejections, unless you are too good and perfect match for the role. This is indeed frustrating times. But this is the time you need to keep calm and continuously try and hone up your skills. Yes, during such times, keeping your confidence high is challenging. You feel that kind of insecurity inside. That is natural and hence don't worry.

However, you should be able to judge your skills & abilities honestly. You be your judge. Never underestimate your abilities and have a complete awareness about what are your strengths and abilities. If you are not confident about yourself and you have self-doubts about your own skills, then that's a red flag. You need to work on your skills & abilities first. Without doing so, you will not be able to clear many more future interviews. So:

- ✈ Understand each interview is different. You will never know what questions will come
- ✈ Be confident about what you know. keep your knowledge structured and simple in your mind. Avoid making your experience overly complex in an attempt to demonstrate that you have knowledge of everything.
- ✈ Have a clear idea about what experience you want to narrate during the interview. For every interview, understand the Job description (JD) and accordingly adapt your experience and explain your experience in alignment with the JD.
- ✈ If the interviewer asks a question about an unknown topic, and if you don't know about it, be honest. If you know something, explain that and say are always ready to learn
- ✈ Be the BOSS! Have a mindset that they require you more than you need them

All the best for your BA Journey!

DISCLOSURE

While writing this book, I have freely referred to contents available in the public domain about various concepts and techniques commonly used during Business Analysis. As an author of this book, I do not own those processes or techniques which are being used universally. I have understood these techniques and implemented them in projects I was part of, at work.

This is an attempt to provide all required information to people new to Business Analysis at one place so that they can learn and adopt these techniques at work. I have tried to blend my experience into the concepts in my own way so that readers can understand the concepts and use them in their work.

Many of those practices have become part and parcel of a BA's way of working, and hence, pinpointing or citing who wrote/conceptualized what principles is indeed tricky. Wherever possible, if required, I have given suitable citations/references to the original author of a work or concept within the vast stream of function called "Business Analysis".

I have tried to jot down my 20+ years of experience as a BA/Consultant so that my corporate experience can become a guide for readers ranging from freshers to experienced IT professionals (from 1+ to 15+ years of Exp) who want to pursue a career as BA.

Citations/Inspirations/References (This is an exhaustive list):

- BABOK & PMBOK
- Agile Manifesto [agilemanifesto.org]
- SCRUM.org
- User Story format by Rachel Davies
- And many online references which I referred for my knowledge.

***

www.ingramcontent.com/pod-product-compliance
Ingram Content Group UK Ltd.
Pitfield, Milton Keynes, MK11 3LW, UK
UKHW041633190726
13854UKWH00006B/2476